CONTENTS

Chapter 6   **The environment**   **163**

Chapter 7   **Education**   **177**

Chapter 8   **Social welfare**   **198**

Chapter 9   **Law and order**   **215**

PREFACE

Every year more and more people are taking Spanish studies in Higher Education. Increasingly, too, those studies are focusing on contemporary Spanish society and the use of language within it. The two aspects are inseparable. An understanding of all but the most trivial of Spanish texts, both written and spoken, requires access to the body of knowledge about their own country and society which is common to all reasonably educated Spaniards. The aim of the Handbook is to allow English-speaking students to access that same body of knowledge.

To illustrate the point, take the following (hypothetical) sentence from a UK newspaper: 'Labour's modernisers will this week tackle head-on two of the thorniest issues facing the party: selective education and electoral reform.' To understand it, the reader requires not only familiarity with English syntax and general vocabulary, but also needs to be aware of the meaning, and connotations, of the specific terms 'Labour's modernisers', 'selective education' and 'electoral reform', all of which form part of the cultural baggage of the educated UK-based English-speaker. The Handbook's primary purpose is to equip English-speaking students of Spanish with the basis of the equivalent body of knowledge and understanding about Spain.

Even more than in general language, culturally defined terminology appears to give rise to problems of interference. Again, to take an example: the party which won Spain's 1996 election habitually figures in the English-language press as the 'Popular Party'. Use of this name, taken directly from the Spanish *Partido Popular*, removes an important element of meaning from the Spanish term and is significantly misleading – as well as faintly ludicrous. It makes no more sense than to say a Spanish text has been 'traduced' into English, merely because in appearance 'traduce' resembles the Spanish word *traducir* (to translate).

The Handbook's second purpose is to help students to avoid some of the more glaring linguistic pitfalls of this type. Here a note of caution must be sounded. In some cases, English usage is too well established to be challenged. Even though 'Committees' would be much more appropriate, the trade union federation *Comisiones Obreras* is already widely known as 'Workers Commissions'. Similarly, although 'coalition' is usually applied to a government, it is already widely used in the English-language names of

Spanish political parties such as *Coalición Popular*, which would be better rendered by 'People's Alliance'.

Another obvious problem in preparing the Handbook was that of selection. I have attempted to cover those concepts and terms which seem to me to occur frequently in texts, together with sufficient background explanation to allow them to be understood. The task was complicated by the change of government which occurred during the final phase of writing. Inevitably there will be increasingly frequent reference to the party and individuals who now run Spain, and less to their predecessors. Nevertheless, the Socialists had been in power for so long and through a period of such rapid development that their names and actions will remain an essential point of reference for many years to come.

The Handbook is arranged in a series of topic-based chapters, each of which attempts to introduce the main features of one facet of Spanish society and its institutions. It is intended for readers without specialist knowledge of any of the subjects concerned, and technical language is kept to a necessary minimum. Although not a reference book as such, the various sections and sub-sections are intended to be self-standing, so that readers can dip into a particular topic or aspects of it. There is frequent cross-referencing, indicated by section numbers in square brackets, to allow threads of interest to be followed across topic boundaries. Inevitably this approach makes for a degree of intrusiveness and repetition, but I have taken the view that it is desirable in the interests of easy usage.

The glossaries included after each chapter are in no sense intended to be comprehensive. They are meant to complement published dictionaries by picking out usages that I have found from experience to be difficult to locate, or potentially misleading, or both. The bracketed Spanish terms inserted in the main text are intended to give an indication of usage in context; there is no suggestion that they are the sole, or even the most usual, equivalent of the preceding English concept or phrase. Where fully assimilated English versions of Spanish terms exist, they are used in the text, e.g. Saragossa, Aragon. Where they do not, the original Spanish form is used, including any accents. This applies in particular to proper names, e.g. Felipe González.

Even more than the text as a whole, the listing of initials and acronyms is, of necessity, selective. I have attempted to include only those which are habitually used to refer to the organisation or concept without further explanation, e.g. PSOE. Where sets of initials have effectively supplanted the full term, e.g. the radio station *Cadena COPE*, they are not included in the list.

A list of further reading is included at the end of the Handbook. It is deliberately brief, including only items which seem to me reasonably accessible to the non-specialist reader. Particular mention should be made of John Hooper's *The New Spaniards*, an outstanding work of journalism that gives an extraordinarily vivid and sympathetic picture of contemporary Spain. There is, of course, no substitute for the quality Spanish press in keeping up with events in the country; a number of titles are now available on the Internet. For more analytical material the best source is the *International Journal of Iberian Studies*, formerly the *Journal of the Association for Contemporary Iberian Studies*.

I owe a sincere debt of gratitude to various people who have helped in the production of this book. First and foremost among them are my wife and parents, for their unfailing support down the years. Second, my former teacher and colleague, Diarmuid Bradley; that I could even think of undertaking such a project is due to his wisdom, inspiration and friendship. Last but very far from least, valued colleagues at Heriot-Watt University, especially Kent Sproule and Ann McFall for support and solidarity beyond the call of duty, and Graeme Lewis for his help in producing the maps. Needless to say, the errors and imbalances of the Handbook have nothing to do with any of them, but are entirely my own responsibility.

Chris Ross
February 1997

LIST OF INITIALS AND ACRONYMS

AEB	*Asociación Española de Banca Privada*	Association of Spanish Banks
AES	*Acuerdo Económico y Social*	National Economic and Social Agreement
AHI	*Agrupación Herreña Independiente*	El Hierro Independents
AI	*Acuerdo Interconfederal*	National Union–Employer Agreement
AIE	*Agencia Industrial Española*	Spanish Industry Agency
AIPF	*Agrupació d'Independents Progrés de Formentera*	Formentera Progressive Independents
AMA	*Agencia del Medio Ambiente*	Environment Agency
AMI	*Acuerdo Marco Interconfederal*	Union–Employer Framework Agreement
ANE	*Acuerdo Nacional de Empleo*	National Employment Agreement
AP	*Alianza Popular*	People's Alliance
APE	*Asociación para el Progreso Empresarial*	Association for Progress in Business
APS	*atención primaria de salud*	primary health care
ASEC	*Acuerdo sobre Solución Extrajudicial de Conflictos Laborales*	Agreement on Out-of-court Settlement of Industrial Disputes
BBV	*Banco Bilbao Vizcaya*	
BCH	*Banco Central Hispano*	
BNG	*Bloque Nacional Gallego*	Galician National Alliance
BOE	*Boletín Oficial del Estado*	Spanish Official Gazette
BUP	*Bachillerato Unificado Polivalente*	old-style baccalaureate
CA	*Comunidad Autónoma*	autonomous region
CAM	*Comunidad Autónoma de Madrid*	Madrid autonomous region
CAMF	*centro de atención a minusválidos físicos gravemente afectados*	unit for care of severely physically disabled
CAMP	*centro de atención a minusválidos psíquicos gravemente afectados*	unit for care of severely mentally handicapped
CAP	*Certificado de Aptitud Pedagógica*	Certificate of Teaching Aptitude
CAV	*Comunidad Autónoma Vasca*	Basque autonomous region

CC	Coalición Canaria	Canary Islands Coalition
CCOO	Comisiones Obreras	Workers' Commissions
CC/RTV	Corporació Catalana de Ràdio i Televisió	Catalan Broadcasting Corporation
CD	Coalición Democrática	Democratic Coalition
CDC	Convergència Democràtica de Catalunya	Catalan Democratic Convergence
CDN	Convergencia de Demócratas de Navarra	Navarrese Democratic Convergence
CDS	Centro Democrático y Social	Social and Democratic Centre
CE	Coalición Extremeña	Extremadura Coalition
CE	Comunidad Europea	European Community
CEAPAT	Centro Estatal de Autonomía Personal y Ayudas Técnicas	National Centre for Personal Independence and Technological Aids
CEC	Centro de Estudios Constitucionales	Constitutional Studies Centre
CEE	Comunidad Económica Europea	European Economic Community
CEE	Conferencia Episcopal Española	Conference of Spanish Bishops
CEE	Consejo Escolar del Estado	National Schools' Council
CEOE	Confederación Española de Organizaciones Empresariales	Spanish Employers' Confederation
CEPYME	Confederación Española de Pequeñas y Medianas Empresas	Spanish Confederation of Small and Medium-sized Enterprises
CES	Consejo Económico y Social	National Social and Economic Policy Forum
CESID	Centro Superior de Información de la Defensa	Defence Intelligence Service
CETA	Centro de Estudios de Tecnologías Avanzadas	Centre for the Study of Advanced Technology
CG	Coalición Gallega	Galician Coalition
CGPJ	Consejo General del Poder Judicial	General Council of the Judiciary
Cha	Chunta Aragonesista	Aragonese Regionalist Committee
CICYT	Comisión Interministerial de Ciencia y Tecnología	Joint Government Science and Technology Committee
CIG	Confederación Intersindical Gallega	Galician Interunion Confederation
CIS	Centro de Investigaciones Sociológicas	Social Research Centre
CiU	Convergència i Unió	Convergence and Union
CNP	Cuerpo Nacional de Policía	National Police Force
CNT	Confederación Nacional de Trabajo	National Labour Confederation
COU	Curso de Orientación Universitaria	one-year pre-university course
CP	Coalición Popular	People's Coalition
CRMF	centro de recuperación de minusválidos físicos	rehabilitation centre for the physically disabled
CSIC	Consejo Superior de Investigación Científica	Higher Council for Scientific Research

CSIF	*Confederación de Sindicatos Independientes de Funcionarios*	Confederation of Independent Public Servants' Unions
DGMA	*Dirección General del Medio Ambiente*	Environment Directorate General
DGPE	*Dirección General del Patrimonio del Estado*	Directorate General of State Assets
EA	*Eusko Alkartasuna*	Basque Solidarity
EE	*Euskadiko Ezkerra*	Basque Left
EGB	*Educación General Básica*	old-style 'basic' education
ELA-STV	*Eusko Langileak Alkartasuna*	Basque Workers' Solidarity
ENP	*espacio natural protegido*	protected countryside area
EPA	*Encuesta de Población Activa*	Official Labour-force Survey
ERC	*Esquerra Republicana de Catalunya*	Catalan Republican Left
ESO	*educación secundaria obligatoria*	new-style compulsory secondary education
ETA	*Euskadi ta Askatasuna*	Basque Homeland and Freedom
ETB	*Euskal Telebista*	Basque Television
ETS	*Escuelas Técnicas Superiores*	Advanced Technical Schools
EV	*Els Verds*	Catalan Greens
FCI	*Fondo de Compensación Interterritorial*	Inter-regional Compensation Fund
FEDER	*Fondo Europeo de Desarrollo Regional*	European Regional Development Fund
FEMP	*Federación Española de Municipios y Provincias*	Spanish Federation of Municipalities and Provinces
FEOGA	*Fondo Europeo de Orientación y Garantía Agrícola*	European Agricultural Guidance and Guarantee Fund
FFAA	*fuerzas armadas*	armed forces
FN	*Frente Nacional*	National Front
FN	*Fuerza Nueva*	New Force
FONAS	*Fondo Nacional de Asistencia Social*	National Social Welfare Fund
FP	*formación profesional*	vocational training
FSE	*Fondo Social Europeo*	European Social Fund
FTN	*Fomento de Trabajo Nacional*	Catalan Development Association
GAL	*Grupos Antiterroristas de Liberación*	Anti-Terrorist Liberation Groups
GIL	*Grupo Independiente Liberal*	Independent Liberal Group
HB	*Herri Batasuna*	People's Unity
IC	*Iniciativa per Catalunya*	Initiative for Catalonia
ICE	*Instituto de Ciencias de la Educación*	College of Education
ICO	*Instituto de Crédito Oficial*	Official Credit Agency
ICONA	*Instituto Nacional para la Conservación de la Naturaleza*	National Nature Conservancy Agency
IF	*Independientes de Fuerteventura*	Fuerteventura Independents

IMAC	*Instituto de Mediación, Arbitraje y Conciliación*	Mediation, Arbitration and Conciliation Agency
INAS	*Instituto Nacional de Asistencia Social*	National Social Welfare Agency
INEM	*Instituto Nacional de Empleo*	National Employment Agency
INH	*Instituto Nacional de Hidrocarburos*	National Hydrocarbons Agency
INI	*Instituto Nacional de Industria*	National Industry Agency
INP	*Instituto Nacional de Previsión*	National Social Insurance Agency
INSALUD	*Instituto Nacional de la Salud*	National Health Agency
INSERSO	*Instituto Nacional de Servicios Sociales*	National Social Services Agency
INSS	*Instituto Nacional de Seguridad Social*	National Social Security Agency
IPC	*Índice de Precios al Consumo*	Retail Price Index (RPI)
IRPF	*impuesto sobre la renta de las personas físicas*	personal income tax
IU	*Izquierda Unida*	United Left
IVA	*impuesto sobre el valor añadido*	value added tax
JJOO	*Juegos Olímpicos*	Olympic Games
JUJEM	*Junta de Jefes de Estado Mayor*	Joint Chiefs of Staff Council
LAB	*Langile Abertzale Batzordeak*	Basque Workers' Commissions
LGE	*Ley General de Educación*	1970 General Education Act
LGS	*Ley General de Sanidad*	1986 General Health Act
LISMI	*Ley de Integración Social de los Minusválidos*	Disabled Persons Integration Act
LOAE	*Ley de Organización de la Administración Central del Estado*	Central Government Structure Act
LOAPA	*Ley Orgánica del Armonización del Proceso Autonómico*	Devolution Standardisation Act
LODE	*Ley Orgánica del Derecho a la Educación*	Right to Education Act
LOFCA	*Ley Orgánica de Financiación de las Comunidades Autónomas*	Autonomous Regions' Funding Act
LOGSE	*Ley de Ordenación General del Sistema Educativo*	Education System Structure Act
LOLS	*Ley Orgánica de Libertad Sindical*	Trade Union Freedom Act
LOPEG	*Ley Orgánica de la Participación, la Evaluación y el Gobierno de los Centros Docentes*	Schools' Participation, Evaluation and Management Act
LOPJ	*Ley Orgánica del Poder Judicial*	Judiciary Act
LRU	*Ley de Reforma Universitaria*	Universities Reform Act
LUCDEME	*Lucha contra la Desertificación en el Mediterráneo*	Campaign against Desertification in the Mediterranean Region
MEC	*Ministerio de Educación y Ciencia*	Ministry of Education and Science
META	*Modernización del Ejército de Tierra*	Army Modernisation Plan

MOPTMA	*Ministerio de Obras Públicas, Transporte y Medio Ambiente*	Ministry of Public Works, Transport and Environment
MOPU	*Ministerio de Obras Públicas y Urbanismo*	Ministry of Public Works and Town Planning
Norte	*Nueva Organización del Ejército de Tierra*	Army Redeployment Plan
ONCE	*Organización Nacional de Ciegos Españoles*	Spanish National Blind Association
ONG	*Organización No Gubernamental*	Non-governmental Organisation (NGO)
OPEP	*Organización de los Países Exportadores de Petróleo*	Organisation of Petroleum Exporting Countries (OPEC)
OTAN	*Organización del Tratado del Atlántico Norte*	North Atlantic Treaty Organisation (NATO)
PA	*Partido Andalucista*	Andalusian Regionalist Party
Par	*Partido Aragonés Regionalista*	Aragonese Regionalist Party
Pasoc	*Partido de Acción Socialista*	Socialist Action Party
PCE	*Partido Comunista de España*	Spanish Communist Party
PCN	*Plataforma Canaria Nacionalista*	Canaries Nationalist Platform
PCPE	*Partido Comunista de los Pueblos de España*	Communist Party of the Peoples of Spain
PDP	*Partido Demócrata Popular*	People's Democratic Party
PER	*Plan de Empleo Rural*	Rural Employment Plan
PHN	*Plan Hidrológico Nacional*	National Water Plan
PIB	*Producto Interior Bruto*	Gross Domestic Product (GDP)
PIL	*Plataforma de Independientes de Lanzarote*	Lanzarote Independents
PL	*Partido Liberal*	Liberal Party
PNB	*Producto Nacional Bruto*	Gross National Product (GNP)
PNN	*profesor no numerario*	temporary lecturer
PNR	*Plan Nacional de Reforestación*	National Reforestation Plan
PNV	*Partido Nacionalista Vasco*	Basque Nationalist Party
PP	*Partido Popular*	People's Party
PR	*Partido Riojano*	Party of the Rioja
PRC	*Partido Regionalista de Cantabria*	Cantabrian Regionalist Party
PRD	*Partido Reformista Democrático*	Democratic Reform Party
PSA	*Partido Socialista Andaluz*	Andalusian Socialist Party
PSC	*Partit dels Socialistes de Catalunya*	Catalan Socialist Party
PSE	*Partido Socialista de Euskadi*	Basque Socialist Party
PSM-NI	*Partit Socialist Mallorquín-Nacionalistes de les Illes*	Majorcan Socialist Party-Nationalists of the Isles
PSOE	*Partido Socialista Obrero Español*	Spanish Socialist Party

PSP	*Partido Socialista Popular*	People's Socialist Party
PSUC	*Partit Socialist Unificat de Catalunya*	Catalan Communist Party
PTE-UC	*Partido de los Trabajadores de España-Unidad Comunista*	Spanish Workers' Party-Communist Unity
pymes	*pequeñas y medianas empresas*	small and medium-sized enterprises (SMEs)
RNE	*Radio Nacional de España*	Spanish National Radio
RTVE	*Radiotelevisión Española*	Spanish Broadcasting Authority
SA	*Sociedad Anónima*	public company
SC	*Sociedad en Comandita*	limited partnership
SEPI	*Sociedad Estatal de Participaciones Industriales*	State Industrial Holding Company
SIDA	*Síndrome de Inmunodeficiencia Adquirida*	Acquired Immunodeficiency Syndrome (AIDS)
SIMA	*Servicio Interconfederal de Mediación y Arbitraje*	Joint Union–Employer Mediation and Arbitration Service
SL	*Sociedad de Responsabilidad Limitada*	private limited company
SME	*Sistema Monetario Europeo*	European Monetary System (EMS)
SMI	*salario mínimo interprofesional*	standard minimum wage
SNS	*Servicio Nacional de Salud*	National Health Service
SOC	*Sindicato de Obreros del Campo*	Landworkers' Union
SOE	*seguro obligatorio de enfermedad*	compulsory health insurance
SOVI	*seguro obligatorio de vejez e invalidez*	compulsory old age and invalidity insurance
TVE	*Televisión Española*	Spanish Television Authority
UA	*Unidad Alavesa*	Alavese Unity
UCD	*Unión de Centro Democrático*	Democratic Centre Union
UDC	*Unió Democràtica de Catalunya*	Catalan Democratic Union
UE	*Unión Europea*	European Union (EU)
UEM	*Unión Económica y Monetaria*	Economic and Monetary Union (EMU)
UGT	*Unión General de Trabajadores*	General Workers' Union
UM	*Unió Mallorquín*	Majorcan Union
UN	*Unión Nacional*	National Union
UNED	*Universidad Nacional de Educación a Distancia*	Spanish Open University
UPC	*Unión para el Progreso de Cantabria*	Cantabrian Progress Union
UPL	*Unión del Pueblo Leonés*	Leonese People's Union
UPN	*Unión del Pueblo Navarro*	Navarrese People's Union
USO	*Unión Sindical Obrera*	Workers' Trade Union
UV	*Unión Valenciana*	Valencian Union

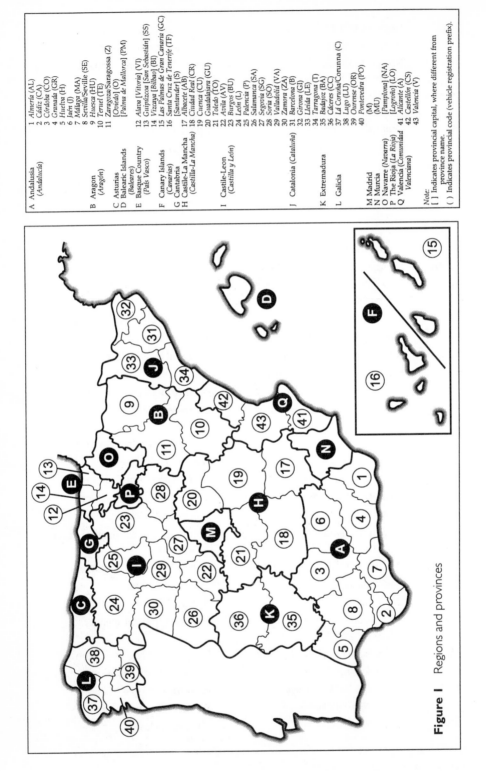

Figure I Regions and provinces

Note:
[ ] Indicates provincial capital, where different from
    province name.
( ) Indicates provincial code (vehicle registration prefix).

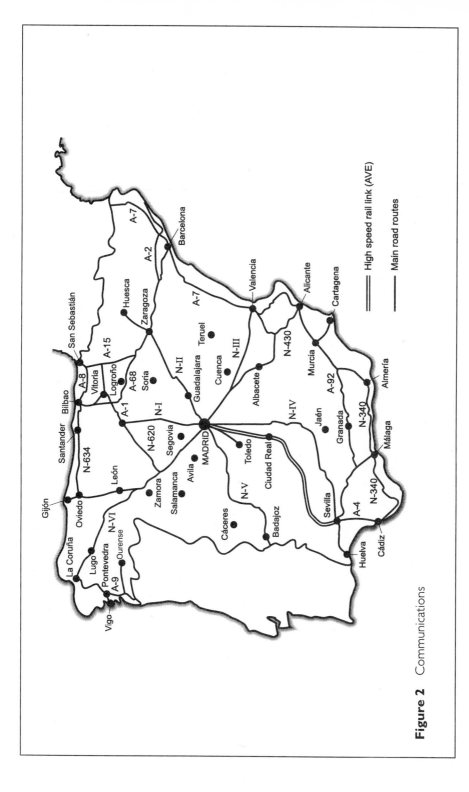

Figure 2 Communications

INTRODUCTION
Contemporary Spain in context

No country can be understood without some knowledge of its history, and none less so than Spain, precisely because its experience has been so different from that of its neighbours. The first section of this introductory chapter attempts to give an overview of that distinct experience over the last two centuries, culminating in the lengthy dictatorship of General Franco and the process by which, after his death, Spain finally joined the mainstream of Western liberal democracy. The second section tries to place Spain in a different sort of context, not historical but geopolitical, by considering the country's changing relations with the outside world.

0.1 THE LEGACY OF HISTORY

Barely had Spain become a united country in 1492 than it emerged as the greatest power the Western world had yet known, controlling vast areas both in Europe and the Americas. From about 1640, however, it entered a period of decline (*decadencia*) that was to last for over three centuries. Not that its people became steadily poorer in real terms, although as recently as the 1940s that was the case. Rather, decline was broad and relative; Spain fell progressively behind other Western countries, politically and socially as well as economically. The crucial phase, during which backwardness (*atraso*) became evident to all with eyes to see, occurred in the nineteenth century.

0.1.1 The nineteenth century and its aftermath

In most of the Western world the nineteenth century saw the great advance into modernity, an advance made possible by the earlier intellectual revolution of the Enlightenment (*Ilustración*). That movement made little impact on Spain. Equally, the country was barely touched by the three phenomena which together brought about modernisation – industrialisation, liberalism and nationalism.

Just as these, where they appeared, were mutually reinforcing, so in Spain their non-appearance was interlinked. The failure to industrialise was both cause and consequence of the weakness of the middle class (*burguesía*), which proved incapable of replacing absolute monarchy (*absolutismo*) with a regime based on the rule of law and individual liberties. The lack of a dynamic middle class also deprived Spain of the key factor in forging a sense of common nationhood as occurred in other European countries. Furthermore, such industrialisation as did take place served to accentuate the distinctiveness of two of the country's disparate regions, the Basque Country and Catalonia. In both it triggered off important political forces whose very essence was denial of Spanish nationhood [3.2.1, 3.3.1].

The result was that, while for other Western countries economic advance went hand in hand with the acquisition of colonial empires, for Spain the loss of most of its American colonies was matched by domestic stagnation. The liberal movement frittered away what little strength it had in fighting three civil wars against the ultra-traditional carlist movement (*carlismo*). From 1820 to 1868 changes in government occurred typically as the result of a military coup (*pronunciamiento*), of which there were frequent examples.

After the disastrous First Republic (1873–4), a further coup restored the monarchy, and put in place a political arrangement known as the Restoration Settlement. Under this, the military was kept out of politics for half a century, but at a high cost. In a caricature of democracy the Liberal and Conservative parties conspired to produce alternation in government (*turno pacífico*). Elections were subject to widespread rigging (*fraude electoral*), of which the main agents were local party bosses (*caciques*).

In 1898 this system was shaken by a graphic demonstration of Spain's international decline. In a few hours the country saw its navy destroyed by a handful of US ships, and lost the remnants of its colonial empire – Cuba, Puerto Rico and the Philippines. This 'disaster' provoked much gloomy analysis of the country's condition. But, outside the field of literature, few results were produced by the ill-defined regenerationist movement (*regeneracionismo*).

Spain's non-involvement in the First World War underlined its negligible weight in world affairs. And, the obvious advantages notwithstanding, it actually served to aggravate the country's problems in one respect. For Spain, alone of the major Western countries, did not experience the surge of unifying national feeling which, for better or worse, the war evoked. Instead, Spain remained deeply split. A tiny, mainly well-off, more or less educated elite had little or nothing in common with the mass of rural poor or the small industrial working class.

Politically the country became ever more sharply divided into what were often called the 'two Spains'. One comprised what we would now call the right, the forces of authority and tradition – the monarchy, the Church and the military, allied with landowners, small farmers and most of the urban middle class. On the left side of the divide was ranged an even more motley collection of industrial workers, landless peasants and urban intellectuals, influenced by ideas that ranged from anarchism through Marxist socialism to liberalism.

After the First World War control over the country swung between these two mutually irreconcilable forces. First, in 1923, General Miguel Primo de Rivera staged a coup with the tacit blessing of King Alfonso XIII, and imposed a mild form of dictatorship (*dictablanda*). When his support crumbled Primo abruptly abandoned Spain in 1930, to be followed a year later by the King. For the second time in 60 years, Spain became a Republic mainly because there was no obvious alternative.

During its five-year life the Second Republic itself underwent regular changes of government. Power was held first by the left, then by the right, during the so-called 'black two years' (*bienio negro*). In February 1936 the combined forces of the left, in the guise of the Popular Front (*Frente Popular*), regained power. Five months later, on 18 July 1936, a military uprising against the elected government plunged the country into civil war. The struggle was an unequal one. The Republic, it is true, could count on considerable support from the masses, and from the strategically vital industrial regions of Catalonia and the Basque Country. But, crucially, it received little backing from abroad. The main Western democracies, France and the UK, stood idly by; the Soviet Union, after initially providing much-needed logistic aid, abruptly withdrew its support in 1938.

The uprising, meanwhile, received considerable supplies of both men and machines from the fascist powers of Italy and Germany. Together with the support of most of the army – as well as significant sections of the people – that proved decisive. In 1939 the republican forces surrendered to the rebels (*nacionales*).

0.1.2 Franco's dictatorship

By 1939 the undisputed leader of the rebels was General Francisco Franco Bahamonde. The personal power of the 'leader' (*Caudillo*) was the first key feature of the regime he created. The second was its basis in the traditionalist ideas of the Spanish right, centred on Spain's glorious military past, the Catholic Church and the desirability of strong central authority. It was this traditionalism that distinguished the Franco regime from the fascist ones of Hitler and Mussolini.

Nevertheless, its third main characteristic was an important fascist element. That derived from the Falange, the party founded by José Antonio Primo de Rivera, son of the country's ex-dictator, and modelled explicitly on Mussolini's fascist one. Conveniently for Franco, the Falange's charismatic leader was killed at the outbreak of the Civil War by republicans, who thus converted a potential rival into a martyr for the francoist cause. While the war was still in progress Franco forcibly amalgamated the Falange with various other groups to form the National Movement (*Movimiento Nacional*).

As well as a powerful instrument of propaganda and social control, the Falange also provided Franco with an ideological basis for his regime, the notion of 'organic democracy' (*democracia orgánica*). In theory this was a purer form of the doctrine than the corrupt liberal democracy of the Western powers, and also more in tune with Spanish traditions. It rejected pluralist party politics and class-based trade unions as the creators of artificial divisions in society. Under francoism the Movement was the sole legal party, and all producers in a given industry, workers, managers and owners alike, belonged to the same trade union (*sindicato vertical*).

In practice, however, these and the other 'natural' organs of the francoist state were instruments of government control. Organic democracy was a cover for an authoritarian and often brutally repressive regime, whose fascist connotations were evident in the name it adopted for its philosophy, 'National Syndicalism' (*Nacionalsindicalismo*) – the parallel with National Socialism was unmistakable.

Franco's closeness to the fascist powers led to Spain's international isolation after their defeat. Most importantly the country was excluded from the American-funded Marshall Plan of economic aid which triggered recovery in the rest of Western Europe. The regime made a virtue of necessity, proclaiming its belief in economic autarky, or self-sufficiency, and itself imposed restrictions on the movement of persons and goods across its frontiers.

In the 1950s isolation was somewhat relaxed. In 1953 a Concordat was signed with the Vatican; later the same year defence agreements were signed by which US air bases were established on Spanish soil. Yet Franco continued to block trade and travel, and even on occasion refused offers of outside economic assistance. By the middle of the decade this course had proved economically disastrous. The country was near bankrupt and living standards remained perilously low. In these dire straits Franco brought into his government a group of technical experts, mainly lawyers and economists. Most were drawn from the conservative Catholic lay group Opus Dei and were unconnected with the Falange.

These experts (*tecnócratas*), of whom the best known were Laureano López Rodó and Alberto Ullastres, brought about a radical change in policy. Often identified with the 1959 Stabilisation Plan (*Plan de Estabilización*), it in fact involved a range of measures adopted during that year and the following one. In essence they allowed foreign trade, tourists and investment into Spain, while allowing out those of its own people unable to find work at home. The result was the prolonged period of economic expansion, lasting up to 1974, which made the word *boom* part of the Spanish language and, allied with continued repression, served to dampen opposition to the regime.

The Franco regime itself also underwent an ideological change in its later stages. Even before the crisis of the 1950s discredited its economic doctrine of self-sufficiency, the defeat of fascism had made National Syndicalism an unhelpful concept with which to be associated. Latterly it was replaced as the regime's official ideology by 'Catholic Nationalism' (*Nacionalcatolicismo*). This lacked the overtly fascist overtones of the earlier concept, but also the more egalitarian and modernising ideas associated with the Falange. Instead, the regime became identified ever more closely with the most conservative brand of Catholic thinking, which placed a dead hand over artistic innovation and free thought of virtually any kind.

Ironically, Catholic elements became one of the sources of discontent with the regime. The dissent of liberal lay Catholics, and some clergy, was fostered by the debates and decisions of the Second Vatican Council (*Concilio Vaticano II*). Another focus of dissatisfaction was the business community, parts of which were increasingly frustrated by the European Community's refusal to countenance Spanish membership so long as the regime lasted [0.2.1].

More active resistance came from two sources, the first being the industrial workforce. Organised with the help of illegal trade unions [4.2.3.1], strikes proved impossible to prevent and regularly escalated into street clashes with the police. Not infrequently the intervention of the army was necessary before they could be suppressed. The second source of active opposition was regional nationalism, which in Catalonia centred on cultural issues and mainly involved the middle classes. In the Basque Country, however, it not only formed an alliance with the workers' movement and the lower clergy; it also developed an armed wing, ETA.

In fact ETA's main significance was as a catalyst which transformed Basque nationalism into a major political force [3.3.1]. Its actions never posed a serious threat to the regime while Franco lived. One, however, did have a significant effect on the prospects of its surviving him. In 1973 an ETA commando blew up the car carrying the first and only man to whom Franco had entrusted the office of prime minister, Admiral Luis Carrero Blanco, and a key element in plans to preserve authoritarian rule after his own death.

Franco's intention was to secure the loyalty of conservative Spaniards, among them the army, by restoring the monarchy in the person of Juan Carlos de Borbón, grandson of Alfonso XIII. To this end the dictator had persuaded Alfonso's son, Juan de Borbón, to renounce his claim in favour of Juan Carlos, whose upbringing Franco had carefully supervised. Despite the monarchy's restoration, however, the machinery of government would remain in the hands of loyal francoists, led by Carrero Blanco. Franco himself seems to have believed that these arrangements would ensure the survival of his regime; famously, he asserted that matters were 'all tied up' (*atado y bien atado*).

0.I.3 Transition to democracy

Even if Admiral Carrero Blanco had survived it is highly doubtful that this confidence would have been vindicated. Like many a dictator, Franco mistook acquiescence with his repressive regime for full-hearted support. That it had never enjoyed except among a small minority; opposition remained muted by fear of another civil war, by the balm of rising material prosperity and because change appeared impossible while Franco lived. His death released the pressures that had built up during the later years of dictatorship, and which rendered virtually unthinkable a continuation of his regime (*continuismo*).

0.1.3.1 Pressures for change

In part, pressure for change derived from the economic progress the regime had itself stimulated. The contacts engendered by incoming tourism and temporary emigration in search of work had shown many ordinary Spaniards that, contrary to the regime's assertions, liberal democracy produced considerably higher living standards than the francoist 'organic' variety [0.1.2]. To the liberal middle classes, for whom economic conditions were easier, democracy offered the attraction of greater intellectual and artistic freedom. To younger Spaniards in general it promised a more relaxed and enjoyable lifestyle.

Powerful external forces also favoured a move towards democracy. The US government had been greatly alarmed at the Portuguese revolution of 1974 and feared that an attempt to prolong dictatorship might result in Spain's 'going red'. More realistically, business interests in Western Europe were eyeing the Spanish market, to which access would only be possible if democracy were restored [0.2.1]. Last but not least, democratic parties in Europe, especially those of the left, provided financial as well as moral support to those working actively for change within Spain.

They were divided, broadly speaking, into two camps. One was made up of individuals who, while working with or for the old regime, had come to accept that some form of meaningful democracy was necessary, even desirable, once Franco was dead. These 'liberalisers' (*aperturistas*) were a disparate, unorganised group whose aims were in a sense negative; while they wished for change, they wished also to keep it within strict bounds.

The genuine opposition, while considerably larger in numbers, also covered a wide spectrum of groups and opinions, ranging from revolutionary Maoists and Trotskyists to enlightened businessmen and liberal Catholics [0.1.2]. Its organised core lay in the umbrella organisations set up by the two historic parties of the Spanish left; the Democratic Council (*Junta Democrática*), headed by the Communist Party, and the Socialist-led Democratic Platform (*Plataforma Democrática*). Their aim was a complete break with the past (*ruptura*). Exactly what that meant was unclear. Certainly it implied that those who had worked with the former regime should not be allowed to shape the country's new form of government. For parts of the opposition, however, it suggested rather more than just political change. Some Socialists and Communists, in particular, expected institutional reform to be accompanied by radical social and economic change involving restrictions on the power of private capital. Such demands were anathema to other supporters of democratisation, both inside and outside Spain.

After a lengthy illness Franco finally died on 20 November 1975 (20-N). Juan Carlos was immediately crowned King, and confirmed in office Carlos Arias Navarro, who had taken over as Prime Minister from Carrero Blanco [0.1.2]. Arias had the reputation of a timid liberaliser; in the event he proved to be more timid than liberal, taking only minimal steps towards democracy. His speeches consistently indicated an essentially authoritarian attitude that gave heart to reactionary opponents of democracy (*nostálgicos*).

Yet Arias was unwilling or unable to clamp down on pressure for change, as he was urged to do by the small group of diehard francoists (*búnker*). Despite still being technically banned, opposition became ever more vocal and visible. In 1976 the Democratic Council and Democratic Platform came together in a Joint Platform (*Platajunta*). Even so, the opposition leaders' control over their followers was tenuous. On the streets, mass demonstrations frequently degenerated into clashes with the police. Widespread industrial unrest reflected workers' growing concern at rapidly rising prices, and at the same time served to worsen economic problems. The situation was getting dangerously out of hand.

0.1.3.2 Adolfo Suárez and political reform

At this crucial juncture, in July 1976, King Juan Carlos and his closest advisers took what proved to be a decisive step. Having encouraged Arias to resign as PM, they used the small room for manoeuvre left to them by Franco's complex arrangements to appoint in his place a high-ranking but relatively unknown francoist bureaucrat, Adolfo Suárez. Their choice provoked consternation and fury from the opposition. In the event, however, it was to prove an inspired one. Effectively Suárez's appointment marks the true beginning of Spain's transition to democracy (*transición democrática*).

It was precisely Suárez's francoist past that allowed him to move the situation forward. A former secretary-general of the National Movement [0.1.2], he had immense knowledge of the operation of the old regime and many of its leading figures. That allowed him to achieve what, on the face of it, seemed impossible; to build a democratic state on francoist laws and institutions. The key to this process lay in the Parliament (*Cortes*), whose members had all been more or less directly appointed by the regime. Using a mixture of procedural manipulation and covert pressure on individuals, Suárez persuaded the existing Parliament effectively to vote itself out of existence. In 1976 it passed the Political Reform Act (*Ley de Reforma Política*) which provided for democratic elections to a new parliament. On 15 December 1976 the Act was overwhelmingly ratified in a national referendum.

Suárez had already ended the ban on political parties, provided they were formally approved by the government. Over the Easter holiday period he took the decisive step of legalising the Communists, thus allowing all significant elements of the opposition to contest the coming elections. They were held on 15 June 1977, Suárez's own party winning a comfortable victory [2.2.1].

Yet the Prime Minister lacked an overall parliamentary majority, and so needed the opposition's support to undertake the further change clearly demanded by popular feeling. Moreover, the economic situation was deteriorating alarmingly. Following the 1973 rise in oil prices, inflation was spiralling out of control [5.1.1]. Many workers were using their newfound freedom to strike for large wage rises, thus further aggravating the situation. Their actions increased rumblings from army leaders unhappy at the legalisation of the Communists. For all these reasons Suárez was anxious to reach agreement with the left-wing opposition.

It was a desire shared by the Socialist and Communist leaders, Felipe González and Santiago Carrillo, who had been taken aback by the results of the two recent polls. In the referendum their joint call for Spaniards to abstain had been almost completely ignored. Then, at the 1977 election, their parties had proved less popular than one led by a former francoist. At the same time, they too were concerned that continued industrial unrest might provoke a coup and so rule out any further elections. And the Socialists especially were under pressure from their foreign allies and financial backers, the most important of whom were the German Social Democrats (SPD), to tone down their more extreme demands.

0.1.3.3 Consensus, disillusion, consolidation

These various pressures on the government and the main opposition leaders produced a willingness on both sides to compromise in order to achieve agreement. The opposition had already done so in its decision to take part in the 1977 election, and so tacitly accept Suárez's gradualist approach. Now it was the Prime Minister's turn to back down. He abandoned his previous plan to base a new constitution on a report from government lawyers and accepted that it must be the task of the newly elected parliament.

How to draft the constitution was one of a set of agreements reached between government and opposition in 1977, known as the Moncloa Pacts (*Pactos de la Moncloa*). The other main thrust of the Pacts was economic. The opposition leaders committed themselves to ensuring that wage demands from their supporters did not push up inflation; the government promised to take measures against unemployment.

In the event, little or nothing was done to create jobs; the opposition, or at least its grassroots supporters, got few direct benefits from the Pacts. The government, on the other hand, gained considerably in the short term. The Pacts did much to restore the confidence of international investors in the Spanish economy, contributing crucially to its gradual improvement and to political stability. Furthermore, Suárez and his allies not only retained the largest say in formal, constitutional change, they also achieved their aim of averting broader socio-economic transformation.

In effect, the Moncloa Pacts marked the left's abandonment of the aim of breaking with the past [0.1.3.1]. Change, it was now clear, was to be restricted to political reform, and even that would proceed in agreement with important elements of the old regime. To cover the extent of these concessions – arguably unavoidable – a new term was coined. The transition was now described as 'a negotiated break with the past' (*ruptura pactada*), which, given the original meaning of '*ruptura*', was a contradiction in terms.

The culmination of this process, the crowning glory of the 'consensus' approach, was the approval of a democratic Constitution in late 1978. From the point of view of constitutional theory, that step marked the end of the transition. Yet in another sense the process still had some way to run. Objectively, the risk of a military coup remained very real. Subjectively, the Spanish people were acutely aware of that danger; democracy had not yet become an established fact of life.

Over the next two and a half years both these factors increased in importance, largely because of the country's continuing economic difficulties. In reality these were only partly due to the political upheaval of transition [5.1.1]. Understandably, however, many Spaniards were dismayed that democracy had not brought immediate material benefits. Their disillusion (*desencanto*) was obvious at the second post-Franco election held in March 1979, when turnout fell sharply.

The apparent loss of enthusiasm for democracy encouraged those who had opposed it all along to harbour hopes of a return to the past. As ever, the key to their fulfilment lay with the military. Its more reactionary elements eventually found the excuse they needed to act, in widespread demands for regional autonomy [3.1.3] and an upsurge in ETA's campaign of violence of which the security forces were the main targets [9.4.2].

On 23 February 1981 (*23-F*) civil guards under the command of Lieutenant-Colonel Antonio Tejero Molina stormed the Spanish Parliament while it was in session. For 36 hours they held its members captive, along with journalists and parliament officials. Simultaneously various army units mutinied, led by their officers; in Valencia, General Milans del Bosch ordered tanks onto the streets.

Most sections of the army, however, remained loyal to the constitutional order. Together with the police they brought the revolt under control and released the captives. Although it was some time before all the leaders of the attempted coup were identified, it was effectively over in a day and a half. Briefly it seemed to confirm all the worst fears that Spanish democracy remained fatally unstable: in the event its effect was to dispel them. For the coup sparked off a massive popular and political reaction. No significant public figure spoke out in its support. Instead, political leaders ranging from the Communists to former francoist ministers headed public demonstrations in support of the new regime. The largest, in Madrid, brought over a million people onto the streets. Spaniards might have been disillusioned with democracy, but they were virtually unanimous in preferring it to the alternative offered by the military extremists.

Eighteen months later a third general election was held, which resulted in an overwhelming victory for the Socialist Party [2.3.1]. Its leader, Felipe González, took over the reins of government in an atmosphere of complete normality. For the first time in Spanish history one freely elected government was replaced by another without any significant section of society seriously questioning the legitimacy of the change. Together with the coup attempt and reaction to it, the Socialists' victory showed that the transition was over and the process of consolidating democracy (*consolidación democrática*) well under way.

0.2 SPAIN AND THE WORLD

Nowadays it is sometimes assumed that the transition marked the end of Spain's distinctiveness. That, naturally enough, is far from being the case. In many ways, the country continues to bear the traces of a history that, for so long, had kept it separate from the mainstream of Western development. In one sense, however, 1975 does mark a decisive turning point, and that is precisely in the country's greatly expanded relations with the outside world. They were spectacularly symbolised in 1992, the Quincentenary of the arrival in the Americas of Spanish ships under the command of Christopher Columbus, when the country hosted three major international events: the Olympic Games (*Juegos Olímpicos* – *JJOO*) were held in Barcelona and the Expo World Fair in Seville, while Madrid reigned as European City of Culture (*Capital Cultural Europea*). In the changes which 1992 marked, three parts of the world are of particular significance.

0.2.1 Spain and Europe

Down the years many commentators have remarked on the tendency in Spain, as in the UK, to refer to 'Europe' as though the country did not form part of the continent. On the other hand, particularly since the 'disaster' of 1898 [0.1.1], there has been another strand in Spanish thinking. Its best-known exponent was the philosopher Ortega y Gasset who, earlier this century, suggested that the remedy for Spain's many problems lay in joining a federal Europe. Not surprisingly, his proposal was regarded as impractical even by those who shared his belief that salvation lay in restoring Spain's links with its neighbours. In the 1980s, however, the notion of closer European integration came to the top of the political agenda throughout the continent. In Spain 'rejoining Europe' had already been an important theme during the transition process. Under those circumstances it is understandable that a general enthusiasm for things European (*europeísmo*) should become such a feature of Spain at all levels.

In fact, the Franco regime had itself made approaches to what was then the European Economic Community. However, the Community made it quite clear that Spain could not be considered for membership so long as it remained a dictatorship, a condition which led business interests inside and outside the country to back democratisation. Once it was met, negotiations on Spain's entry were begun during the premiership of Adolfo Suárez. Since they proved difficult it was Suárez's successor, Felipe González, who reaped the considerable kudos of concluding the talks successfully. In 1985 the Treaty of Accession (*Tratado de Adhesión*) was signed, and on 1 January 1986 Spain became a member of what had become the European Community. Because of the problems of adaptation to EC rules and regulations a number of these were applied in stages over a seven-year transitional period (*período transitorio*).

It was accordingly not until the beginning of 1993 that Spain, technically, became a fully-fledged member state (*estado miembro*) of the renamed European Union. However, although some of the matters involved were of considerable economic significance, in the public mind and for most practical purposes Spain's membership dates from 1986. Its full participation was underlined by assumption of the Community presidency in 1989, a position it again occupied in 1995.

Right up to the end of its time in power the socialist government remained firm in its enthusiasm for continuing European integration (*unión europea*). Nor does its conservative successor led by José María Aznar appear to have any doubts on that score, despite the considerable economic costs for Spain [5.1.3]. Those costs have led to a marked cooling of popular enthusiasm for the EU. Yet no voice of any political importance in the country has even contemplated withdrawal from the EU. Such positive feelings about its European neighbours reflect the reality that Spain's fate is now inextricably bound up with theirs.

0.2.2 Spain and Latin America

Perhaps precisely because Spaniards are aware of such interdependence, enthusiasm for 'Europe' has been accompanied by a marked determination to preserve Spain's distinctiveness. On one level, it is a crucial tool for marketing the vital tourist industry. On another, it is reflected in renewed interest in distinctively Spanish traditions, such as flamenco-style dance. Within the EU it has often taken the form of emphasis on Spain's special links with its former colonies, above all those in Latin America.

The Spanish empire was never a commercial enterprise in the same sense as the British one. Its ex-colonies have arguably had greater economic significance for Spain since independence, as an outlet for the country's unemployment. Emigration to Latin America was particularly marked from the country's poorer regions; in some parts of the New World all Spaniards are referred to as Galicians. Many Spaniards have family ties in the Americas, and the wealthy returning emigrant (*indiano*) continues to feature strongly in popular consciousness.

Highest at the start of this century, trans-Atlantic emigration received a fresh boost when restrictions on leaving the country were relaxed after 1960 [0.1.2]. As well as allowing the Franco regime to export its unemployed, Latin America also provided one of its few sources of foreign support. Most notably, the Argentinean populist dictator Juan Perón provided invaluable food aid during the early 1950s, when famine was a real possibility in Spain.

In that sense, francoist enthusiasm for 'Spanish America' (*Hispanoamérica*) had a basis in reality. Yet any idea that it might provide his regime with a world role was fanciful. Itself officially classified as a Third World country until the 1960s, Spain could not begin to compete for influence in Latin America with the region's powerful northern neighbour, the USA.

The success of Spain's post-1975 transition led some democratic politicians to portray it as a political model for the country's former colonies. More realistically the country can aspire to reforge some of its former links as part of a powerful European trading bloc. Recognising this, the Spanish government has ostentatiously defended Latin American interests in the EU and tried to portray itself as a bridge between the two continents. It has also promoted an updated version of 'Spanish America'.

In 1991 the first Conference of Iberian American States (*Conferencia Iberoamericana*) was held, at Guadalajara in Mexico. The Conferences have subsequently become regular events. The neologism 'Iberian America' (*Iberoamérica*) was chosen to include Portugal and its own ex-colony, Brazil, in a conscious avoidance of the tendency in Spanish to use 'the (Iberian) peninsula' to mean Spain. As much the larger of the two European partners, however, Spain clearly regards itself as the driving force of the 'Iberian American community'. Whether that role will provide any material benefits for Spaniards in general, as opposed to the rulers who attend the Conferences, is perhaps doubtful.

0.2.3 Spain and the USA

Part and parcel of closer links with Western Europe is, inevitably, a growing US influence, both economic and cultural. That is a thorny issue in part because, like France, Spain is the homeland of a great world language whose status is threatened by American English. But in the Spanish case there are other, historical factors to be considered – inevitably conditioned by the Franco era.

For one thing, the Spanish right contains a deep strand of anti-American feeling quite without parallel in Western Europe. The United States was instrumental in depriving Spain of its last significant colonies [0.1.1], and actively supported the earlier independence struggles of those on the South and Central American mainland. The Franco regime swallowed the resultant resentment to sign the 1953 Defence Agreements [0.1.2]. Yet for many

Spaniards who shared its traditionalist ideals, such bitterness was reinforced by the sight of their country reduced to the status of a US client.

On the other hand, American sustenance of a regime which had backed
Hitler and Mussolini against the Western powers had much the same
impact on Franco's opponents. To that were added later the effects of the
1968 movement of student unrest which, as elsewhere in Europe, had a
strongly anti-US tone. A considerable proportion of those who came to
occupy leading positions during and after the transition were involved in,
or influenced by the events of 1968.

Among these were Felipe González and a number of his Socialist colleagues. Their anti-Americanism was expressed, most obviously, in opposition to Spain's entry into NATO, a move favoured by Suárez and his
short-lived successor as prime minister. When, in 1981, it became clear that
the PSOE would soon come to power, Leopoldo Calvo Sotelo took pre-
emptive action and negotiated Spanish entry behind Parliament's back. In
the 1982 election campaign the PSOE savagely attacked his decision.
However, once in power the Socialists changed tack so dramatically that in
1986 González fought and won a referendum called to confirm Spanish
membership of NATO [2.3.2].

The Socialists' change of heart did not mark the end of anti-US feeling,
which resurfaced during the Gulf War with the revelation that US aircraft
en route for the combat zone had used their bases in Spain. When the
González government negotiated the bases' withdrawal, as it had promised
in the complex proposal put to voters in the 1986 referendum, the step was
generally welcomed. By then, though, the end of the Cold War had caused
a general rethinking of attitudes throughout the West. In the new climate
Spain's effective full integration into NATO has provoked virtually no reaction within the country.

The extent of change was underlined when, in December 1995, Foreign
Minister Javier Solana was appointed NATO Secretary General. Solana's
Socialist colleagues portrayed his elevation not as a betrayal but as a feather
in the country's, and party's, cap. Polls indicated that most Spaniards
shared that view; even the Communist-led left-wing opposition tacitly
admitted as much, attacking Solana's appointment as an ill-deserved
reward. Today American cultural and political influence continues to evoke
adverse reactions in Spain, but on a scale much closer to that elsewhere in
Europe than was the case 20 years ago.

0.3 GLOSSARY

20-N m	20 November 1975 (death of Franco)
23-F m	23 February 1981 (attempted coup)
absolutismo m	absolute monarchy, rule
acuerdos para la defensa mpl	1953 defence agreements with USA
adhesión f	accession (to EC)

alzamiento m	uprising (francoist term for rebellion of 18 July 1936)
aperturista mf	liberaliser (at end of Franco era)
atraso m	backwardness
autarquía f	autarky, policy of economic self-sufficiency
bienio negro m	'two black years' of right-wing government, 1934–6
búnker m	diehard francoists
burguesía f	middle classes, bourgeoisie
cacique m	(corrupt) local party boss
carlismo m	Carlist movement
Caudillo m	'Leader', title assumed by Franco
consolidación democrática f	consolidation of democracy
continuismo m	(support for) continuation of Franco regime after 1975
crisis del petróleo f	oil crisis (esp. that of 1973)
decadencia f	decline
democracia orgánica f	'organic democracy', francoist term for regime philosophy
desencanto m	disillusion (with democracy, esp. c.1978–81)
desmantelamiento m	removal (of US bases)
estado miembro m	member state (of EU)
estraperlo m	black market (during Franco era, esp. 1940s and 1950s)
europeísmo m	enthusiasm for Europe/EU
familias (del régimen) fpl	factions within Franco regime
fraude electoral m	election-rigging, electoral fraud
Frente Popular m	Popular Front (left-wing alliance in 1936 election)
Hispanoamérica f	Spanish America (francoist term)
Iberoamérica f	Iberian America, Spanish and Portuguese America
indio m	(rich) returning emigrant from Latin America
integración f	integration; entry (into EC)
intentona (golpista) f	attempted coup (esp. that of 23 February 1981)
movida f	Madrid 'scene' of late 1970s and 1980s
Movimiento Nacional m	National Movement, single party of Franco regime
Nacionalcatolicismo m	'Catholic Nationalism', ideology of later Franco regime
nacionales mpl	francoist forces (in civil war)
Nacionalsindicalismo m	'National Syndicalism', ideology of earlier Franco regime
nostálgico m	reactionary
período transitorio m	transitional period (following Spain's accession to EC)
regeneracionismo m	post-1898 regenerationist movement
Restauración f	Restoration of monarchy (in 1876)
ruptura (democrática) f	clean break with past (i.e. Franco regime)
ruptura pactada f	'negotiated break with the past'
sindicato vertical m	francoist government-controlled trade union
tecnócrata mf	expert (adviser to Franco regime post-1960)
tejerazo m	attempted coup of 23 February 1981
transición democrática f	transition to democracy

turno pacífico m	system of alternation in power based on electoral fraud
unión europea f	European integration
Unión Europea (EU) f	European Union
vecino del norte m	USA (as seen from Latin America)

1

THE SPANISH STATE

The basis of a country's public life lies in the institutions and mechanisms by which it is governed, the state. The equivalent Spanish term (*estado*) is often used specifically to refer to Spain's own central government as opposed to the country's various regional governments. That distinction is followed here. The present chapter will examine the main central institutions – the monarchy, the Parliament, the political executive made up of the Prime Minister and his cabinet, and the administrative apparatus subordinate to it – leaving regional government to be studied in Chapter 3. Also dealt with in Chapter 1 is local government. Although clearly distinct from the central institutions, it shares with them one essential feature. Unlike the regions, which are the product of an open-ended process of development, the structures of both central and local government derive from the Constitution adopted by Spain after Franco's death.

1.1 THE 1978 CONSTITUTION

For some time after 1975 the outcome of Spain's transition to democracy remained unclear [0.1.3]. In particular, it was uncertain whether the new Spain was to be built on a new constitutional foundation. This uncertainty was resolved by the first democratic general election, held in 1977, at which advocates of minimal change to the old regime suffered a shattering defeat [2.4.1]. Nor was Prime Minister Adolfo Suárez in a position to carry through his original intention, that a new constitution be drafted by government lawyers. Instead he was forced to concede the opposition's demand that the task be undertaken more openly, by the democratic representatives of the Spanish people.

1.1.1 Constituent process

As a result, the newly elected parliament became a constituent assembly (*cortes constituyentes*), that is, one charged with drawing up a new constitution. The

Parliament, in turn, encharged the bulk of the drafting process to a seven-man, cross-party committee whose members became known collectively as the 'fathers of the Constitution'. The draft they produced in January 1978 was then further debated and amended in both Houses of Parliament. On 31 October an agreed text emerged.

On 6 December 1978 (6-D) this text was submitted to a referendum; it received the support of 88 per cent of those who voted, representing 59 per cent of the total electorate. Only in the Basque Country was the result less clear. There, although just over three-quarters of the votes cast were favourable, the low turnout (49 per cent) meant that these represented only just over a third of the region's electorate. This fact, together with the circumstance that there had been no Basque representation on the drafting committee, was to provide an unfortunate excuse for some to question the legitimacy of the new constitutional order in the region [3.3.2].

Formally the constituent process was not completed until some three weeks later, with the King's ratification of the agreed text and its official publication on 29 December. Nevertheless, the date most closely associated with the 1978 Constitution is that of its popular approval, now commemorated by a public holiday, Constitution Day.

1.1.2 Structure and principles

The Constitution is divided into 11 parts or titles; the first is an Introductory Title (*Título Preliminar*), while the remaining ten are substantive and denoted by Roman numerals. The areas covered are mainly typical of previous Spanish Constitutions and other similar documents, the main original feature being the specification in Title VII of the principles on which the Spanish economy is to be run.

The titles are themselves subdivided into a total of 169 numbered articles, organised where appropriate into chapters and sections. The major concerns of those who framed the Constitution are apparent in the number of articles devoted to different topics. Well over half of them cover just three areas: basic rights and liberties (46 articles), the role of Parliament (31) and provisions for regional self-government (23).

In addition to the main text the Constitution includes a number of dispositions. The last, or Final Disposition, established the date when the Constitution would take effect. A single Revocatory Disposition (*disposición derogatoria*) revoked the Fundamental Laws of the Franco regime, a series of measures which had effectively acted as its constitution. Nine transitional dispositions (*disposiciones transitorias*) covered questions relating to the introduction of various of the Constitution's provisions.

Of the four additional dispositions, the last three clarify points relating to the age of legal majority (*mayoría de edad*), the special situation of the Canary Islands and the court system. The first declares that the Constitution 'protects and respects the historic rights' of the Basque provinces and Navarre. This seemingly anodyne statement hinted at the complex issues bequeathed by history in those two regions [3.1.4, 3.3.1, 3.4.3].

Returning to the text itself, the three fundamental principles of the Constitution are set out in Article 1.1. First, Spain is defined as a democracy. This principle is reflected not only in the central role accorded to a Parliament elected by regular popular vote, but also in provision for various forms of direct participation in the operation of the state (*participación ciudadana*). Such provision, however, is often cautious – for example, half a million signatures are required before a proposed law can be presented to Parliament by a 'people's initiative' (*iniciativa popular*). In other cases, for example, direct participation in the judicial process through the institution of the jury [9.1.2], the necessary detailed legislation has been long delayed.

Second, Article 1.1 defines Spain as a state under the rule of law (*estado de derecho*). On the one hand, this principle means that all actions of public authorities are subject to legislation, which in turn must conform to the principles set out in the Constitution itself. On the other, it is reflected in a lengthy catalogue of rights set out in subsequent articles. They include not only basic human freedoms but also other economic and social rights whose protection poses clear problems, most notably the 'right to work' (Article 35).

In such cases the text is regarded by experts as establishing an aspiration; it is seen not as a delimiting constitution (*constitución muro*), freezing the country's institutional development at a particular moment in time, but as an enabling one (*constitución cauce*). Thus, even if the state cannot be forced to provide work, it is considered that the Constitution's provisions would prevent removal of public support for the unemployed. Equally, while discrimination of various types undoubtedly exists, by proscribing it, the Constitution allows action to be taken against its overt practice by any social or economic body.

Similar considerations apply to the Constitution's third basic principle, one which has no direct English equivalent. The definition of Spain as a 'social state' (*estado social*) was inspired chiefly by the post-1945 (West) German socio-economic model, known in English as the 'social market economy'. One aspect of Spain's adoption of this model is precisely the inclusion in the Constitution of social rights, such as that to work.

The other is explicit constitutional authorisation to state institutions of an active role in the country's economic affairs. Most famously, this role includes redistribution of income more fairly not just between the country's regions, but also between its individual citizens. As with a number of the rights it purports to guarantee, the imprecise nature of the text in this area poses obvious problems of implementation, but also interpretation.

1.1.3 Interpretation

The need for a means of interpreting the Constitution's often imprecise language is foreseen in the text itself, Title IX of which provides for creation of a Constitutional Court (*Tribunal Constitucional*). The details of its membership and operation are laid down in legislation passed in 1979. This Act establishes that the Court shall consist of 12 members, all of whom must be experienced and respected jurists.

Of these, two are appointed by the government of the day, eight elected by Parliament with at least a three-fifths majority, while two are named by the governing body of the legal profession [9.1.1]. Like their nine-year term of office this balance was designed to ensure the Court's independence of direct government influence. As in other areas, the efficacy of these legal safeguards has subsequently been called into question by political developments [1.4.1].

The Court, against whose decisions there is no appeal, is empowered to resolve three types of conflict over the Constitution's meaning. First, it adjudicates in disputes between the central government and the other bodies which enjoy legislative powers in Spain – the country's autonomous regions – over which of the two is competent to make law governing particular matters (conflictos de competencias). Because of their scope and, in many cases, the sensitive political issues involved, such disputes represent an important aspect of the Court's work, although they constitute only a small percentage of its cases.

The second way in which the Court interprets the Constitution is by deciding whether a particular act passed by the central or regional parliaments, or decree issued by the government, contravenes the Constitution. To this end the Court acts only on the initiative of certain authorised agencies. On the one hand, the central government, regional authorities and groupings of at least 50 Members of Parliament may, within three months of a law's coming into effect, request the Court to rule on whether it complies with the Constitution (recurso de constitucionalidad). On the other, judges may question the constitutional status of a law applicable to any case with which they are concerned (cuestión de inconstitucionalidad).

Since judges may act on behalf of litigants, this second procedure allows members of the public access to the Constitutional Court, albeit indirectly. Direct public access to the Court exists in that all Spaniards may make application to it for protection of certain of the rights and freedoms established by the Constitution, where these have allegedly been infringed by a public authority (recurso de amparo). The rights concerned are those contained in Articles 14 to 29, as well as the right of conscientious objection to military service. Application to the Court may be made only once all other forms of legal redress have failed. It is one of the positive signs of genuine public participation that, contrary to many predictions, this type of dispute has made up the vast majority of those coming before the Constitutional Court.

Although lacking the powers of authoritative interpretation bestowed on the Constitutional Court, a further institution helps defend Spaniards' rights, along with the Court and the Constitution itself. The Ombudsman (Defensor de Pueblo) is charged with monitoring the activities of all public authorities for possible contraventions of individuals' constitutional rights. In practice he acts in response to complaints; in doing so he has the right to priority assistance from those authorities whose alleged maladministration he chooses to investigate. The Ombudsman is also the only agent outside government and parliament empowered to request a judgement from the Constitutional Court on new legislation. He is required to present periodic reports to Parliament, by whom he is appointed.

1.1.4 Amendment

The rules governing amendments (*reformas*) to the Constitution are laid down in Title X. They may be introduced by the same agencies as ordinary legislation [1.3.3]. However, in a reflection of the overriding concern with stability felt by the Constitution's architects, the conditions attached to their passage are extremely strict. In most cases a two-thirds majority is required in both Houses of Parliament. In addition, a referendum must be held should a group comprising a tenth of the membership of either House demand it within 15 days of such parliamentary approval.

However, an even more exacting procedure is set out for any 'fundamental' amendment affecting the text as a whole or its most important provisions: those relating to the role of the monarch and individual rights and liberties, as well as the basic principles set out in the Introductory Title [1.1.2]. Such amendments must first be approved by a two-thirds majority in both Houses, which must then be dissolved immediately and a general election held. The newly elected Parliament must then confirm its predecessor's decision, again with a two-thirds majority in both Houses. Finally, a referendum must ratify Parliament's approval of the amendment.

It is thus hardly surprising that as yet only one attempt at change has been made, and that in response to obligations acquired by Spain as a member of the European Union. Given the overwhelming pro-European feelings of the country's political class [0.2.1], the success of that particular amendment, which allows citizens of other EU member states to vote at local elections, is equally unsurprising – and far from indicative. There can be no doubt that more contentious changes will prove much less easy. On the other hand, it may be that few amendments prove necessary, given the Constitution's imprecision in many areas [1.1.3].

1.2 THE MONARCHY

The central constitutional role of the monarchy, or Crown as it is called in the text, is apparent from its inclusion among those aspects whose amendment is subject to especially demanding procedures [1.1.4]. The relative ease with which this role was accepted by the traditionally republican left was seen at the time as a key aspect of the consensus achieved during the transition [0.1.3.3]. Moreover, both then and more recently there has been a tendency to play up the contribution of King Juan Carlos and his closest advisers to the transition's success, not merely in the period up to approval of the 1978 Constitution but also thereafter. It is therefore important to stress that the Constitution also specifies the essentially subordinate nature of the monarch's role – and that the course of events since 1978 has repeatedly borne this out.

Thus, despite being Spain's Head of State, the monarch exercises only negligible powers of initiative in that role. Formally, operation of the state at the highest level depends largely on his signature. It is the monarch that makes senior official appointments, including that of the Prime Minister; laws are issued and justice carried out in his name. However, these, like all his actions, require the endorsement (*refrendo*) of another important constitutional figure – the government, its head, or Parliament – from which the actions in practice emanate. Similarly, the monarch's endorsement of their decisions, such as legislation or the appointment of ministers, is a purely formal act.

This is not to say that the monarchy lacks significance, but rather that its importance is not real but symbolic. On one level, the monarch's formal involvement in key aspects of public life represents the principle of national unity; that the state acts on behalf, and in the common interest, of the Spanish people as a whole. On another, certain specific actions serve to present a particular image of the country both to the outside world and to its own citizens.

It is generally agreed, for instance, that Juan Carlos's official visits abroad (*viajes oficiales*) have been a highly effective form of 'marketing' for Spain. Internally, the deliberately ostentatious exercise of his right to vote has reminded any Spaniards who harboured lingering doubts about democracy that the contemporary monarchy is a pillar of that form of government, not an alternative to it. Perhaps, too, maintenance of a relatively modest lifestyle and royal household (*casa real*) serves to underline the constitutional aspiration to greater equality.

There are two areas in which the monarch's influence might be seen as real. The first is his role in appointing a Prime Minister following a general election. Under normal circumstances the monarch has no discretion in this regard; he calls on the leader of the largest party to form a government and, once they have received the requisite parliamentary vote of confidence, swears them in. It has been argued that after a close election, where no party enjoyed a clear parliamentary majority, the monarch's role could acquire greater importance. However, there is no evidence that this was the case after either the 1993 or the 1996 general elections, neither of which produced a decisive result.

The second way in which the monarch is seen as possibly exercising real influence is through his role as Commander-in-Chief of the Armed Forces (*Mando Supremo de las Fuerzas Armadas*). Here again there is no question of the King's exercising planning or operational control; these functions lie clearly with the appropriate institutions (government and Parliament) and, like others, require only formal endorsement by the head of state. Nevertheless, it does seem clear that Juan Carlos has been able to exercise a degree of authority over military – especially army – officers, thereby preventing their hostility to democracy from spilling over into active opposition, most famously on the night of the 1981 coup attempt [0.1.3.3].

Yet, in so far as such authority exists, it would appear to derive less from the provisions of the Constitution than from the particular traditions of the Spanish military, and from Juan Carlos's upbringing and experience. After all, there seems little reason why officers suspicious of the constitutional order should feel loyalty to the monarch because of the role it assigns to him. More generally, the undoubted esteem enjoyed by the monarchy in Spain today has essentially been earned in political practice rather than bestowed through constitutional theory. To a significant degree it is not so much enthusiasm for monarchy as an institution as respect for Juan Carlos's personal exercise of the monarch's role (*juancarlismo*).

At the same time, the fact that Juan Carlos and his consort Sofia perform many duties together, as the royal couple (*los reyes*), means that popular respect is not restricted to the King himself. It extends also in some degree to their children, who have been schooled in the same downbeat approach to monarchy. The two eldest are daughters, the Princesses Elena and Cristina. The youngest, Prince Felipe, has the title of Prince of Asturias. As the Constitution specifies the primacy of male offspring, he is also heir to the throne (*heredero*).

1.3 PARLIAMENT

Both the monarch and his heir – on coming of age – must swear an oath of loyalty. Its wording expresses the Crown's subordination to the law of the land and, above all, to the Spanish people as a whole. It is they who wield sovereignty under the 1978 Constitution, which ascribes the central role in the state to the body which makes law and represents the common will; Parliament. Indeed, the political form of the state is defined as not just a constitutional but a 'parliamentary' monarchy (Article 1.3).

1.3.1 Election, structure and composition

The key role of Parliament (*Cortes*) in securing the fundamentally democratic nature of the state [1.1.2] derives from its method of election. This is by universal suffrage of all Spaniards aged 18 and over at a general election (*elecciones generales*). The maximum period between elections is set at four years.

The Constitution states that the Parliament (*Cortes*) should be organised in the form of two chambers (*Cámaras*), or Houses. The official title of the Lower House (*Cámara Baja*) is the Congress (*Congreso de los Diputados*); its members are deputies (*diputados*). The Upper House (*Cámara Alta*) is known as the Senate (*Senado*), its members being senators (*senadores*). In line with British usage deputies are sometimes referred to in English as MPs, but strictly speaking the term 'members of parliament' (*parlamentarios*) applies to both Houses in the Spanish case.

As in the UK, the Upper House is the less powerful of the two. Indeed, in Spain it is especially impotent, effective parliamentary influence lying with the Congress. According to the Constitution, this should have between 300 and 400 members; current legislation sets the total at 350. After the 1996 election just over one-fifth of these were women.

The constituencies (*circunscripciones*) which deputies are elected to represent are Spain's 50 provinces; in addition, the North African enclaves of Ceuta and Melilla each elect one deputy. The numbers of deputies returned by the various provinces are reviewed regularly. They are broadly proportional to the size of a province's electorate, subject to a minimum of three. This arrangement means that the smaller, rural provinces are significantly over-represented. The most populous province, Madrid, currently elects 34 deputies, roughly one for every 120000 voters. That is over four times the figure for Soria, the province with the smallest electorate.

Rural over-representation is one reason why the results produced by the Spanish electoral system are less proportional than in any Western country except those which, like the UK, use majority systems in single-member constituencies. The others are the relatively large number of constituencies, most of which return five or fewer deputies, and the requirement for a party to win at least 5 per cent of the votes to gain representation even in the larger provinces. Together these arrangements seriously disadvantage small parties, or at least those which operate throughout the country as opposed to within a particular province or region.

Thus, in practice, the constitutional requirement that the electoral system for the Congress should 'respect the principle of proportionality' is met only partially, if at all. However, most criticism has focused not on this point, but on the limited ability of voters to influence exactly who represents them, since they can choose only between lists of candidates presented by the competing parties. And, while the number of seats (*escaños*) allocated to a list depends on the number of votes it receives, the particular candidates elected are determined purely by their placing on the list, which is decided by the party. A number of proposals have been made recently to change this system of closed, blocked lists (*listas cerradas y bloqueadas*), by allowing voters either to adjust the order of candidates within a list or to choose candidates from several. As yet, however, no agreement has been reached.

In any case, experience at elections for the Upper House, which are held concurrently with those to the Congress, suggests that the changes proposed would have little effect. At Senate elections voters may indeed cast their votes for candidates of several parties: in practice they opt overwhelmingly not to do so. In most constituencies, that is in the mainland provinces, voters cast three votes each for the Senate, and the four best-placed candidates are elected. Ceuta and Melilla elect two Senators each, while in the Canaries and Balearics the constituencies are individual islands or groups of islands, each of which returns a single Senator.

This system favours the rural provinces even more clearly than that used for the Congress. However, again debate about its reform has not centred chiefly on such bias. Instead it has been concerned mainly with the Senate's constitutionally defined role as a chamber of 'territorial representation'. At present that is achieved through the representatives of the various regional governments, which each designate one Senator, plus one more for each complete million of regional population. These indirectly elected Senators – currently there are 48 – are heavily outnumbered by their 208 directly elected colleagues. The question of whether, and how, to redress the balance forms part of wider debates on the Senate's general impotence and the developing relationship between central and regional government in Spain [3.5.3].

1.3.2 Organisation and procedure

The internal organisation of the two Houses follows similar lines. In each case overall responsibility for the running of day-to-day business and the maintenance of discipline lies with the Speaker of the House (*presidente de la Cámara*). He – up to now there has been no female speaker – is assisted in this task by a presiding committee (*mesa*), which he chairs. It establishes general rules of procedure for the House and the order of business for each day, that is, its agenda. Speaker and committee enjoy the support of legally trained parliamentary clerks (*letrados*).

The speaker is elected by the House as a whole at the beginning of a new parliament (*legislatura*), i.e. after a general election, together with the remaining council members. These are his four deputies (*vicepresidentes*) and four secretaries. As a rule their election is in fact the product of consensus between the main parties, which agree on a share-out of the posts.

These arrangements are typical of those in contemporary Western legislatures. The second internal organ of each House of the *Cortes* is, by contrast, a peculiarly Spanish institution. This is the Standing Council (*Diputación Permanente*), which traditionally acted as a watchdog over the powers of the House while it was not in session. With the increasing unlikelihood of coup attempts, this role seems happily now to be outdated. In practice the Council's main function is to ratify government regulations issued after a parliament has been dissolved.

The *Cortes* differs from the British Parliament in another, more significant way. That is the extent to which it operates – both formally and in practice – not as an assembly of individually elected representatives but of political parties. This characteristic reflects a general constitutional recognition of the role of parties [2.1.1]. In terms of parliamentary procedure it is apparent in the formalised role accorded to the parliamentary parties, or groups (*grupos parlamentarios*), made up of all of the House's members belonging to a single political party. These are represented on the Standing Council in proportion to their size. More importantly, it is the groups which elect representatives to the spokespersons' committee (*junta de portavoces*).

This body is chaired by the Speaker, and acts as an interface between the House as a whole and the presiding committee. In particular it enables the latter to take into account the wishes of members in organising the House's business. The workings of the chairpersons' committee again reflect the importance attached to the parliamentary groups, since the voting power wielded by representatives on it is proportional to the size of their groups.

For these and other reasons the conditions under which such groups may be formed are crucial. In the Congress a minimum of 15 deputies are required, or five if their party obtained at least 5 per cent of the votes cast throughout Spain at the previous general election. In order not to disadvantage regionally based parties who have, in practice, no hope of satisfying either of these conditions, five members may also form a group provided the lists on which they were elected obtained at least 15 per cent of the votes cast in constituencies where they were presented. In addition, parties may band together to form groups if they so desire. In the Senate the minimum group size is ten, and cross-party groups may be formed by those Senators representing a particular autonomous region, whether directly or indirectly elected [1.3.1].

In both Houses those members who are not in a position to join a party group, or choose not to do so, automatically form part of the Mixed Group (*Grupo Mixto*). This group enjoys the same rights as others but naturally tends to lack the political cohesion to make full use of them. None the less, both individual members of the Mixed Group, and the group as a whole, have on occasion played significant parts in parliamentary life.

In both Congress and Senate the full House (*pleno*) meets to exercise important symbolic functions, such as 'electing' the leader of the largest parliamentary group as Prime Minister. Plenary sessions are also held regularly for substantive matters. However, most substantive debate takes place in committees of various types. Some standing committees (*comisiones permanentes*) may themselves pass laws. Also important are committees of investigation – known in the Senate as 'special committees' – set up to inquire into particular issues. Joint committees (*comisiones mixtas*) have members drawn from both Houses. In all cases representation on committees is in proportion to the size of parliamentary groups. A verbatim record of proceedings (*diario de sesiones*) is published for all committees, as well as for the Houses themselves.

1.3.3 Legislation

The Spanish Parliament's legislative work encompasses various different types of measure. Of these, only the most common has a direct British equivalent – the Act of Parliament (*ley ordinaria*). Spanish framework acts (*leyes marco*) and foundation acts (*leyes de base*) both set out objectives and principles to guide subsequent detailed legislation. Framework legislation relates to fields in which this latter is the responsibility of autonomous regions. Foundation acts lay down rather more specific guidelines for central government regulations (*decretos legislativos*).

In all these cases, parliamentary approval depends on a simple majority of those voting. However, for legislation dealing with certain issues of outstanding importance, such as the status of autonomous regions and the ratification of international treaties, stricter conditions apply. In these cases, which are specified in the Constitution, legislation must receive the approval of a majority of members, not just of those actually voting. The same condition applies to the subsequent amendment or repeal of such entrenched legislation (*leyes orgánicas*).

A further category of legislation consists of the 'royal decree-law' (*real decreto-ley*). Such decrees may be issued by the government to deal with urgent matters excluding certain fundamental areas such as individuals' rights and liberties and the basic institutions of the state. In this case Parliament's role is restricted to debating the measure within 30 days of its issue and deciding whether to ratify or overturn its provisions.

With the exception of this last case, the procedure followed by the various forms of legislation in their passage through the *Cortes* is similar. Legislation is usually initiated by the government, in which case it is often preceded by a White Paper (*Libro Blanco*) intended for public consultation. It then becomes a draft bill (*anteproyecto de ley*), which is subjected to preliminary scrutiny by the presiding committees of the two Houses. If accepted for debate this becomes a government bill (*proyecto de ley*).

Non-government bills (*proposiciones de ley*) may emanate from a number of sources, including a people's initiative [1.1.2], as well as the various regional parliaments or either House of the *Cortes*. In the last case the initial proposal may come from a parliamentary group or an individual member with the support of 15 colleagues; this latter option provides the nearest equivalent to a British Private Member's Bill.

Non-government bills are subject to several handicaps relative to government ones. They may not refer to matters requiring organic legislation or to tax affairs. Nor can they ever be accorded priority or emergency status. Indeed, any government with an effective majority can prevent their ever being debated, since that depends on their first being accepted by a vote of the full Congress.

Once admitted for debate, bills of both types pass first to the Congress and then to the Senate. Most discussion takes place in the appropriate committee; it in turn generally appoints a working party (*ponencia*) which prepares a report (*dictamen*) for the full committee. The bill, incorporating any amendments in committee, returns to the full House for further debate and possible amendment. In the Upper House the starting-point for this process is the bill as passed, and possibly amended by the Congress. Senate approval for this text completes the bill's passage through Parliament.

Alternatively, the Senate may introduce amendments of its own or reject the measure in its entirety. In either case the bill is returned to the Congress which may overturn Senate amendments merely by voting in favour of its original text. Even outright rejection by the Senate has little practical effect, since the Congress may approve its original proposal immediately with the support of a majority of its members; once two months have expired, a majority of those voting suffices. Even this meagre blocking power of the Upper House is reduced to a timespan of 20 days if either the government or the Congress itself declares the legislation concerned to be urgent.

Once a bill has successfully surmounted these various hurdles it is passed to the monarch for his endorsement [1.2]. Having thus become law, the measure – like other state documents – is published in the Official Gazette (*Boletín Oficial del Estado*).

1.3.4 Parliamentary control

The second main task of the *Cortes* is to exercise parliamentary control over the government of the day. In order to do so, both Houses have the right to demand from it any information they consider necessary and to require government members to appear before them. Indeed, parliamentary committees of investigation [1.3.2] may require the appearance of any witnesses they think fit. However, the most frequently used mechanisms are those which allow Parliament to demand a government response to two types of interrogation.

Questions on specific matters (*preguntas*) may be presented only by individual Members of Parliament; they may require an oral reply from a government minister. 'Interrogative motions' (*interpelaciones*) may also be presented by individual members. However, they may in addition be asked by parliamentary groups [1.3.2]; they relate to the general conduct of government and they may result in the presentation, and possible adoption, of a resolution by the House. In these latter respects they are similar to British opposition motions.

In addition to these, and the establishment of investigative committees, Parliament has two further devices by which to exert control over the government of the day. The first is the censure motion (*moción de reprobación*) condemning the actions of a particular government member. Such motions have purely moral force, as the Constitution establishes that Parliament can only require the resignation of the government as a whole, not of individual members.

This restriction also applies to the second device, the motion of no-confidence (*moción de censura*). In addition, and following the German model, such motions must be constructive in nature, that is they must not only condemn the Prime Minister in office but also propose the name of an alternative candidate. Moreover, to be approved they require a majority of all members of the Congress, not just of those deputies actually voting, which they must do in public.

Given these restrictions it is scarcely surprising that only two such motions have been presented, neither successfully. In both cases (in 1980 and 1987) the focus of the debate fell on the alternative candidate presented in the motion rather than on the record of the incumbent and his government. Politically this proved advantageous to the opposition on the first occasion but disastrous in the second. In constitutional terms it undoubtedly meant that, to a considerable degree, the intended purpose of the no-confidence motion was distorted.

1.4 THE EXECUTIVE

Under the 1978 Constitution executive power lies with Spain's government, in the narrow sense – that is, the political head of the country's governmental body, made up of the Prime Minister and his cabinet of ministers. Conscious of their country's history, the Constitution's authors had two conflicting concerns about the executive's status. On the one hand, they wished to ensure government's subordination to Parliament. On the other, they wished to avoid paralysing its power to act. In the event, they were much more successful in achieving the second of these aims than the first.

1.4.1 Pre-eminence of government

Effective domination of Parliament by the government of the day is a cause for growing concern in a number of Western democracies. In Spain, certain features of the state mean that the executive's domination is especially marked. To some extent this pre-eminence can be traced to constitutional and legal arrangements. Thus government bills enjoy a privileged position in the legislative process [1.3.3]. Similarly, stringent conditions attach to the presentation and passage of a parliamentary motion of no-confidence in the executive [1.3.4]. By contrast, a vote of confidence (*moción de confianza*) requested by the Prime Minister himself requires merely the support of a majority of deputies actually voting in order to pass.

However, the fundamental reasons for government pre-eminence have less to do with the Constitution itself than with subsequent developments unforeseen by those who drew it up. One is the arguably lax way in which the constitutional requirement for a proportional electoral system was interpreted [1.3.1]. This has produced not the minority or coalition governments envisaged by the Constitution's architects but a succession of single-party administrations. Moreover, the leading political parties have proved to be considerably more tightly disciplined than expected [2.1.2].

In conjunction, these factors have enabled the government to establish a high degree of influence over the *Cortes*, and also to some extent over the judiciary [9.1.1]. This was especially so during the period 1982–93, when the Socialist Party enjoyed an overall majority in the *Cortes*. Then Parliament's legislative role effectively became a mere rubber-stamp, as the government steam-rollered measures through the *Cortes* irrespective of opposition views [2.3.2].

At that time, too, Parliament's theoretical powers to scrutinise the government's actions and call it to account for them were largely neutralised, since their exercise depends on the opposition's ability to muster a majority in at least one of the Houses. This applies, for example, to establishment of committees of investigation, which was repeatedly blocked by the government majority. Similarly, censure motions against individual ministers were not only lacking in effective force [1.3.4]; they were also doomed to inevitable defeat and thus risked reinforcing the standing of their target rather than undermining it. The then Prime Minister made no secret of how little importance he attached to parliamentary control over him and his colleagues; at one stage he attended the Congress only twice in one year.

In the late 1980s the Parliament's manifest loss of power and prestige became a cause for concern about the health of Spanish democracy. In part as a result, the government showed decidedly greater attention at least to the formal aspects of its relations with the legislature. Again, however, this development owed more to political realities than to constitutional theory, in the sense that this period saw the emergence of a more coherent and effective opposition [2.4.2]. Only with the Socialists' loss of their overall majority after 1993 did real changes become apparent, and even then they were limited.

One example was the opposition's success in forcing the establishment of a Senate special committee to investigate the government's alleged involvement in counter-terrorism during the 1980s [9.4.3]. However, the success was short-lived, since the committee's work was effectively stymied when the main Catalan regionalist party abruptly resumed its previous support for the government. Equally, it was another about-face by the same grouping that effectively forced the Socialists from office [2.3.4].

Neither before nor after their replacement – by another minority administration bolstered by Catalan support – did Parliament succeed in channelling obvious public concern about corruption and other executive abuses of power. At no time did it place real pressure on the government. Indeed, so subordinate had its role become that it barely attempted to do so.

1.4.2 The Prime Minister

Just as the Spanish executive occupies a pre-eminent position among the country's institutions, so it in turn tends to be dominated by its head. Since adoption of the 1978 Constitution, four men have held the post of Prime Minister (*presidente del gobierno*). Leopoldo Calvo Sotelo (1981–2) faced political problems that were so great and so numerous as to make him the servant rather than master of events [2.2.2]. In the case of the present incumbent, José María Aznar (1996–), it is too early to reach clear conclusions, but the signs are that his own role is central to the success or failure of the government he leads.

The other two elected Prime Ministers of the post-Franco era both bestrode the Spanish political scene during their respective terms of office. It is true that Adolfo Suárez (1976–81) was eventually forced to resign for reasons which have never been entirely explained [2.2.2]. Yet it is also the case that, at least during his first three years in office, he dominated Spanish

politics under far from easy circumstances. However, it was during the premiership of Felipe González (1982–96) that the PM's ascendancy (*presiden-
cialismo*) was most marked.

As with executive dominance of the state, the reasons for this ascendancy, and its accentuation under González, derive to a large extent from
political factors, particularly those relating to the PM's own party base
[2.3.3]. As in other countries the increasingly personalised media coverage
of politics in general, and elections in particular, plays a role too. However,
the power of the Spanish PM is also due in part to certain provisions of the
1978 Constitution which were specifically designed to prevent his becoming a lame-duck figure, as so often had happened in the country's previous
history.

Thus it is the Prime Minister personally who is given the support of a
new Parliament in the form of a vote of investiture. Should a change of government occur as the result of a successful no-confidence motion, then the
requirement for this to be constructive means that a candidate to the post
must be named [1.3.4]. If a PM were to be removed by a failed vote of confidence or a successful motion of no-confidence, then the entire government
would have to resign with him. Moreover, although the Constitution dic-
tates that certain matters of major importance must be discussed by the
government as a whole, it does not specify any method of decision-making
– and it is the Prime Minister who is responsible for presenting the government's view to Parliament or otherwise acting on it.

Above all, certain decisions are effectively taken by the PM alone, subject
only to the formal endorsement of the monarch [1.2]. In particular this
applies to ministerial appointments [1.4.4]. It applies also to the decision to
call a vote of confidence, or to dissolve Parliament and thus force an early
general election (*elecciones anticipadas*). Both privileges give the PM an obvious means of control over recalcitrant colleagues and his own political
party.

Finally, the PM's power is further bolstered by the support he receives
from two institutions. One is the separate ministry encharged with managing his own and the cabinet's business [1.4.5]. The other is his group of
political advisers (*gabinete del presidente*). Together with this entourage, the
Prime Minister represents a sort of 'government within the government',
often referred to obliquely by the name of his official residence, the
Moncloa Palace.

1.4.3 Deputy Prime Minister

Other than in the case of the Prime Minister the Constitution makes no distinction between the members of the cabinet. It does provide for the
appointment of one or more Deputy Prime Ministers (*vicepresidentes*). Yet it
specifies neither their specific functions, nor the method of their appointment and dismissal, assumed to be the same as for other ministers, that is, at
the PM's behest.

During Adolfo Suárez's term of office as PM, his practice of this right tended to confuse the situation still further. Each of his cabinets contained several deputy premiers, none of whom was explicitly charged with deputising for him under specified circumstances. Nor were they given responsibility for a specific ministry. Instead, they had special coordinating powers in a field covering several ministries (e.g. economic affairs, the military).

On his election in 1982 Felipe González appointed Alfonso Guerra his sole deputy. The following year the Central Government Structure Act [1.5.2] gave legal definition to the role of Deputy PM, implicitly now a single post. As would be expected from the title, its functions were stated to consist essentially of assuming the PM's responsibilties should he die, be indisposed through illness or leave the country.

These provisions formalised the Deputy PM's primacy over ordinary ministers in such special circumstances. The 1983 Act further strengthened his position by specifying that he, like the PM, was automatically a member of all cabinet committees [1.4.4]. Between 1982 and 1996 the Deputy PM was also distinguished from his cabinet colleagues by having no specific subject responsibility. In practice, however, this apparent resolution of the Deputy PM's position proved to be a function of the special relationship between González and Guerra, and the latter's role as link between government and the ruling party [2.3.3]. In the later González governments, in which Guerra was replaced as Deputy PM by the less influential Narcís Serra and Joaquín Almunia, the post's role again lost definition.

When Aznar became PM in 1996 he reverted to earlier practice in the sense that he appointed two deputies – Francisco Alvarez Cascos and Rodrigo Rato. However, these each headed a ministry in their own right, Rato the joint Economics and Finance Ministry and Alvarez Cascos the Prime Minister's Office [1.4.5]. Given the nature of this latter post it seemed likely that Alvarez Cascos was destined to play a role similar to that of Guerra, as the politically crucial link between government and ruling party.

1.4.4 Cabinet and ministers

The 1978 Constitution allows for the government to include members other than ministers. However, the mechanism for doing so has never received the necessary definition through legislation, and thus does not as yet exist in practice. As a result the government, in the strict constitutional sense, consists of the cabinet of ministers (*consejo de ministros*). Important parts of its work are carried out in cabinet committees (*comisiones delegadas del gobierno*), of which the Prime Minister and his Deputy are automatically members.

In effect, the Prime Minister makes cabinet appointments, and dismisses ministers, although officially this is done by the monarch on his recommendation. Indeed, ministers are clearly subordinate to the PM, since their position is totally dependent on his [1.4.2]. On the other hand, they are relatively immune from parliamentary pressure, as they cannot be forced to resign by a censure motion [1.3.4].

Ministers are not necessarily members of the *Cortes*, although they have the right to appear before both Houses, and the obligation to do so if required. Nor are they necessarily members of the party in power; successive governments have included non-party 'independents', although typically these have subsequently entered Parliament attached to a party list. Another difference from UK custom is the absence of a ministerial team in the Upper House, an indication of the Senate's relative powerlessness [1.3.1].

Technically, a change of government is considered to have taken place in the event of a general election, the replacement of an incumbent Prime Minister, or a cabinet reshuffle (*crisis de gobierno*). According to that definition there have been 23 governments between Franco's death in 1975 and 1996, four of them appointed prior to approval of the 1978 Constitution. Thereafter Adolfo Suárez presided over four cabinets in little over two years, Leopoldo Calvo Sotelo five in one and a half, figures which reflect the political uncertainty of the time.

By contrast, Felipe González headed only 11 different teams during his 13 years in office; his first alone lasted over two and a half years. Latterly, however, González's cabinets too became more short-lived, largely due to the frequent ministerial resignations caused by allegations of political impropriety or corruption [2.3.4]. To date, José María Aznar has appointed only one cabinet.

The overall size of cabinets has been very stable since 1981, never falling below 16 or exceeding 19. The Suárez governments of 1979–81 tended to be slightly larger, having between 22 and 24 members, almost all male. Not until 1981 was a woman appointed to cabinet office, when Soledad Becerril became Arts Minister.

After González's election the following year there was a six-year period of all-male cabinets, until Rosa Conde became Government Spokesperson. Only in 1990 was a woman again entrusted with a subject portfolio. Between then and the 1996 election cabinets included either two or three women, although their ministries were all relatively low-ranking ones. Aznar's first cabinet broke new ground; it included four women, one of whom was given the relatively high-ranking Justice portfolio.

1.4.5 Ministries

Within the cabinet, each minister – except the PM and, prior to 1996, his Deputy [1.4.3] – is charged with responsibility for a particular portfolio (*cartera*), or area of policy, and heads the corresponding ministry. There is constitutional provision for appointment of ministers without portfolio but it has not been used since the 1970s. The Constitution also requires the government to obtain Parliament's approval before making changes to the number of ministers or the distribution of their responsibilities. This injunction, however, has been repeatedly ignored in the frequent restructuring of ministries since 1978 (see Tables 1.1–1.3).

Table 1.1 Cabinet composition, 1979–96: cabinet formed 6 April 1979 (first after 1978 Constitution)

Cartera	Portfolio
Vicepresidente primero/Seguridad y Defensa Nacionales	First Deputy PM/National Security and Defence
Vicepresidente segundo/Asuntos Económicos	Second Deputy PM/Economic Affairs
Asuntos Exteriores	Foreign Affairs
Defensa	Defence
Interior	Home Affairs
Hacienda	Finance
Trabajo	Employment
Relaciones con la CEE	Relations with the EEC
Industria	Industry
Educación y Ciencia	Education and Science
Administración Territorial	Local and Regional Government
Cultura	Arts
Justicia	Justice
Sanidad y Seguridad Social	Health and Social Security
Obras Públicas y Urbanismo	Public Works and Town Planning
Transportes y Comunicaciones	Transport and Communications
Agricultura	Agriculture
Comercio	Trade
Economía	Economy
Investigación y Universidades	Research and Universitities
Presidencia	Prime Minister's Office
Relaciones con las Cortes	Relations with Parliament
Adjunto al presidente (sin cartera)	PM's personal adviser (without portfolio)

Notes: Order of portfolios as given by government sources; generally assumed to indicate status within Cabinet.
Prime Minister = Adolfo Suárez. Total membership including Prime Minister = 24 (no women).

Of the three great departments of state in British terms, the Foreign Office (*M. de Asuntos Exteriores*) has existed as a separate portfolio throughout the constitutional era. The same has applied to the Home Office or Interior Ministry (*M. de Interior*), with the brief exception of González's last two governments in 1994–95. In these the Interior portfolio was combined with that of Justice [9.1.2]. This amalgamation was highly controversial, coming at a time when senior Interior Ministry officials had themselves been indicted for involvement in covert anti-terrorist operations [9.4.3]. The motivation seems to have been political – desire to give a high profile to the Justice Minister Juan Alberto Belloch, one of the few cabinet members untainted by corruption allegations [2.3.4]. In his first government, formed in 1996, José María Aznar once again separated the two portfolios.

Similar considerations played a role in an earlier amalgamation which created a ministry equivalent to the British Treasury. Up to 1982 the portfolios of

Table 1.2 Cabinet composition, 1979–96: cabinet formed 5 May 1994 (final González cabinet)

Cartera	Portfolio
Vicepresidente	Deputy PM
Asuntos Exteriores	Foreign Affairs
Justicia e Interior	Justice and Home Affairs
Defensa	Defence
Economía y Hacienda	Economics and Finance
Obras Públicas, Transportes y Medio Ambiente	Public Works, Transport and Environment
Educación y Ciencia	Education and Science
Trabajo y Seguridad Social	Employment and Social Security
Industria y Energía	Industry and Energy
Agricultura, Pesca y Alimentación	Agriculture, Fisheries and Food
Administraciones Públicas	Public Administration
Presidencia	Prime Minister's Office
*Cultura	Arts
*Sanidad y Consumo	Health and Consumer Affairs
*Asuntos Sociales	Social Affairs
Comercio y Turismo	Trade and Tourism

Notes: Order of portfolios as given by government sources; generally assumed to indicate status within Cabinet.
Prime Minister = Felipe González. Total membership including Prime Minister = 17 (3 women).
* = portfolio held by a woman.

Table 1.3 Cabinet composition, 1979–96: cabinet formed 5 May 1996 (first Aznar cabinet)

Cartera	Portfolio
Vicepresidente/Presidencia	Deputy PM/PM's Office
Vicepresidente/Economía y Hacienda	Deputy PM/Economics and Finance
Asuntos Exteriores	Foreign Affairs
*Justicia	Justice
Defensa	Defence
Interior	Home Affairs
Fomento	Development
*Educación y Cultura	Education and Arts
Trabajo y Asuntos Sociales	Employment and Social Affairs
Industria, Energía y Turismo	Industry, Energy and Tourism
*Agricultura, Pesca y Alimentación	Agriculture, Fisheries and Food
Administraciones Públicas	Public Administration
Sanidad	Health
*Medio Ambiente	Environment

Notes: Order of portfolios as given by government sources; generally assumed to indicate status within Cabinet.
Prime Minister = José María Aznar. Total membership including Prime Minister = 15 (4 women).
* = portfolio held by a woman.

Economy (*Economía*) and Finance (*Hacienda*) were kept separate, as is common practice in a number of Western countries. However, when Felipe González came to power that year he wished to deploy his party's leading financial expert, Miguel Boyer, to best effect. He accordingly merged the two, and made Boyer a 'super-minister' in charge of the new, joint Ministry. This arrangement has subsequently been maintained.

In other cases, changing political circumstances have given rise to alterations in the titles and responsibilities of individual ministries. Thus Suárez's first, pre-constitutional government included ministers for each of the armed services, posts which have not figured in any cabinet since 1977. Between 1979 and 1986 all cabinets included a Minister for Local and Regional Government (*Ministro de Administración Territorial*), responsible for the delicate process of devolving power to the regions. With the process complete, the title was changed to Minister for Public Administration (*Ministro para las Administraciones Públicas*).

More recently, the term 'environment' has come to figure in ministry titles [6.3.1]. Initially it was appended to the title of what had originally been the Ministry of Public Works (*Ministerio de Obras Públicas – MOP*) before adding first Town Planning (*Urbanismo*) and then Transport to its name. In 1996 Aznar finally set up a separate Environment Ministry. The remaining functions were given to a new Development portfolio (*Fomento*), a title with distinctly francoist overtones.

The other major change in the structure of responsibilities took place in 1980. In that year the vast Health and Social Security Ministry set up in 1977 was divided into two smaller, more manageable units – Health and Consumer Affairs (*Sanidad y Consumo*) and Employment and Social Security (*Trabajo y Seguridad Social*). Interestingly, this split foreshadowed that which took place in the UK some years later.

Also worthy of note from a British perspective are two other ministerial portfolios. The first, that of Government Spokesperson (*Portavoz del Gobierno*), was created by González in 1985. Initially linked with Arts (*Cultura*), it acquired a separate ministry three years later. The post's creation represented an unusually overt recognition of the importance of media management in modern politics.

In 1992, however, the spokesperson's functions were assumed by another ministry lacking a UK equivalent; the Prime Minister's Office (*Ministerio de la Presidencia*). This had itself been absorbed into a Public Administration super-ministry in 1986, before being re-established in its own right in 1992. The considerable powers exercised by the Office's Head (*Ministro de la Presidencia*) are not due primarily to its formal responsibilities for protocol and the premier's personal security. Rather, they derive from control over the PM's schedule of appointments, the arrangement of cabinet business and, in the role of government secretary, the recording of its deliberations and decisions. With the further addition of the spokesperson's responsibilities, this minister is a key figure in Spanish government.

Spanish practice frequently refers to ministries by their portfolio title (e.g *Presidencia* for 'the Prime Minister's Office'). In addition, the Foreign Office is sometimes known by the official residence of its minister, the Holy Cross Palace (*Palacio de Santa Cruz*).

1.5 ADMINISTRATION

Clearly running a modern country involves much more than the passage of laws or the operation of the cabinet. Below this top level of government there is necessarily a much larger apparatus, responsible for detailed implementation of policy and day-to-day administration. This is the task of Spain's public service (*función pública*) and its staff (*funcionariado*). The first thing to note about this machinery is that, unlike the upper echelons of public life, its structure and personnel were relatively little affected by the transition after Franco's death in 1975.

1.5.1 Franco's legacy

To a considerable extent this was inevitable. After 1975 not only was there an overwhelming desire to avoid opening old wounds. Under Franco the state machinery had simply become too large and too complex to allow the sort of wholesale purge of public administration typical of previous regime changes in Spain; such dramatic change would have brought the country to a standstill. Yet, while it may have been desirable for that reason alone, relative continuity within the public service has undoubtedly had serious implications for administration in post-1978 Spain.

One was the extraordinarily complex arrangements which had grown up in a number of areas of government activity. Their most obvious symptom was the typically Spanish phenomenon of innumerable public counters (*ventanillas*), each with its narrowly defined area of business and idiosyncratic, often apparently arbitrary, opening hours. Another was the complex and outdated career structures of public servants (*funcionarios*), based on a series of corps which bore little relation to contemporary needs. Moreover, the public service as a whole was imbued with attitudes typical of an authoritarian state, which were often inappropriate for dealing with citizens enjoying constitutionally guaranteed rights.

Reforms and the passage of time have done much to reduce, although not completely eliminate these problems. Others have been more difficult to deal with. The lack of public scrutiny under the Franco regime encouraged practices such as the filling of jobs on the basis of contacts rather than merit (*enchufismo*) and influence-peddling (*tráfico de influencias*), that is, the allocation of lucrative public works contracts in return for money and favours. The succession of corruption scandals in the late 1980s were in part a reflection of how hard such habits die.

The conditions of the Franco regime also blurred almost entirely a distinction which is notoriously difficult to draw in any democratic country – that between the government of the day and the permanent administration. The three features which distinguish elected politicians and civil servants in the UK barely applied. Leading members of the regime moved back and forward between cabinet posts and senior ones in the public service; in both cases they were not merely permitted but obliged to join the governing party; and in both they were equally subject to removal at Franco's behest.

This blurring of the boundary between the political and administrative spheres has, to a considerable extent, been maintained in contemporary Spain. It is, for example, apparent in Spain's quangos [1.5.3], senior appointments to which are regularly made on political grounds by national and regional governments. The same applies to institutions with constitutional status, such as the governing bodies of the judiciary [9.1.1] and the public television service [4.3.1], for which Parliament is the appointing authority.

1.5.2 Civil service

Perhaps most importantly of all, the overlap between government in the strict sense and the administration is also evident within the ministries themselves. There, most senior civil servants (*altos cargos*) are in fact political appointees (*cargos políticos*). It should be stressed that such a system is not peculiar to Spain and is designed quite deliberately to provide an adequate link between two apparatuses that can otherwise become undesirably separated. Without it, many would argue, it is impossible to ensure that the government policy which reflects the democratically expressed will of the people is transmitted into administrative practice.

Spain's attempt to resolve this dilemma of democracy was given a formal basis by the series of administrative reforms introduced by the Suárez and González governments of the early 1980s. These were brought together in the 1983 Central Government Structure Act (*Ley de Organización de la Administración Central del Estado – LOAE*). This Act introduced two grades new to the Spanish civil service, both of which are filled by political appointees rather than career administrators.

The higher of the two, containing the most senior non-cabinet posts, is that of Secretary of State (*secretario de estado*). It exists only in the larger ministries, and its role corresponds broadly to that of a British junior minister. That is, Secretaries of State may attend cabinet meetings but only to provide information, not to participate in discussion. That is a privilege denied to the other new grade, that of general secretary (*secretario general*), which also exists only in certain ministries. Holders of both types of post head sections of a ministry (*secretarías*), and have responsibility for a particular policy area or areas.

Intermediate between these two grades in seniority is another also filled by political appointees. Unlike the two grades created by the LOAE, however, that of Under-Secretary of State (*subsecretario de estado*) is a long-standing feature of the Spanish public service. While the post may carry responsibility for a policy area within a ministry, it has others which give it particular importance. One is the internal running of the ministry concerned, including personnel, financial and legal matters.

However, the crucial point is that it is in the interministerial Under-Secretaries' Committee (*Comisión General de Subsecretarios*) that two key types of decision are taken. The first is the allocation of budgets to the various ministries. The second is preparation of the cabinet agenda, which in practice means effectively predetermining its decisions on all but the most politically sensitive of issues. As a result, Under-Secretaries play a key role both in translating a ministry's projects into government action and in securing the financial means to implement them. In those ministries where the post has been abolished, the responsibilities have been assumed by a Secretary of State.

In addition to these political appointees at the head of the ministries' administrative structures (*organigramas*), all ministers, including the Prime Minister and his Deputy, have a private staff of political advisers (*gabinete*). As in the UK, these provide their masters with strategic and political advice on the work of the Ministry as a whole, rather than on particular subject fields. Unlike the British case, they are technically civil servants, the office's Director having the grade of Secretary of State.

Below these various tiers of political appointees – whose titles, it should be noted, are mostly potentially misleading for English speakers – begins the administrative structure proper. Its highest grade is that of director general (*director general*). Such posts have tended to grow in numbers and importance in recent years with the expansion of government activity in the 1980s. They carry responsibility for a directorate general, a particular section or sub-section of the ministry's organisation.

By contrast, the grade of professional general secretary (*secretario general técnico*) has declined in importance, even though every ministry continues to have at least one such post. Its task is to provide advice and support across the whole range of a ministry's responsibilities, a function now largely usurped by the minister's political advisers.

These grades, and those below, are staffed by career civil servants (*funcionarios de carrera*). Unlike their political superiors, their initial appointment is by competitive public examination (*oposición*). Subsequent promotion tends to be based on a points system, in which seniority plays a role but so also do other factors, such as in-service training.

1.5.3 Central government agencies

In addition to the ministries, two other types of institution can be seen as forming part of Spain's central administration. The first is a wide range of bodies which are attached to ministries without forming part of their structure. What these quangos have in common is that appointments to their governing bodies are made by the Madrid government, and so are susceptible to political criteria.

The quangos are numerous and have widely varying natures and functions. They include the Royal Academies of the arts and sciences, as well as the Cervantes Institute, charged with promoting the Spanish language world-wide. The Higher Council for Scientific Research (*Consejo Superior de Investigación Científica* – CSIC) is meant to encourage and oversee research activity, a task in which it has enjoyed strictly limited success.

Some quangos operate in fields where in other countries the initiative is taken not by the state but by civil society. Examples are the National Youth Bureau [8.4.2] and National Women's Bureau [8.4.3]. Others control very considerable budgets, including the procurement agencies (*Juntas de Compras*) attached to various ministries. A number of quangos have been involved in the influence-peddling scandals of recent years, including the national railway board, RENFE, and the agency responsible for producing the Official Gazette [1.3.3].

Of particular interest are the Constitutional Studies Centre (*Centro de Estudios Constitucionales* – CEC) and the Social Research Centre (*Centro de Investigaciones Sociológicas* – CIS). Both of these are attached directly to the Prime Minister's Office [1.4.5]. As a result, the very heart of government's political machinery enjoys privileged access to sensitive information which has been assembled with public money, in particular the results of regular opinion polls carried out by the CIS. This situation has given rise to justified concern.

The second category of central government agency is a relic of the past. Its origins long pre-date the Franco regime, which merely accentuated an already established tradition of centralisation. However, the considerable expansion of government activity under the dictatorship, as well as its desire to control directly national life at all levels, led to a rapid growth of the state's apparatus at local and provincial level. This outlying administration (*administración periférica*) came to encompass a vast network of offices directly responsible to Madrid ministries or other central institutions. With the transition to democracy the situation has changed radically, above all because of the devolution of power to the regions. Nevertheless, certain responsibilities continue to be discharged by branches of the outlying administration.

The key institution of this apparatus is the provincial civil authority (*Gobierno Civil*), whose head is the civil governor (*Gobernador Civil*). The two titles derive from the fact that in the past this branch of outlying administration was parallelled by a military structure also based on the provinces [4.1.1.1]. Since the major rationalisation carried out in 1983, the civil authority has overall responsibility for all central government administration in its province.

The process of devolution has, ironically, given rise to one further arm of outlying administration. This is the central government representative (*delegado del gobierno*) in each autonomous region. This post, unlike that of the provincial governors, is enshrined in the Constitution. As well as representing the state at official events in the region, the representative's role involves coordinating the work of the various governors within it; in single-province regions the two posts have effectively been combined. Informally, but perhaps more importantly, the representative may also act as a channel of communication between central and regional governments. This part of his role is particularly significant in those regions where regionalist parties are strong, notably Catalonia and the Basque Country.

1.6 LOCAL GOVERNMENT

In Spanish, local government is often referred to as 'local administration'. This usage reflects the conditions of the Franco regime, under which local government effectively became part of the central government's outlying administration [1.5.3]. Its role was to impose central decisions locally rather than to allow local responses to local issues, far less democratic ones. Further back in time, however, Spain enjoyed a tradition of relatively independent local government, a tradition re-established by the 1978 Constitution and confirmed by the holding of democratic local elections in 1979.

1.6.1 Municipalities

The Spanish local government unit with the longest tradition is also the smallest; the municipality (*municipio*). The country's municipalities vary widely in size and nature, from the largest cities, through medium-sized towns down to single villages or rural areas containing various hamlets. They are run by municipal councils (*ayuntamientos*). Councillors (*concejales*) are elected at four-yearly municipal elections held on a single day for the whole of Spain, coinciding with those for most of the autonomous regions [3.1.4]. As in parliamentary polls, electors vote for a list of candidates [1.3.1].

The mayor (*alcalde*) is not a mere figurehead as in the UK, but the council's leader. He is formally elected by the councillors; in practice the post is almost always filled by the leading candidate on the list receiving most votes. In the largest authorities the mayor normally works closely with one or more deputy mayors (*tenientes de alcalde*), and with a 'cabinet' of senior councillors (*equipo de gobierno*). Within this, individual councillors have responsibility for the different departments (*áreas*) into which the council's administrative structure is divided. They are referred to by the name of the department concerned (e.g. *concejal de vivienda*) and correspond broadly to the committee chairpersons of UK local authorities.

Another feature of the larger authorities, with their extensive administrative structures, is the prevalence of political appointments to senior posts [1.5.2]. Apart from the very smallest councils almost all are now politicised, in the sense that councillors are elected on party lists. In the smaller ones only some, or none, of the institutions listed above are to be found. There the main weight falls on the mayor, and on the clerk to the municipality (*secretario municipal*).

The range of services which a municipality is required by law to provide is smaller the lower the population for which it is responsible. Many are very small indeed – out of 8,000 more than 60 per cent have fewer than 1,000 inhabitants – and significant numbers lack the resources to provide even the most basic of services. One solution to this problem has been to amalgamate several councils into one. In such cases, villages deprived of their council usually retain an honorary mayor (*alcalde pedáneo*) for ceremonial purposes. Because of the difficulties posed by traditional loyalties, however, such rationalisation of municipal boundaries (*concentración municipal*) has been relatively rare. As an alternative, in some areas councils have banded together in voluntary federations (*consorcios, mancomunidades*).

Structural problems are also apparent at the other end of the scale, in the largest population centres. There urban growth has meant that traditional municipal boundaries often make little administrative sense, cutting through what are now effectively single settlements. One potential means of addressing this problem would be creation of metropolitan area authorities with responsibilities across entire conurbations. Such a solution was attempted in the Barcelona area. However, political rivalry with the Catalan regional government led to dissolution of the experimental authority.

Another way in which the largest authorities have sought to promote their distinct interests is by creating an association to do so. This is known as the Group of Seven, its members being the mayors of Spain's seven largest cities (Madrid, Barcelona, Seville, Saragossa, Valencia, Malaga and Bilbao). The Group operates alongside the organisation which represents all the country's local authorities, the Spanish Federation of Municipalities and Provinces (*Federación Española de Municipios y Provincias – FEMP*).

1.6.2 Provinces

Whereas Spain's municipalities date from the Middle Ages and even earlier, the country's 50 provinces were created only in the early nineteenth century. They also differ from the smaller units in that they were originally intended as a means of extending central government control down to local level. It is at provincial level that the last remnants of the central government's outlying administration continue to operate [1.5.3]. These factors inevitably lend a touch of anomaly to the position of the provinces in post-Franco Spain.

Their continuing existence is due to the fact that, after 1975, they were given a new role as the upper tier of a democratised system of local government. In part this was done by handing over to them some functions formerly exercised by the outlying administration. However, it was also a response to the problems posed by the small size of many municipalities [1.6.1]; in such areas responsibility for some service provision was taken over by the provinces.

The body which exercises these responsibilities is the provincial council (*diputación provincial*), made up of provincial councillors (*diputados*) and headed by a council chairperson. In most cases council members are elected indirectly, that is by the various municipal councils within the provinces. There are two exceptions to this procedure, the first being the island councils (*cabildos*) of the various Canary Islands.

The second is that of the three Basque provinces – Alava, Guipúzcoa and Vizcaya – where, uniquely in Spain, the provinces date back to the Middle Ages. There the administrative authority (*diputación foral*) is controlled by a directly elected provincial council (*Juntas Generales*). The Basque Country, where the provinces also enjoy relatively strong powers, displays in extreme form a problem apparent throughout Spain; the proliferation of administrative tiers and the overlap of functions between them [3.5.3].

Given their ambiguous historical role and relatively minor functions, the provincial authorities are the most obvious candidate for elimination in any attempt to simplify the situation. Indeed, this has already effectively occurred in the five single-province regions (*comunidades uniprovinciales*). There the provincial councils have been absorbed by the respective regional governments. Elsewhere, especially in Catalonia, there has been pressure to replace the provinces by districts (*comarcas*) with greater relation to traditional sentiment and/or contemporary population patterns, as well as the needs of service delivery. Yet not everywhere are there obvious alternatives to the provinces. And, in any case, their abolition would not solve the underlying problems posed by the small municipalities.

1.7 GLOSSARY

6-D m	6 December 1978 (date of referendum on 1978 Constitution)
administración periférica f	outlying administration (of central government)
alcalde m	mayor; leader of municipal council
alcalde pedáneo m	honorary mayor (of former municipality)
alto cargo m	senior public servant
anteproyecto de ley m	draft bill (for parliamentary scrutiny)
área f	department (of local authority)
asesor m	adviser
ayuntamiento m	municipal council
bicameralismo m	(system of) two-chamber Parliament
Boletín Oficial del Estado m	Spanish Official Gazette
cabildo m	island council (Canaries only)
Cámara Alta f	Upper House (of Parliament)
Cámara Baja f	Lower House (of Parliament)
cargo político/de confianza m	political appointee
Carta Magna f	constitution
cartera (ministerial) f	(ministerial) portfolio; ministry

casa real f	royal household
circunscripción f	constituency
comarca f	district
comisión delegada del gobierno f	cabinet committee
comisión especial f	special committee (of Senate)
comisión de investigación f	committee of investigation (of Congress)
comisión mixta f	joint committee (of both Houses)
comisión permanente legislativa f	standing legislative committee
comisión permanente no legislativa f	standing non-legislative committee
comunidad uniprovincial f	autonomous region consisting of a single province
concejal m	municipal councillor
concentración municipal f	rationalisation of municipal boundaries
conflictos de competencias mpl	central–regional government disputes over legislative competence
Congreso (de los Diputados) m	Congress; Lower House of Spanish Parliament
consejo de ministros m	cabinet
consorcio m	federation of adjoining municipalities to provide services
constitución cauce f	enabling constitution
constitución muro f	delimiting constitution
constitucionalización f	inclusion in the Constitution
cortes constituyentes fpl	constituent assembly
Cortes Generales (las) fpl	Spanish Parliament
crisis de gobierno f (cf. *crisis en el seno del gobierno*)	cabinet reshuffle (government crisis)
cuestión de inconstitucionalidad f	challenge by a judge against legislation on grounds that it contravenes the Constitution
decreto legislativo m	government regulation
Defensor del Pueblo m	Ombudsman
delegado del gobierno m	central government representative in an autonomous region
desarrollo m	detailed provision for feature envisaged in Constitution
Día de la Constitución m	Constitution Day
diario de sesiones m	verbatim record of proceedings
dictamen m	report (from parliamentary committee)
diputación foral f	provincial administrative authority (Basque Country and Navarre only)
Diputación Permanente f	Standing Council (of the Spanish Parliament)
diputación provincial f	provincial council
diputado m	deputy/MP; provincial councillor
director general m	director general (highest career public service grade)
disposición adicional f	additional disposition (to Constitution)
disposición derogatoria f	revocatory disposition (to Constitution)
disposición transitoria f	transitional disposition (to Constitution)
elecciones anticipadas fpl	early election
elecciones legislativas fpl	general election

elecciones municipales fpl	municipal/local elections
enchufe m	well-placed contact (in an organisation)
enchufismo m	practice of filling jobs on basis of contacts
equipo de gobierno m	'cabinet' of leading councillors in local authority
escaño m	seat (in Parliament)
estado m	state; (Spanish) central government
estado de derecho m	state under the rule of law
estado social m	state whose economy is run on (German) social market lines
función pública f	public service
funcionariado m	public servants
funcionario m	public servant
funcionario de carrera m	career public servant
gabinete m	private office (staff)
Gobernador Civil m	provincial governor
Gobierno Civil m	provincial civil authority
Grupo Mixto m	Mixed Group (of deputies/senators)
grupo parlamentario m	parliamentary group/party
heredero m	heir (to the throne)
iniciativa legislativa f	right to initiate legislation
iniciativa popular f	people's initiative (procedure by which a proposed law can be presented to Parliament)
interpelación f	interrogative motion (requiring government response to Parliament)
juancarlismo m	support for/loyalty to King Juan Carlos
junta de portavoces f	(parliamentary) spokespersons' committee
Juntas Generales fpl	directly elected provincial council (Basque Country only)
legislatura f	legislature; Parliament (period between elections)
letrado m	legally trained parliamentary clerk
ley de base f	foundation act (basis for subsequent government regulations)
ley marco f	framework act (guidelines for regional legislation)
ley ordinaria f	Act of (Spanish) Parliament
ley orgánica f	organic act (entrenched legislation)
Libro Blanco m	White Paper (for public consultation)
listas cerradas y bloqueadas fpl	closed, blocked lists (electoral system)
mancomunidad f	federation of adjoining municipalities to provide services
Mando Supremo de las Fuerzas Armadas m	Commander-in-Chief of the Armed Forces
mayoría de edad f	age of legal majority
moción de censura f	no-confidence motion (against PM)
moción de confianza f	vote of confidence
moción de reprobación f	censure motion (against individual minister)
municipio m	municipality
oposición f	opposition (party); competitive public examination
organigrama m	structure (of an organisation)
padres de la Constitución mpl	fathers of the 1978 Constitution; members of Constitution drafting committee

parlamentarios mpl	members of (Spanish) Parliament
participación ciudadana f	direct participation (by individuals, in machinery of government)
pleno m	plenary session; meeting of full House/municipal council
ponencia f	committee set up for a special purpose
pregunta f	question (to government minister, by individual MP)
presidencialismo m	presidential system; pre-eminence of PM in Spanish politics
presidente del Congreso/Senado m	Speaker of Congress/Senate
presidente del gobierno m	Prime Minister
proposición de ley f	non-government bill
proyecto de ley m	government bill
rango m	grade (in public service)
real decreto-ley m	royal decree-law (urgent legislation)
recurso de amparo m	application for protection of constitutional rights and freedoms
recurso de constitucionalidad m	request for ruling on compliance of a law with the Constitution
reforma (constitucional) f	amendment (to the Constitution)
refrendo m	endorsement (of action of one state institution, by another)
reyes (los) mpl	the King and Queen; the royal couple
rodillo m	(practice of) steamrollering legislation through Parliament
secretaría f	section (of ministry)
secretario de estado m	Secretary of State (approx. equivalent to UK junior minister)
secretario general m	general secretary (ministry post, grade below Under-Secretary)
secretario general técnico m	professional general secretary (senior career public servant)
secretario municipal m	clerk to municipality
Senado m	Senate; Upper House of Spanish Parliament
senador m	senator
subsecretaría f	section (of ministry) headed by Under-Secretary
subsecretario de estado m	Under-Secretary of State (Civil Service grade below Secretary of State)
teniente de alcalde m	deputy mayor
término municipal m	area run by a municipal council; municipality
título m	title (primary divisions) of the Constitution
Título Preliminar m	Introductory Title
tráfico de influencias m	influence-peddling
Tribunal Constitucional m	Constitutional Court
ventanilla f	counter (in government office)
viaje oficial m	official visit
vicepresidente m	deputy (for full title see corresponding *presidente*)

2

POLITICAL PARTIES

Throughout the Western world political parties are central to public life. They set the framework within which debate on issues takes place, at national level and often locally as well. In contemporary Spain they have acquired a particular significance, due to the nature of society and state institutions, and also to that of the parties themselves. This chapter begins by examining certain features of Spanish parties in general, features which to a degree distinguish them from their counterparts in other Western democracies. The remaining sections then consider the development of each of the country's main parties in turn, before looking briefly at some of the minor players on the political stage.

2.1 GENERAL FEATURES OF SPANISH PARTIES

Political parties are crucial to modern notions of democracy. They are supposed to channel public opinion, in all its variety and even contradiction, into a manageable number of alternative visions of how to run the country in the form of election manifestos (*programas electorales*). When Spain returned to democracy in the 1970s this model had already come to appear dubious as a description of reality, even in countries where parties were well established. Since then, the doubts have increased. In the case of Spain, tardy modernisation, and the Franco regime's ban on democratic politics, meant that in 1975 no parties existed with experience of such activity. The result was to accentuate even more than elsewhere the divergence between the functions and behaviour of parties as predicted by the classic democratic model and in practice.

2.1.1 History, status and popular standing

The most obvious difference between Spanish parties and those in almost all other Western countries is their relative lack of historical tradition. The

point is of contemporary importance. It is known that loyalty to a
party, not just over the lifetime of a voter but over generations, ofter
significant part in determining voting habits. In Spain parties have
yet, little chance to build up a reservoir of loyalty. Indeed, in the per
to 1936 Spain remained so politically backward that there was little opportunity for the development of parties as they are normally understood
[0.1.1].

On the one hand, those forces which favoured only gradual change or
opposed it altogether – those we would today broadly term the right – controlled the country by means other than winning fair elections. As a result
the parties they formed remained mere groups of notables, based in
Madrid, with links to corrupt political bosses at local level (*caciques*). None
developed a mass membership, and none re-emerged to play a significant
role in politics after 1975. The only party permitted under the regime, the
government-run National Movement (*Movimiento*), was dissolved the year
after the dictator's death.

On the left, the position was rather different. By the 1930s both the
Socialists and the Communists were established political forces, with genuine party organisations and, in the former case, considerable electoral
strength. Because of Spain's late and patchy economic development, however, these were restricted to some of the few regions where industry had
developed: the Basque Country, Asturias and Madrid. What is more, for
almost 40 years both parties of the left were banned and vilified by the
Franco regime. In so far as they operated at all, it was in exile or underground.

As a result, of all the myriad political parties which emerged after they
were legalised in 1976 – the media talked of an 'alphabet soup' (*sopa de
siglas*) – none had in existence a normal structure of organisation and membership. And neither they nor voters themselves had recent, or, indeed, any
experience of democratic politics. Moreover, in the case of the Communists,
who in 1976 were widely expected to emerge as a leading if not the largest
political force, there were understandable doubts about their commitment
to observe the rules of democracy.

For all these reasons, those who framed the 1978 Constitution were anxious to foster the growth of democratic parties. Their concern was expressed
through recognition, in the Constitution's Introductory Title [1.1.2], of parties as a 'basic mechanism of political participation'. It was again demonstrated by the speed with which this special status was regulated in greater
detail. Before the end of 1978, at a time when many major matters required
urgent attention, a Political Parties Act was passed. Under this law parties
were given certain privileges, in particular the right to public funding once
registered officially as such [2.1.3]. In return, they were required to satisfy
certain conditions. In essence, parties' statutes, their own internal 'constitutions', had to conform to certain rules. Thus their stated aims must not be
contrary to the Constitution itself, and their internal structure and operation must be democratic in nature.

The first provision has on occasion been applied to regionalist parties who aspire to break away from Spain, thus infringing the country's territorial unity stipulated in Article 2. It would also appear to allow a refusal to register – effectively a ban on – fascist or other anti-democratic groups. The second has also been mentioned as a possible ground for deregistering Basque parties linked to terrorism. In general, however, the conditions imposed by the 1978 Act have had virtually no practical application.

Moreover, developments have belied the widespread fear that Spanish parties would prove sickly creatures in need of careful nurture. One indication of their robust health is the turnout at general elections (*participación electoral*) or, to use the term usually adopted in Spain, the abstention rate. After rising sharply in 1979 due to popular disillusionment with the results of democracy, abstention fell to just 20 per cent in 1982 as a wave of popular enthusiasm swept the Socialists to power [2.3.1]. And, although turnout dropped sharply later in the 1980s, during the 1990s it has once again risen to levels of which many older democracies would be proud.

Yet at the same time popular esteem for parties as institutions has sunk, with the involvement – to a greater or lesser degree – of all the major ones in the corruption scandals of recent years. In fact, corruption allegations formed the main, indeed, almost the only plank of the campaigns mounted by the conservative opposition in both 1993 and 1996. On both occasions the response of the Socialist government was to brand their main opponent as Franco's heir. In other words, high turnout followed extremely negative campaigns, which both reflected and aggravated the low standing of parties in general.

2.1.2 Leaders and members

A key factor in shaping public perceptions of parties has been the way in which they have operated. Central to that is the relationship between their upper echelons (*cúpula*) and rank-and-file membership (*bases*). In Spain, this has been crucially affected by the context in which parties rapidly developed after 1976.

The two parties which already had some form of organisation, the Socialists and Communists, were used to the secrecy and discipline required by underground operation. On the right and in the centre, parties were initially little more than groups of public figures; such organisation as they had was inherited, unofficially, from Franco's National Movement [0.1.2]. As a result, they shared two features with their opponents. One was the high degree of control exercised by the leadership. The other was a low level of party membership (*afiliación*), with the percentage of the population belonging to parties among the lowest in Europe. Even today the largest parties, the Socialists and the People's Party, have no more than 300 000 individual members (*militantes*). In 1979 both Socialists and Communists claimed around 100 000, while no force on the centre-right had any significant membership at all.

Quite apart from general concerns about the health of democracy, the lack of members posed a very practical problem for the new parties. As well as building up their own organisations, those that enjoyed success had somehow to fill elected posts, such as MPs and councillors, as well as numerous political appointments in national, regional and local government [1.5.2]. The solution adopted by the country's first ruling party was to absorb a considerable number of politicians and bureaucrats from the former regime [2.2.1]. However, when the parties of the left took over control of many local authorities after the 1979 municipal elections, they were faced with a major difficulty.

The Socialists were particularly affected; they won more votes and thus had more posts to fill, but had fewer members and activists than the Communists in many areas. Moreover, within four years the party gained control over central government and most of the new autonomous regions [2.3.2]. Its response was, in part, to expand its membership by incorporating potential ministers, local councillors and political appointees. The reverse also applied; the enormous patronage wielded by the Socialists during the 1980s attracted new members for reasons often only tenuously connected by political beliefs.

Towards the end of the decade, as the People's Party captured control over many local and regional authorities [2.4.3], it was affected by a similar process. The result is that the membership of both Spain's main parties, which between them run the vast bulk of government in the country, is made up to an extraordinary degree of political office-holders (*cargos*). This phenomenon, in turn, has had two main consequences.

It means, first, that a very high proportion of party members have a strong personal, often financial interest in obtaining and holding onto public office. Not surprisingly, administrations formed by the main parties at all levels of government often appear more interested in holding on to power than in using it to implement their election manifestos. Even more seriously for parties' collective standing, the situation is a significant factor in corruption.

It also leads to another form of impropriety – opportunistic party-hopping (*chaqueteo*). During the transition period, when parties were still in the stage of formation, the practice of individuals moving between them was a frequent and even understandable one. Nevertheless it caused sufficient disquiet that its most visible form – MPs crossing the floor in Parliament (*transfuguismo*) – was made the subject of strict controls; if an MP leaves his party group he must either resign or join the Mixed Group [1.3.2]. Switches of allegiance at lower levels are less easy to prevent. Their effect, in terms of public cynicism about politics and politicians, can be readily surmised.

Second, the make-up of the main parties has tended to strengthen the degree of control exercised by their leaderships. It is they that decide on the placing of individual candidates on the party lists presented to voters [1.3.1], and they who make political appointments to senior administrative posts [1.5.2]. It is party leaders who play the key role in media-centred election campaigning, especially important in Spain precisely because of low

party membership. And, as elsewhere, such campaigning tends to place a heavy emphasis on party unity; dissidents can expect scant rewards.

The electoral impact of national leaders is important even at lower levels, since local and most regional elections take place on a single day and the campaign for them is to a large extent a national affair [3.1.4]. Yet local and, especially, regional leaders also play a significant role and, perhaps more importantly, now control a considerable amount of patronage in their own right. Likened on occasion to Spain's pre-democratic party bosses [2.1.1], the more powerful of these city and regional leaders provide the only real counterweight to the leadership's power within the main parties.

2.1.3 Party funding

The fear of those who drew up the 1978 Constitution was that Spain's fledgling parties would prove too weak to ensure the state's democratic nature. In so far as the strength of parties is concerned, these fears have proved wildly exaggerated. Not only do parties monopolise participation in politics, in the sense that only the candidates they present have any realistic chance of election to public office, the widespread system of political appointments means that their influence over the machinery of government goes far further than merely the elected sphere.

As a consequence, the most commonly voiced concern today about the health of Spanish democracy is that the country has become a party-run state (*partitocracia*). The description needs to be severely qualified, in two ways. First, within parties it is the leadership, not the membership as a whole, who exercise effective power [2.1.2] – and as elsewhere, leaders tend to pragmatism rather than ideology. Second, particularly in the case of parties in power at national or lower levels, there is a considerable degree of contact and overlap between party leaderships and those who control the machinery of government. Arguably, rather than parties controlling the state, it is the executive that exercises a decisive influence over parties.

Ironically, one of the measures taken in the 1970s to strengthen parties has, in practice, served to increase their subordination to the executive. That is the state funding (*financiación*) introduced by the 1978 Political Parties Act [2.1.1]. As in other countries, reservations were expressed in Spain about the provision when it was introduced. However, given the country's highly unusual circumstances, there was no viable alternative; parties, in so far as they existed, lacked both funds and the means to generate them. Consequently the money they received from the state immediately became the main source of income for all parties of any significance, and remains so today.

During the 1980s there was growing public concern about the operation of party funding in general. In response, measures were introduced in 1987 to regulate it in greater detail. Under them parties receive an annual sum from the state, based on their performance (votes and seats won) in the most recent election. In addition they receive special support for election campaigns on the same basis, including access to television time as well as finance. One effect of this arrangement is to intensify even further parties' concern with electoral success [2.1.2].

The 1987 legislation covers not only public funding but also income from other sources. Under this heading come, first, membership dues (*cuotas de afiliación*) and other income generated by the party itself. Given the low level of membership and activism this source is inevitably of only minor significance.

The second means by which parties may raise money themselves is through bank loans (*créditos bancarios*). That clearly places a premium on good links with the banking sector, and has proved a controversial issue on occasion, most notably in 1986. Then the notorious antipathy between Adolfo Suárez and the country's leading bankers – the ex-premier referred to them as the 'evil godmother' of Spanish society – seems to have led them to discriminate in granting loans against the party he was leading at the time [2.2.3]. Interestingly, their action seemed to have little impact on its results.

Finally, parties may receive private donations. These are subject to limits on their quantity and to stringent conditions on how they are made. While this strict control has decided advantages in terms of clarity – it would, for example, render illegal the vast majority of the private and company donations which have proved controversial in the UK – it also poses problems of its own. These arise because, perhaps inevitably, parties find the level of funding they receive, public and otherwise, to be inadequate in practice. As a result, many of the influence-peddling scandals of recent years [1.5.1] have been concerned not with personal but with party enrichment. The most notorious example was the 'Filesa affair' of the 1980s, named after a company set up by the Socialist Party specifically to channel the proceeds of such activities into party coffers. To a greater or lesser degree, however, all the major parties have financed themselves in this way, which represents yet another incentive, this time collective rather than individual, for parties to cling to office at all cost.

As a result of these problems, there have been discussions between the two largest about relaxing the strict controls on private contributions to parties. So far these have not borne fruit. The main differences have been over whether to retain the anonymity of private donors, and whether to permit companies to make political contributions. Whether or not it becomes easier for parties to receive private donations, however, they are certain in the medium term to remain dependent on state contributions as their main source of funding.

2.2 THE CENTRE: UCD AND ITS SUCCESSORS

To some contemporary observers, the brief history of the first political party to govern Spain after 1975 confirmed fears about the country's ability to sustain viable parties. The Democratic Centre Union (*Unión de Centro Democrático – UCD*) existed for a mere six years. Like the party itself, however, its fate was essentially a product of the general instability of the transition period. It is also the case that UCD – the initials are usually given without any article in Spanish – occupied a part of the political spectrum, the centre, to which no significant party in the 1990s belongs. None the less, UCD still figures frequently in discussion, because of its key role during the transition and because its experience illustrates a number of issues that continue to affect parties today.

2.2.1 Suárez and the rise of UCD

UCD emerged by a process of clustering from the bewildering array of tiny parties that sprang up after Franco's death [2.1.1]. Its nucleus was the People's Party (*Partido Popular*), founded in 1976 by José María Areilza. Areilza had occupied various senior official posts under the Franco regime but had latterly been prominent among those working for limited change from within it [0.1.3.1]. He was considerably better known at the time than the young man recently appointed Prime Minister by King Juan Carlos, Adolfo Suárez, and widely seen, not least by himself, as a suitable successor.

In January 1977 Areilza's formation absorbed another similar group, changing its name to Democratic Centre. Thereafter it swallowed up or allied with a steady stream of smaller parties. In the spring came the decisive step when Suárez climbed aboard the bandwagon, imposing two conditions for his support. First, he became the grouping's leader, Areilza being summarily ditched. And many of his closest colleagues, like him former Francoist bureaucrats, also assumed leading positions within UCD as the expanded electoral alliance was now rechristened.

Suárez's burgeoning personal standing, which he skilfully and ruthlessly promoted through privileged access to state-run television, was crucial to UCD's success at the 1977 general election (*see* Table 2.1). To the surprise of many, it won the largest share of the vote, some distance ahead of the longer established parties of the left. So swift had this process been that it was not until later the same year that UCD formally converted itself into a party in its own right.

Its 1977 victory allowed UCD, and above all Suárez, to steer the process of transition over the next few crucial years. In particular it had the largest representation – three members out of seven – on the committee which drafted the Constitution [1.1.1]. Yet there as in other forums the government genuinely consulted with the chief opposition parties. In part this was forced, as UCD never enjoyed an overall parliamentary majority. But its willingness to compromise was also in part voluntary, motivated by awareness among its leaders of the delicacy of the transition process. In that sense it set the tone of consensus which marked the key period of the transition [0.1.3.3].

Table 2.1 Results of principal parties in general elections, 1977–96

		1977	1979	1982	1986	1989	1993	1996
Turnout	%	79	68	80	71	70	76	78
Democratic Centre	V	6310	6289	1385				
Union (UCD)	P	36.4	35.0	6.5				
	S	166	168	11				
Social and Democratic	V			601	1839	1618	413	
Centre (CDS)	P			2.9	9.2	8.0	1.8	
	S			2	19	14	0	
Spanish Socialist	V	5372	5470	10127	8902	8116	9076	9319
Party (PSOE)	P	29.3	30.5	48.4	44.6	39.9	38.7	37.5
	S	110	121	202	184	175	159	141
People's Party (PP)[1]	V	1505	1068	5543	5248	5286	8170	9659
	P	8.3	6.0	26.5	26.3	26.0	34.8	38.9
	S	16	9	107	105	107	141	156
Spanish Communist	V	1710	1911	845				
Party (PCE)	P	9.4	10.7	4.0				
	S	19	23	4				
United Left (IU)	V				892	1859	2246	2630
	P				4.5	9.1	9.6	10.6
	S				7	17	18	21
Convergence and Union	V	522	484	773	1012	1030	1162	1144
(CiU)[2]	P	2.8	2.6	3.7	5.1	5.1	5.0	4.6
	S	11	8	12	18	18	17	16
Basque Nationalist	V	296	275	396	309	252	290	317
Party (PNV)[3]	P	1.7	1.5	1.9	1.6	1.3	1.2	1.3
	S	8	7	8	6	5	5	5

Notes: [1] In 1977 and 1982 – People's Alliance (AP); in 1979 – Democratic Coalition (CD); in
1986 – People's Coalition (CP).
[2] Leading Catalan regionalist party.
[3] Leading Basque regionalist party.
V = votes (in thousands); P = per cent poll; S = seats.

2.2.2 UCD:decline and disintegration

At the next general election in March 1979, the first held under the new
Constitution, UCD again emerged victorious. However, by then divisions
within the party were already apparent. At one level they were personal.
UCD's origins meant that it was a party of factions headed by one or more

powerful 'barons', each jealous of their own status and many resentful of Suárez and his closest advisers, a group referred to as the 'plumbers'. Since the party had virtually no organisational structure or mass membership the leadership was highly dependent on the barons at election times, and even to control its own MPs. It was in the parliamentary party that divisions between supporters of different barons came together, explosively, with those between the party's four main ideological factions.

The first was closely linked to the Catholic Church, which none the less had denied it support in forming a separate party [4.1.2.1]. These Christian Democrats were correspondingly conservative on social issues, but favoured the state intervention in the economy typical of the German 'social market economy' [1.1.2]. The liberal faction, by contrast, favoured a greater degree of social change, being less influenced by the Church if not mildly anticlerical. Economically they were concerned to remove the many restrictions imposed on business by the former regime. They were accordingly much less enthusiastic about the 'social' aspects of the German model. The Social Democrats, the third main grouping, were largely in agreement with the liberals on social issues but strongly opposed to them on economic ones. There they wanted to see not reduced state intervention but an expansion in welfare state provision and economic planning.

The last of UCD's factions was a group of former francoist bureaucrats. Apart from Suárez himself its most prominent member was Rodolfo Martín Villa, a key figure in successive UCD cabinets. Not known as liberalisers before Franco's death [0.1.3.1], their concern seems to have been above all with avoiding insurrection by either the left or the military – with the process of transition rather than with its ends. By 1979 that process was largely complete in terms of institutional changes. With the rules of political play established in the Constitution, attention moved to more detailed and controversial issues. This change was fatal for UCD. In particular, the attempt to regulate divorce opened up splits between the Christian and Social Democrat factions which proved unbridgeable. Lacking strong discipline, the parliamentary party began to disintegrate, with individual deputies, or small groups led by a particular baron, defecting to parties to both right and left.

In the midst of this disintegration, in January 1981, Suárez resigned, for reasons which seem to have been connected with pressures from the various 'barons'. Thereafter UCD was kept in power, indeed in being, only by the opposition's fear that overthrowing the government would provoke a second coup attempt like that which took place during the inauguration of Leopoldo Calvo Sotelo as the new Prime Minister [0.1.3.3].

Under his leadership UCD's collapse continued inexorably. By summer 1982 it had lost a third of its deputies; Calvo Sotelo was forced to call an early election at which UCD suffered a catastrophic defeat. Reduced to a mere 11 seats in the Congress it had previously controlled, UCD survived for only one year before it was dissolved.

2.2.3 Collapse of the centre

Suárez himself had abandoned UCD before the 1982 election to set up a new party, the Social and Democratic Centre (*Centro Democrático y Social – CDS*). The 'and' is important; the oft-repeated intention of UCD's former leader was not to found a left-of-centre 'social democratic' party but to re-occupy the centre ground of politics he felt his old one had latterly abandoned. The CDS fared very poorly at the 1982 election, but considerably better four years later (*see* Table 2.1). With the right-wing People's Alliance in seemingly endless crisis [2.4.1], the CDS appeared to have a real chance of replacing it as the main opposition party.

However, in 1988 Suárez made a crucial tactical error. In a number of major cities the CDS joined with the Alliance to oust Socialist administrations which lacked an overall majority. This step effectively undermined its claim to represent a 'pure centre' (*centro-centro*), distinct from both left and right. Thereafter its electoral fortunes deteriorated rapidly; at the 1993 general election it failed to win a single seat. By then Suárez himself had admitted defeat and retired from active politics. Without its founder the party effectively withered away.

The CDS's relative success at the 1986 election was won in the face of competition for the centre-ground. The Democratic Reform Party (*Partido Reformista Democrático – PRD*) was set up in 1983. Although it contained a number of leading figures from UCD's liberal faction, the driving force behind the new party's creation was the Catalan regionalist party Convergence and Union [3.2.2], whose deputy leader, Miquel Roca, was the PRD's effective head. Roca, one of the 'fathers of the Constitution' [1.1.1], enjoyed considerable prestige throughout Spain. However, the PRD was unable to capitalise on this, or on the favourable treatment it received from the banks when granting loans for the 1986 campaign. It captured only 1 per cent of the votes, failing to win any seats, and was thereafter quietly dissolved.

The demise of the PRD and the CDS has left Spain without a specifically centrist party. Today the country appears to have an established two-party system (*bipartidismo*), in which both major contenders themselves continually seek to occupy the centre ground. In those circumstances it is unlikely that a successor to UCD will emerge. None the less, the party remains an important point of reference in Spanish politics for a number of reasons. First, its fate serves as an awful warning to others of the dangers of factionalism, a warning that has clearly been taken to heart by the country's leading parties in their insistence on strong internal discipline. On a more positive note, the consensual approach to politics associated with UCD is often compared positively to more recent experience, both by commentators and in responses to opinion polls. Indeed, during its rise to power in the mid-1990s, the People's Party made much of the notion that it was UCD's heir [2.4.3].

However, while such comparisons may be electorally useful they are misleading. In UCD's day the 'centre' had a meaning specific to the period;

it was occupied by those who wished to bring about democracy without the radical change desired by the left. Later, in effect, the centre was associated with the person of Suárez. Neither of these definitions retains any meaning today.

2.3 THE SOCIALIST PARTY

Without doubt the party that has exercised greatest influence over the contemporary development of Spain, which it governed from 1982 to 1996, is the Spanish Socialist Party (*Partido Socialista Obrero Español – PSOE*). The PSOE is also by some way the country's oldest party, having been founded in 1879. Long associated with the strict personal integrity and rigid Marxist beliefs of its first leader, the Madrid printer Pablo Iglesias, the PSOE was changed as much by its lengthy period in office as was Spain itself.

2.3.1 From underground to office

During the Franco era the PSOE's leadership went into exile, and largely refrained from promoting underground opposition to the Franco regime. Its attitude provoked growing resentment among members within Spain. In 1974 a group of these took control over the party at its 25th Congress, held at Suresnes in southern France. A young lawyer, known by the codename of *Isidro*, was elected leader. Together with his closest colleagues – most of them either from the Basque Country or, like himself, from Seville – *Isidro*, whose real name was Felipe González, was to dominate the PSOE's development for the next two decades.

The strength of his grip on the party became quite clear in 1979. At that year's 28th Congress delegates rejected a proposal to drop the term 'Marxist' from the party's self-description, a step its leader considered vital if the party was to avoid scaring off potential voters. González promptly resigned. Before the year was out he had been overwhelmingly re-elected, and his proposal approved, at a special Congress hastily convened when it became clear that his opponents could offer no alternatives.

By 1979 the Socialists had already established themselves as Spain's second largest party, having clearly won the struggle with the more fancied Communists for left-wing votes (*see* Table 2.1). That same year they won control over most of Spain's important towns and cities at the first democratic local elections. In many councils their control depended on a mutual-support agreement with the Communists (*pacto municipal*). This agreement indicated the thrust of the PSOE's strategy at the time; to harness the support of all those who felt that under the then UCD government social and economic change had been too slow and too limited. Already, in 1977, the PSOE had absorbed the smaller People's Socialist Party (*Partido Socialista Popular – PSP*), whose leader Enrique Tierno Galván was a highly successful Mayor of Madrid from 1979 to his death in 1986. When UCD's social democratic faction broke away in 1980 [2.2.2], it too was absorbed into the PSOE. Its leader, Francisco Fernández Ordóñez, who had served under both Franco and Suárez, later concluded his career as González's Foreign Minister.

The Socialists also received a steady flow of prominent defectors from the Communists, by now in seemingly permanent crisis [2.5.1]. Crucially, the PSOE also now attracted a large proportion of their voters, particularly young, educated professionals previously influenced by the Communists' role in opposition to the Franco regime. Such voters proved highly susceptible to the PSOE campaign at the 1982 general election. Its slogan – *Por el cambio* (Vote for change) – captured perfectly the image of non-ideological radicalism assiduously cultivated by González.

Along with the collapse of UCD [2.2.2], the attraction of former Communist voters was the key to the PSOE's sweeping 1982 victory; the ten million votes it received remains the highest total ever achieved at a Spanish election. With the help of the electoral system [1.3.1], they were sufficient to provide a handsome overall parliamentary majority. The election date, 28 October 1982 (*28-O*), marks a watershed in Spanish politics. Not only did it confirm that the transition was over [0.1.3.3]. It also ushered in a period of 14 years during which the PSOE dominated Spanish government and politics to an extraordinary degree.

2.3.2 A party of government

The PSOE's dominance was strengthened in 1983, when it increased its hold on local government and also won control of most of the newly created autonomous regions. Thereafter, the collapse of UCD [2.2.2], and the troubles of the main opposition party [2.4.1, 2.4.2], meant that for some years the PSOE faced no effective nation-wide opposition. In any case, the country's new institutional structure, and specifically the relationship between parliament and government [1.4.1], had been designed on the assumption that no party would enjoy an overall parliamentary majority. Even a strong opposition would have been hard pressed to exercise effective control over a party as disciplined and dynamic as the PSOE of the 1980s.

In that situation, the PSOE leadership fell into practices that verged on the anti-democratic, showing scant regard for any opinions other than its own. On the other hand, it also provided the sort of 'strong', active government UCD had so patently been incapable of providing after 1979. During the 1980s enormous, and badly needed progress, was made on a variety of fronts; taxation [5.2.3] and education [7.2] were reformed, industry was restructured [5.1.2], the welfare state overhauled [8.1.2, 8.2.1] and infrastructure, especially new roads, constructed. In effect, the PSOE presided over Spain's belated modernisation.

Indeed, Spain's socio-economic modernisation came to be the party's central concern, along with another for which modernisation was the prerequisite; entry into the European Community. The successful completion of this process came with Spain's accession on 1 January 1986. The architects of entry were the Foreign Minister, Fernando Morán, and Manuel Marín, for whom the success proved to be a springboard to higher things – he subsequently became a senior member of the EU Commission.

The emphasis on modernisation and EC entry brought a considerable change in the PSOE's image. The party increasingly sought to portray itself as the defender of national interests, as the 'party of Spain'. This was very different from its traditional claim to represent the interests of manual workers, for many of whom the González governments' economic policies had severe consequences [5.1.2]. Their resentment was reflected in the progressive estrangement between the PSOE and the Socialist trade union confederation, the UGT, which reached crisis proportions with the 1988 general strike [4.2.3.3].

An important milestone in the PSOE's transformation was its abandonment of opposition to Spanish membership of NATO [0.2.3]. Once the party was in power, its leaders became convinced that withdrawal from the Atlantic Alliance was incompatible with their new goals, in particular entry into the EC. By the time that González fulfilled its promise to call a referendum on the issue, he and his party had reversed their stance and advocated continued membership. The comfortable victory of their 'yes' campaign, in defiance of opinion polls, provided striking evidence of the influence which the PSOE had come to exercise not just over government but also over Spanish public opinion.

The NATO U-turn, and the direction of government economic policy caused considerable concern in the party. In 1985 Morán, who opposed the move, was removed as Foreign Secretary. At the same time the Economics and Finance Minister Miguel Boyer also left, as an apparent sop to the party's left. Yet left-wing dissidents in the party, organised in the faction Socialist Left (*Izquierda Socialista*), never became more than a minor irritant to the leadership. Indeed, Boyer's successor, Carlos Solchaga, was equally firm in pursuing policies closer to Thatcherite neo-liberalism than traditional socialist ideas.

In any case, his personal success at the NATO referendum allowed González to crush easily any dissent apparent in 1986. His prestige was further enhanced by a comfortable triumph in that year's general election. In 1989 González again led the PSOE to victory, in an election called almost a year early to benefit from the economic boom that followed EC entry [5.1.2]. By then the PSOE's vote had been eroded to the extent that it won exactly half the Congress seats, thus technically losing its overall majority. Nevertheless, with the opposition split, this was a purely academic consideration. The PSOE ended the 1980s as it had spent most of the decade – in unassailable command of the political scene.

2.3.3 *Felipismo* and the González–Guerra partnership

Just as in the UK, domination of politics in the 1980s by one party and its leader brought a new word into the language. Unlike Thatcherism, however, *felipismo* is not associated with a clearly defined political or economic doctrine. To its supporters it suggested dynamic pragmatism, untrammelled by outdated ideology: to its opponents, unprincipled opportunism. For both groups, the term is associated above all with the person of Felipe González.

The other key feature of *felipismo* was the strong control exercised by González over his party. This hold was the result of the party's tight discipline and strong organisational base. In the main industrial areas, where the PSOE branch office (*Casa del Pueblo*) had long been a feature of local life, this was well established. Elsewhere, it was rapidly built up during the 1980s. Especially in these areas of newer Socialist activity, the increasing proportion of members dependent on the party for their political future and even livelihood made it relatively easy for the leadership to exercise control [2.1.2], especially when it proved so successful electorally. As a result, and with the partial exception of the Catalan and, to a lesser extent, the Basque regional sections [3.2.2, 3.3.3], the PSOE is a highly centralised party. Firm control is exercised by the National Executive (*Comisión Ejecutiva*), and above all by González as its general secretary. Particularly in the early years of his leadership, however, he was heavily dependent on a close partnership with one colleague, Alfonso Guerra.

Like González from Seville, Alfonso Guerra became deputy general secretary of the party in 1974. He soon proved himself a consummate party manager; it was his manipulation of the party apparatus which ensured González's victory in the second 1979 Congress [2.3.1]. In 1982 Guerra was appointed Deputy Prime Minister, with no ministerial portfolio [1.4.3]. This left him free for another task; ensuring that party and government worked together, under the orders of their common leader. It also gave Guerra access to unprecedented powers of patronage, which he used to strengthen even further his vice-like grip over the PSOE.

The other aspect of Guerra's key importance was electoral. On the one hand, he masterminded all the PSOE's election campaigns from 1977 to 1989. On the other, he himself was a major electoral asset, adept at appealing to traditional Socialist voters with biting attacks on the better-off. Such rhetoric provided a vital counterbalance to González's talk of modernisation and Europe. In this as other respects, the PSOE's two leading personalities complemented each other in a well-matched partnership (*binomio*).

Hence the importance for the PSOE of the breakdown in this partnership. It began with a scandal involving one of Guerra's brothers. Despite holding no government or even party post, Juan Guerra had used official premises in Seville while acquiring a considerable fortune with suspicious ease. When this 'Guerra affair' first broke, González threatened to resign if his deputy were obliged to do so. However, as political and media pressure increased, the premier backtracked. In 1991 he accepted Guerra's resignation as Deputy PM.

As a result, even though Guerra remained deputy general secretary of the party, he lost his key role of link between it and the government. What is more, relations between the two partners deteriorated rapidly. Guerra increasingly aligned himself with those in and close to the PSOE who were unhappy with the government's policies, especially in the economic sphere [2.3.2]. At the same time, his break with González prompted those who resented Guerra's hold over the party apparatus to challenge it. The resultant internal struggles pitted this group, known as modernisers (*renovadores*), against those loyal to Guerra (*guerristas*).

The situation was complicated by the fact that some modernisers were also worried about the PSOE's apparent lack of ideological direction. They accordingly became involved in a grandiose review of party policy, carried out under Guerra's overall direction. However, the product of this process, the so-called 'Programme 2000', proved to contain little in the way of new ideas. Thereafter the modernisers' aim was increasingly seen to be control over the party apparatus.

For that González's personal support was crucial, and the general secretary long refused to give it. However, in early 1993 criticism of the government from Guerra's supporters became so overt that it forced González to act. He exercised his power to dissolve Parliament and call a general election. This in itself forced the party to unite behind the government, especially given the concentration of Guerra's supporters in elected or other political posts. Moreover, in an unprecedented step, González took personal command of the campaign, bypassing Guerra's traditional election-time role.

The surprise victory won by the Socialists in 1993 [2.3.4] was thus, even more than the 1986 NATO referendum, a personal triumph for González. Thereafter he threw his enhanced prestige behind Guerra's opponents. At the 33rd party Congress later in the year they lost their control over the party executive; the same process was later repeated at regional and local level throughout most of the country. Even though Guerra himself was still deputy general secretary his power had been broken.

2.3.4 Corruption and crisis

In the early 1990s the PSOE faced mounting problems. In addition to the rift between González and Guerra it had effectively split with its traditional trade union ally [4.2.3.3]. The economy was entering a severe downturn [5.1.3]. Most importantly the Juan Guerra affair [2.3.3] had proved to be only one in a continuing line of damaging corruption scandals. These successive affairs (*casos*) involved mainly the abuse of public funds but also security matters. They forced the resignation not only of senior administrators linked to the Socialists, but also of several ministers. The PSOE's own apparatus was also directly implicated, because of its involvement in a number of related party-funding scandals [2.1.3].

Corruption formed the focus of opposition attacks at the 1993 election, by which time an economic recovery was under way. González's response was to distance himself from the party apparatus, both through the tone of his speeches and by running the campaign personally [2.3.3]. He also offered a public and personal apology for party and government misdeeds, and promised a 'new beginning' if re-elected. He further infuriated Guerra and the party apparatus by placing on the PSOE's slate of candidates a number of 'independents', public figures previously unconnected with the party, the most prominent being the jurists Juan Alberto Belloch and Baltasár Garzón.

These star 'signings' (*fichajes*) apparently boosted the PSOE's appeal. Defying the opinion polls, the party once again emerged victorious from the election, for the fourth time in succession. However, its latest success was won at a considerable cost. This was less because González's approach to the campaign had widened the breach with Guerra; in fact, his victory allowed him finally to break his old partner's hold over the party apparatus [2.3.3]. More important was the subsequent behaviour of one of his star 'signings'.

Both were immediately given important government posts. Belloch was put at the head of a new 'super-ministry' formed by merging the Interior and Justice portfolios [1.4.5]. His rapid rise inevitably provoked jealousies among some of his colleagues. Nevertheless he remained a considerable asset for the party, which he soon joined.

Garzón proved more problematic. Spain's best-known judge, he had become famous through his success in breaking up Galician drug-smuggling rings. Young and photogenic, Garzón played a central role in the PSOE's 1993 campaign, since González indicated that he would be given a free hand to deal with corruption if the party were returned to power. With the election won, however, the hand turned out be less free than the public, and Garzón himself, had been led to expect.

Despite being given a senior post in Belloch's new ministry with 'special' powers of his own, Garzón found his investigations blocked once they threatened senior figures in the PSOE. This applied in particular to alleged government involvement in the 'dirty war' waged against ETA by the so-called Anti-terrorist Liberation Groups (GAL). A frustrated Garzón resigned, and resumed his former career as an examining magistrate attached to the High Court [9.1.3]. His subsequent investigations brought the GAL affair into the very heart of the government, culminating in the 1995 arrest of former Interior Minister, José Barrionuevo [9.4.3]. Speculation mounted that the 'Mister X' with ultimate control over the GAL had been González himself.

In another respect, too, its 1993 election victory proved a poisoned chalice for the PSOE. For the first time the party was forced to govern without an effective overall majority, and thus to seek parliamentary support from other parties. One option, favoured by Guerra and his supporters, was to renew the Communist alliance of the late 1970s [2.3.1]. However, not only was this effectively ruled out by the attitude of the Communists themselves [2.5.2]. It would also have meant changes in economic policy which González was not prepared to contemplate.

The Prime Minister opted instead for an agreement with the principal Catalan and Basque parties. The former became the government's main bulwark over the next two years. Although Convergence and Union (CiU) refused to enter a coalition, as González would have preferred, a parliamentary pact secured the regular support of its votes in Congress, which together with the PSOE's own represented an overall majority.

Even so, the PSOE government was forced to submit itself to much more rigorous parliamentary control of its actions than before. CiU's backing on general policy matters did not extend to preventing creation of various committees of investigation [1.4.1], whose work provided further evidence of financial and other irregularities by senior Socialists. Moreover, CiU itself became increasingly concerned at the implications of associating with an ever more unpopular government. In autumn 1995 it moved to distance itself by refusing to support the following year's budget estimates.

2.3.5 Return to opposition

As a result of his allies' defection, González was forced to call an election for the following spring, which saw his party finally defeated. Yet its defeat proved to be much less comprehensive than generally expected [2.4.3]. In large measure this could be attributed to González himself. Having previously stated that he would not stand for election again, he was eventually obliged to do so by a party conscious that he continued to be its main electoral asset. Even with the GAL allegations hanging over him [2.3.4], he once again proved a formidable campaigner, enormously popular with wide sections of the electorate.

The other main reason for the PSOE's surprisingly strong showing in 1996 was its solid support in certain regions and among particular social groups. This base was very different from that on which its 1982 triumph had been built. Then it had relied above all on two groups; the industrial workforce, anxious for better living conditions, and younger urban dwellers, attracted by the Socialists' progressive image. The PSOE's record in power had ultimately proved disappointing for both these groups. Material prosperity had risen, but workers, especially in older industries, had not been among the main beneficiaries. Since the legalisation of abortion, under strict conditions, in 1983 the party had undertaken few major social reforms. In the 1990s its progressive image was tarnished by controversial law and order legislation [9.4.3]. Corruption scandals [2.3.4], as well as its long hold on power, made it appear to many voters as an old party, the party of the establishment.

During its period in office, however, the PSOE had built up new pillars of support. On the one hand, it could now rely on many votes from employees of a public sector vastly expanded under its rule, and possibly threatened by a right-wing government. On the other, the elderly have come to form a very significant part of the Spanish electorate, and one which the PSOE had been careful to cultivate through allocation of state benefits [8.4.1]. The same applies, on a lesser scale, to the rural poor of the south [5.2.4].

Only in the three southern regions of Extremadura, Castile-La Mancha and Andalusia did the PSOE emerge victorious in 1996. In Andalusia it even won a resounding victory in a regional election held on the same day. These regions remain the most economically backward in the country. Thus, although the Socialists could be encouraged by their 1996 showing in one way, in another the election results were deeply worrying for them. In the 1980s it was the party of modernisation and progress: in the 1990s the PSOE has come to rely electorally on Spain's least dynamic regions and social groups.

Over and above these electoral trends, returning to opposition inevitably proved traumatic for a party so used to power. In the aftermath of its 1996 defeat, voices in the PSOE were heard demanding a 'complete overhaul' of the party (*renovación total*). The demand proved problematic, however. For one thing, it implied admission of past financial irregularities on a scale far greater than the party's upper echelons were prepared to concede. Such change also implied replacement of González as leader – at a time when the 1996 results suggested he remained the party's prime electoral asset, and when the only obvious successor had been ruled out by Javier Solana's appointment as NATO Secretary-General [0.2.3]. As González himself had pointed out before the election, and repeated thereafter, he was 'both a problem and a solution' for the party. Its inability to resolve this dilemma rendered the PSOE a surprisingly ineffectual opposition during its first months out of office.

2.4 THE PEOPLE'S PARTY AND ITS FORERUNNERS

The People's Party (*Partido Popular – PP*) is currently Spain's ruling party. It was elected to power at the general election of 1996, having been previously the largest opposition party; it is not to be confused with the short-lived party of the same name which formed the nucleus of UCD [2.2.1]. In direct contrast to its predecessor in power, the present-day PP is an extremely young party, having adopted its current name only in 1989. Even its direct forerunner, People's Alliance (*Alianza Popular – AP*), was founded little more than 20 years ago. None the less, in many ways the past has been as important for PP as for its Socialist rival, and perhaps even more so.

2.4.1 People's Alliance and People's Coalition

The reason lies in the origins of AP. This was set up in 1976 as an alliance of seven small right-wing groups, none of which was a party in any meaningful sense. Instead they were the personal followings of their respective leaders, parodied as the 'magnificent seven', all of whom had been prominent in the previous regime. Their leader was Manuel Fraga Iribarne, who had served in various of the dictator's cabinets.

One of the regime's 'liberalisers' [0.1.3.1], Fraga none the less favoured a strictly controlled form of democracy. His party campaigned for the 1977 election on a platform of minimal change. Its crushing defeat showed clearly that this line was out of touch with popular feeling (*see* Table 2.1). Thereafter AP and its few deputies took part in the process of drawing up the 1978 Constitution, of which Fraga himself was one of the 'fathers' [1.1.1]. Yet despite this, doubts remained about its commitment to democracy. All its leading figures were wont to express reservations about the changes under way and a number of its MPs failed to vote for the Constitution.

In an attempt to moderate its image, AP formed a new alliance for the 1979 election, incorporating a number of groups and individuals unhappy with or excluded from UCD. This Democratic Coalition performed even worse than AP had done in 1977. The setback prompted Fraga to abandon the idea of trying to compete with UCD as a centre-right option. Over the next few years he set about building a 'great party of the right' (*gran derecha*). His model was the British Conservative Party and his aim to turn AP, like the Tories, into a natural party of government (*mayoría natural*).

Considerable efforts were made to improve AP's organisation, and, indeed, to create a party structure for the first time in much of Spain, with limited success. In fact, the crucial factor in changing the party's fortunes was the disintegration of UCD [2.2.2]. AP profited from this process, first by a steady stream of defections in Parliament, then by a large increase in its vote at the 1982 election. As a result it was transformed from a minor player in the political spectrum into the main, indeed, virtually the only national opposition to the triumphant Socialists.

This in itself allowed AP to reap further benefits, such as the effective support of the Spanish Employers' Confederation, the CEOE [4.2.2]. AP also attracted into a new electoral alliance two splinter parties which had emerged from the wreckage of UCD. They were the Christian Democrat People's Democratic Party (*Partido Demócrata Popular – PDP*), led by Oscar Alzaga, and José Antonio Segurado's tiny Liberal Union, later Liberal Party (*Partido Liberal – PL*). Together with AP these made up the People's Coalition (*Coalición Popular – CP*). These recruits gave a modest boost to CP's appeal, but they also imported into it the problems that had destroyed UCD [2.2.2]. From the outset CP had within itself organised currents of opinion with differing political beliefs and mutually suspicious leaders. It proved unable to fix on a coherent line of opposition to a government whose unpopular economic policies were broadly in line with its own views. Most notoriously, in the 1986 NATO referendum [2.3.2] Fraga called on his supporters to abstain, even though he and his party were staunch supporters of Spanish membership.

Such inconsistency made it easy for the government to play down attacks from CP as opportunistic. At the same time, CP suffered from a lingering impression among large sections of the electorate that it would seek to return to the policies of the Franco regime, especially by restricting individual freedoms. These reservations were linked particularly to the person of Fraga. When CP failed to advance at the 1986 election, commentators spoke of an 'electoral ceiling' (*techo electoral*). By this they meant a level of support (around 25 per cent of the electorate) through which no party led by Fraga could hope to break.

Almost immediately following the 1986 election PDP withdrew from CP. Its leaders criticised CP's policies for being too right-wing, and declared that only a more moderate line offered hope of defeating the PSOE. When, in November, CP performed disastrously in a Basque regional election, Fraga resigned, publicly and emotionally, as AP leader. In January 1987 CP effectively ceased to exist when the PL also abandoned it, leaving AP alone as well as leaderless.

2.4.2 From AP to PP

It was widely expected that Fraga would be succeeded as party chairman by his deputy, Miguel Herrero de Miñón, who before joining AP had been one of UCD's representatives among the 'fathers of the Constitution' [1.1.1]. However, at a special party congress held in January 1987 Herrero's supporters were outmanoeuvred by those of a younger, relatively unknown challenger. Previously AP regional leader in Andalusia, Antonio Hernández Mancha was elected chairman, his choice clearly reflecting a desire among delegates for a fresh start.

This the new leader of the AP attempted to provide by changing the line of its attacks on the government. Whereas Fraga had concentrated on opposing liberal social policies, in areas such as abortion and education, Hernández Mancha focused on the impact of the Socialists' economic policies on less well-off voters [5.1.2]. For an essentially conservative party this was a radical departure which could only have been carried off by a strong, established leader, which Hernández Mancha was not. In addition, his populist line alienated the CEOE leadership [4.2.2].

Given these continuing travails, AP's poor results in the 1987 regional elections were predictable. They also added a further problem for the party – the advance of a number of regionally based parties of the right and centre-right [3.4.3]. In some areas – notably Aragon and Navarre – these even threatened to eclipse AP completely, and so undermine its credibility as a truly national party.

By 1989 Hernández Mancha's support had vanished and he did not even stand for re-election as leader. In desperation, it seemed, the party turned again to Fraga as its chairman. The impression of stagnation was reinforced at the 1989 election, when AP again failed to improve on its 1982 performance, despite the PSOE's deteriorating support. However, two significant changes had indeed taken place. AP no longer existed, having adopted the name of People's Party. And for the first time Fraga had not been his party's candidate for Prime Minister.

Both changes had been agreed, on Fraga's recommendation, at the foregoing party Congress. Their first intention was to remove the 'ceiling' imposed by his own past [2.4.1]. But they also aimed to resolve the dilemma addressed by UCD and CP in different ways but with equal lack of success, the question of how to bring together the three main strands of the Spanish centre-right: elements of the francoist old guard, liberals and Christian Democrats [2.2.2, 2.4.1].

The change in party name was a clear sop to the latter, 'People's Party' being the designation adopted by Christian Democrats in many Western European countries, and in the European Parliament. There AP's representatives had previously sat together with the British Conservatives; now Fraga agreed that they would enter the Christian Democrat group, by far the largest on the centre-right. He also brought into the party leadership an internationally known Christian Democrat, Marcelino Oreja, formerly chairman of the Council of Europe and later a European Commissioner.

These various moves were intended to give the newly-born PP the image of a modern, mainstream European party, linked to the highly successful Christian Democratic parties in Germany and other EU countries. In terms of economic policy, if anything the PP shifted away from Christian Democrat ideas towards more liberal ones, a move which enabled it to regain the support of the CEOE. The resultant mix of social conservatism and economic liberalism brought the PP ideologically close to the British Tories, but in their contemporary, Thatcherite guise rather than the traditional brand Fraga had always admired.

The problem of Fraga's own person was solved by removing him with honour from the national political scene. In 1989 he headed the PP's slate at the Galician regional election; winning an overall majority he withdrew to govern his own home region. At his party's 1990 Congress – the first held under the initials PP – he was elected to the special post of 'founding chairman' (*presidente fundador*). He was replaced as party leader by José María Aznar, the man Fraga himself had chosen to be PP's candidate for Prime Minister the previous year.

2.4.3 Aznar and the PP's rise to power

Under Aznar the PP began a slow but steady recovery. The new leader had three factors in his favour. The party's disastrous financial situation had been greatly eased by the new provisions for state funding introduced in 1987 [2.1.3]. The PP's main rival for centre-right votes committed a fatal tactical error [2.2.3]; its subsequent decline into obscurity left the PP as the only real alternative to the PSOE. Finally the Socialists' increasing problems made them much more vulnerable than before [2.3.4].

On the debit side, Aznar experienced considerable difficulty in establishing himself as a credible leader in his own right. Although he 'won' the first of his televised debates with González in 1993, he continued to lag behind the Prime Minister in popular esteem. Given the highly personalised focus of Spanish politics, this inevitably made it hard for the PP to turn itself into a genuine alternative government (*alternativa de poder*). That factor was crucial in its failure to confirm opinion poll forecasts and win the 1993 general election. Even so, its results were by far the best achieved by the party or any of its predecessors.

The other main factor in the narrow 1993 defeat was the PSOE's tactic, orchestrated by Deputy PM Alfonso Guerra, of insinuating that the PP was still closely linked to the Franco regime, in its ideas and also in its personnel. In response, Aznar stepped up his efforts to bring forward a new generation of leaders, like himself too young to have been involved with the previous regime. At the same time, he continued working to give the PP the strong, nation-wide basis AP had never fully established.

In conjunction with PP general secretary Francisco Alvarez Cascos he achieved considerable success in this task. Party membership rose markedly and the party's youth wing, New Generation (*Nuevas Generaciones*) flourished. At the same time, the PP succeeded in marginalising many of the regional centre-right parties which had emerged in the mid-1980s. With the two largest, in Aragon and Navarre, it reached agreements to present joint lists for general elections. As a result of these moves, by the mid-1990s the PP had become the first truly national, truly democratic, genuine party of the right in Spanish history.

Even so, the fact that a basically conservative party remained stronger in the large cities, especially Madrid, than the rural areas and small towns pointed to continuing gaps in the party's organisation relative to that of the PSOE. Ironically, the effect has been similar; whereas the PSOE's dense organisation enables the leadership to exert a high degree of internal control [2.3.3], the PP's less developed structure makes it hard to organise effective opposition to the party elite.

In 1994 Aznar's efforts began to bear fruit. At that year's European election it outpolled the PSOE for the first time in a national contest. At the following year's regional and municipal elections it enjoyed further success, taking control of 12 out of 17 regions, and all the large cities except Corunna and those in the Basque Country and Catalonia. This triumph also had a knock-on effect, in that it brought to public notice a whole series of the party's regional leaders who had previously been largely anonymous. Unlike the old UCD barons [2.2.2], they are clearly subordinate to the party's Madrid leadership.

Avoiding the errors of both AP and UCD has been a clear priority for Aznar. On the other hand, in the run-up to the 1996 general election – a time when the twentieth anniversary of Franco's death brought the transition into the spotlight – he was at pains to identify his party with positive memories of UCD. Its Congress held in January of that year was dominated by the notion of the PP as a 'centre' party. While that may have had positive effects, it also allowed the PSOE once more to exploit the past in the subsequent campaign. On this occasion the focus of Socialist innuendo was the influence allegedly exercised over the PP by the Opus Dei organisation, whose close involvement with the Franco regime is notorious [4.1.2.2].

That may have been one reason why the PP's victory in the 1996 election turned out to be much narrower than expected. In the event, the party failed to win an overall majority. It was over two months before Aznar was able to negotiate the necessary parliamentary support to form a government. To do so he was forced to make a number of concessions to the Catalan CiU which had previously maintained the Socialists in power [2.3.4].

After two months of negotiations Aznar was able to announce his first government. Apart from his two deputies, Alvarez Cascos and Rodrigo Rato [1.4.3], the other key figures were two experienced politicians. Abel Matutes, a former European Commissioner, became Foreign Minister, while Jaime Mayor Oreja, a Basque whose uncle replaced Matutes in that role after helping found the PP [2.4.2], was given the task of dealing with ETA as Interior Minister.

In policy terms, Aznar immediately stated his intention to maintain and even intensify efforts to ensure Spain met strict criteria for European Monetary Union [5.1.3]. Partly to help make the necessary savings, partly from free market principles, he also moved to reduce direct state intervention in the economy [5.4.1]. Irrespective of its economic validity, his action soon provoked public disquiet, since signs soon emerged of a close connection between the PP and business interests favoured in the sell-off of former state assets. Such signs were a disappointment to voters who had hoped that the change in government would bring a solution to the problem of interest-peddling, whether for personal or party advantage [2.1.3].

2.5 THE COMMUNIST PARTY AND UNITED LEFT

The third largest force in Spain's Parliament is United Left (*Izquierda Unida – IU*). IU is in fact an alliance involving both parties and individual members. By far its largest component, however, is the Spanish Communist Party (*Partido Comunista de España – PCE*). Indeed, it is fair to say that IU is to a large extent a vehicle for the PCE, the existence of which reflects the latter's failure to make a significant impact on Spanish politics in its own right.

2.5.1 Communist failure

This failure contrasts with expectations at the time of Franco's death. Both the PCE and outside observers believed that the party would emerge as a major political force – that was why its legalisation by the Suárez government before the 1977 election was such a delicate moment in the transition [0.1.3.2]. The PCE had been the only force to undertake significant opposition activity throughout Spain and had close links to the Workers' Commissions, the strongest trade union federation [4.2.3.1]. Many younger educated Spaniards outside its traditional working-class base had been attracted by its activism. However, these advantages proved illusory, for a variety of reasons.

The emergence of so-called Euro-communism in the 1970s caused turmoil in Western Communist parties. At the very time of Spain's transition to democracy the PCE was hit by deep internal divisions. Furthermore, it had been portrayed for 40 years by the regime propaganda as the incarnation of evil and chiefly to blame for the Civil War; even many on the left had bitter memories of its behaviour then. Alone of the major party leaders, the PCE's Santiago Carrillo was old enough to have participated in that conflict.

The desire felt by most Spaniards to bury the memory of the Civil War was a lesson read by many into the results of the 1977 election (*see* Table 2.1). Both then and in 1979 the PCE performed poorly. In 1982 it suffered a further catastrophic defeat; many former supporters, especially those who had seen the PCE essentially as a means of opposing Franco, now opted to cast a tactical vote (*voto útil*) for the Socialists in order to ensure a government of the left.

In the mid-1980s the PCE was racked by internal dissent, and suffered several splits [2.6]. After the 1982 débâcle Carrillo resigned and was replaced as general secretary by the much younger Gerardo Iglesias. But he proved unable to turn the party's fortunes around, at a time when the euphoria of the PSOE's arrival in power rendered a left-wing opposition seemingly superfluous. The 1986 NATO referendum gave the PCE a fresh opportunity since it was the only major party to oppose the government outright, and was strongly represented on the Citizens' Platform (*Plataforma Ciudadana*) which coordinated the 'no' campaign. Although this campaign was ultimately unsuccessful [2.3.2], it did attract considerably more support than the PCE had proved able to do at elections. The party's leadership attempted to capitalise on this, by forming a broad grouping of those involved in the Platform to fight the 1986 general election.

2.5.2 United Left: division and isolation

The new grouping was christened United Left (*Izquierda Unida*), and succeeded in marginally improving on the Communists' vote four years before. Later in 1986 IU was given a more formal structure. Originally seven parties formed part of it, but, other than the PCE, only one proved of any lasting importance – the Socialist Action Party (*Partido de Acción Socialista – Pasoc*), made up of PSOE dissidents.

During the late 1980s the collapse of Communist regimes in Eastern Europe made it difficult for IU to make electoral headway, given its domination by the PCE. On the other hand, it received a fresh impulse from the same direction in the shape of a new, more dynamic leader. This was Julio Anguita, the Mayor of Cordoba and known as the 'Red Caliph' because of his success in turning the city into a Communist electoral bastion. Elected PCE general secretary in 1988, the following year he took over as IU's 'general coordinator', or effective leader. Along with the unpopularity of the government, Anguita's high standing among voters was the main reason why, after relatively disappointing election results in 1989, IU harboured hopes of better ones in 1993.

The heart attack Anguita suffered during the campaign was accordingly especially damaging for IU, which again failed to perform up to its hopes. On the other hand, Anguita's rapid recovery brought re-emergence of the problems caused by his intransigence in two respects. One was his refusal to allow dissolution of the PCE into IU, as a step into making the latter a party in its own right. The other was Anguita's insistence on pursuing an unrelentingly hard line against the PSOE, refusing absolutely to cooperate with the Socialists unless they radically changed their economic policies. He was especially harsh in his criticism of the various corruption scandals which affected the Socialists in the 1990s.

In Andalusia IU went so far as to join with the conservative PP in forcing the Socialist regional government to resign. This step gave substance to damaging accusations from the PSOE, who claimed that IU was involved in a 'pincer movement' (*pinza*) on the party, an unholy alliance of left and right that favoured only the latter. IU's strategy backfired at the resultant regional election, held on the same day as the 1996 general one, since the PSOE was returned with an increased majority.

The Socialists' criticisms were mirrored by widespread concern within IU, embracing dissidents in the PCE itself, Pasoc and the faction known as New Left (*Nueva Izquierda*). These modernisers (*renovadores*) wished to see IU take a more flexible attitude to possible alliances with the PSOE, and to place more stress on new issues, such as feminist and environmentalist ones. Their main leaders were ex-Socialist Pablo Castellano, Cristina Almeida, a combative and popular Madrid lawyer and Diego López Garrido.

However, the modernisers have been unable to break the grip on IU of those loyal to the Anguita leadership (*oficialistas*). Ultimately the reason for this is that, of the groups within IU, only the PCE has a well-established organisation. Moreover, like other Communist Parties it is strongly centralist in operation. IU's own structure is weak and ill-defined, a fact that not only makes change more difficult but presents problems at election times.

An exception to this general picture is the situation in Catalonia, which has traditionally had its own Communist Party, the PSUC [3.2.1]. Similarly, Initiative for Catalonia (IC), of which the PSUC is the main component, remains semi-independent of IU [3.2.2]. Under the leadership of Rafael Ribó, IC and the PSUC have moved towards complete integration. They have also gone much further than IU's national leadership in cooperating with environmentalist groups [2.6]. Although IC's results in Catalonia remain below those of IU in Spain as a whole, they have shown a stronger upward trend in recent years.

On the other hand, Ribó's refusal to heed the wishes of the PCE leadership have opened up yet another division within IU, this time along territorial lines. In 1996 these internal problems were again decisive in preventing IU from capitalising on the discredit into which the Socialist government had fallen. Even so, a modest advance consolidated IU's position as Spain's third party which, given the poll's indecisive result, made a PSOE–IU coalition mathematically possible. Yet so poor were relations between the two main parties of the left that this possibility was barely broached. In effect, its intransigent line meant that IU's influence on the new government's shape and policies was negligible.

2.6 MINOR PARTIES

Some smaller parties were heavily involved in the negotiations that preceded the formation of a new government after the 1996 election; indeed, it was their support which enabled Aznar finally to assemble the requisite majority in the vote of investiture. However, they were all regionally based. Apart from the three largest nation-wide parties (PP, PSOE and IU), none won a seat in either House of Parliament. In recent years the most successful minor parties have in fact been two maverick formations led by controversial business figures: the Grouping (*Agrupación*) set up by José María Ruiz Mateos and the Independent Liberal Group (*Grupo Independiente Liberal – GIL*) led by Jesús Gil y Gil.

A general lack of awareness about environmental issues [6.3.2] has meant that Spain has as yet not experienced a phenomenon apparent elsewhere in Western Europe; the emergence of a significant environmentalist party. In 1986 and 1989 no less than five such groupings stood, none receiving more than 2 per cent of the votes. In 1993 both the number of parties and their support fell, the two largest groupings – the Greens and the Ecologists – winning less than 1 per cent between them. Three years later the largest purely environmentalist grouping, the European Greens won under 60000 votes throughout Spain (just 0.2 per cent of those cast).

In 1996, admittedly, some environmentalists stood in a loose alliance with United Left [2.5.2]. In Catalonia these links are much closer than elsewhere in Spain. For the 1995 regional election there the Catalan Greens (*Els Verds – EV*) stood in formal electoral alliance with IC, the semi-autonomous Catalan section of IU [2.5.2]. The venture was repeated at the 1996 general election, when IC–EV won 8 per cent of the votes in the region. Relative to the previous such poll, that represented a considerably better result for both partners than those achieved in Spain as a whole.

Nor have the extremes of either right or left made any significant impact on Spanish politics since 1975. Both have been divided into numerous tiny groupings (*grupúsculos*), many ephemeral. This has been particularly true on the left. Immediately following the legalisation of parties in 1976 an enormous number of small revolutionary groups professing Trotskyist, Maoist and other revolutionary ideas sprang up. In total these received some 3 per cent of the votes cast at the 1979 general election. Subsequently they have all sunk into insignificance or disappeared altogether.

So too have two parties which in the 1980s split off from the Communist Party (PCE), and which were briefly of minor importance. The Communist Party of the Peoples of Spain (*Partido Comunista de los Pueblos de España – PCPE*), led by Ignacio Gallego, left the PCE in disagreement with its abandonment of strict Communist orthodoxy under Santiago Carrillo [2.5.1]. The PCPE later joined United Left [2.5.2], before falling into oblivion. The second such party was formed by Carrillo himself, after he too left the PCE. The ironically titled Spanish Workers' Party-Communist Unity (*Partido de los Trabajadores de España-Unidad Comunista – PTE-UC*) was eventually dissolved by its leader, who advised his few remaining followers to join the PSOE.

The far right has, if anything, been even less successful, although National Union (*Unión Nacional – UN*) did win a seat in Congress, in 1979. Yet even then UN, which explicitly advocated to a return to Franco-style authoritarian rule, won only 1.9 per cent of the votes. More recently UN's leader, Blas Piñar, has been associated with the groupings New Force (*Fuerza Nueva – FN*) and National Front (*Frente Nacional – also FN*). The latter was consciously modelled on Jean Marie Le Pen's party of the same name in France, but has failed to achieve anything like the same level of support. Indeed, in view of its lack of success, the Spanish extreme right has largely withdrawn from electoral politics since 1986. It does, however, have a presence in the worrying problem of quasi-organised youth violence, associated especially with skinhead gangs [8.4.2].

2.7 GLOSSARY

28-O m	28 October 1982 (first PSOE general election victory)
3-M m	3 March 1996 (first PP general election victory)
6-J m	6 June 1993 (fourth and final PSOE general election victory)
abstencionismo m	tendency to/practice of abstaining; abstention rate
afiliación f	membership
agrupación local f	local (party) branch
alternativa de poder f	alternative government
barón m	party baron, powerful faction leader
base electoral f	electoral support (of a party)
bases fpl	rank and file members
binomio m	partnership
bipartidismo m	two-party system
cacique m	(corrupt) local party boss
campaña electoral f	election campaign
cargo m	post, office; office-holder
caso m	affair, scandal
centro-centro m	pure (political) centre
chaqueteo m	party-hopping
coalición electoral f	electoral alliance
Comisión Ejecutiva f	National Executive (of party)
Congreso Federal m	National Conference (of party)
consenso m	consensus, spirit of compromise
cristiano-demócrata m	Christian Democrat

cuota de afiliación f	membership fee
cúpula f	upper echelons (of party)
democristiano m	Christian Democrat
desgaste m	loss of popularity (as a result of holding office)
elecciones anticipadas fpl	early election
elecciones generales/legislativas fpl	general election
electorado m	electorate, voters
federación f	regional section of PSOE
felipismo m	personalised leadership style of F. González
Ferraz	Madrid street, location of PSOE headquarters
fichaje m	signing; prominent personality incorporated onto party's slate of candidates
financiación f	funding
fontaneros mpl	'plumbers', A. Suárez's group of political advisers
Génova	Madrid street, location of PP headquarters
gobierno de coalición m	coalition government
gran derecha f	great party of the right
grupo parlamentario m	parliamentary party
grupúsculo m	microparty
guerrista m	supporter of A. Guerra in PSOE internal disputes
independiente m	non-party member brought onto party slate or appointed to political office
Juventudes Socialistas fpl	Young Socialists (PSOE youth wing)
mayoría natural f	natural party of government
militante mf	(party) member, activists
Movimiento m	Franco regime's state-party
Nuevas Generaciones fpl	New Generation (PP youth wing)
obrerismo m	traditional working-class socialism
oficialista mf	supporter of J. Anguita in IU internal disputes
pacto municipal m	mutual support pact in local government
participación electoral f	(election) turnout
partido de cargos m	party largely made up of office-holders
partitocracia f	state dominated by parties
pinza f	pincer movement; tacit alliance of IU and PP to attack PSOE
presidente fundador m	founding chairman (of PP), honorary title given to M. Fraga
programa electoral m	election manifesto
referéndum de la OTAN m	1986 NATO referendum
renovación total f	complete overhaul (of a party, or other organisation)
renovador m	moderniser (in PSOE or IU)
siete magníficos mpl	'magnificent seven', founders of AP
sopa de siglas f	'alphabet soup', myriad small parties which appeared after legalisation in 1976
tasa de abstención f	abstention rate
techo electoral m	electoral ceiling, level of support party unable to break through
tendencia f	current of opinion, faction (in party)
transfuguismo m	practice of crossing the parliamentary floor, i.e. switching parties
voto útil m	tactical vote/voting

3

REGIONS AND REGIONALISM

Spain is a famously diverse land, partly because of topography and climate. Yet diversity is also the result of the country's belated and partial economic development which, in the late nineteenth century, led to political regionalism, in the form of demands for self-rule in the Basque Country and Catalonia. From then on regional tensions became a running sore in Spanish politics, which Franco's attempts to repress only served to aggravate. This chapter will examine the very different response of the democratic regime installed after his death, as well as the new tensions which it threw up and the further institutional changes they, in turn, have brought about.

First, however, a point of terminology. Throughout, the term 'region' is used in a purely geographical sense, to mean a part of Spain. It is in no sense contrasted with nation, which is understood to be a political and social concept. 'Regionalism' is used to describe political activity based on the notion that the people of a particular region have shared interests best met through some form of self-rule. Movements and parties of this type are often called, by themselves and others, 'nationalist'. Avoidance of that term here is not a comment on the validity of their claims; it merely reflects the fact that the areas in which they are based are regions of Spain, not independent states.

3.1 THE INITIAL ROUND OF DEVOLUTION

Probably no part of the 1978 Constitution has attracted so much interest and praise, inside and outside Spain, as its provisions for regional self-rule. However, it is a mistake to see the regionalised form of state known as the *Estado de las Autonomías* as a major achievement by those who drafted the Constitution – and not only because it is by no means clear that devolution has been an unequivocal success [3.5.3]. Quite simply, the Constitution's architects did not set out to establish a new form of state but to solve a specific political problem.

3.1.1 Regions in the Constitution

High among the concerns of those who drew up the Constitution was the pressure for self-rule in Catalonia and the Basque Country. A major issue in its own right [3.2.1, 3.3.1], this pressure was also closely linked to the danger of military insurrection, since the army was highly sensitive about Spanish national unity and because the security forces were bearing the brunt of terrorism in the Basque Country. The purpose of the Constitution's provisions for the regions was accordingly to strike a delicate balance between satisfying Basque and Catalan demands and provoking the army.

These provisions were contained in the lengthy Title VIII, and it is little wonder that they provided anything but a precise blueprint for nation-wide devolution. In fact they did none of the things that would normally be expected from such a blueprint. They did not define the powers of regional authorities; they did not specify how these were to be funded; they did not even establish a set of regional boundaries.

What the Constitution did do was to stipulate that regions might accede to a degree of limited self-rule if they chose to do so. Any province or group of provinces which could demonstrate the existence of popular demand for devolution would have the right to become an autonomous region (*Comunidad Autónoma – CA*). The mechanism for achieving such status was defined as a Statute of Autonomy. A region's Statute would serve as a sort of 'mini-constitution', establishing institutions of regional government and defining the policy fields in which they could exercise powers, either legislative or executive.

Title VIII also defined upper and lower limits to the extent of such powers. Article 148 listed subject areas in which powers would be assumed by any region becoming autonomous, while Article 149 defined those in which powers were to be reserved to the central government. This arrangement left open the possibility of regions acquiring powers in areas appearing on neither list. There was also provision for central government to devolve its own powers to particular regions by decree.

The complex and imprecise provisions of Title VIII contrasted with those of the Constitution's second Transitional Disposition [1.1.2], devoted to regions which had previously 'approved by referendum a draft Statute of Autonomy'. The formulation was designed to single out the so-called 'historic nationalities' – a term invented to avoid the use of either 'nations' or 'regions' – of Catalonia, the Basque Country and Galicia. These three regions were authorised to assume immediately any powers other than those set out in Article 149, without having to meet the demanding conditions laid down for other regions who wished to do so [3.1.2].

Also separate from the main text of the Constitution was an indication of the particular problems presented by Basque regionalists, who regarded the province of Navarre as an integral part of their national homeland. Yet majority opinion in Navarre was known to oppose incorporation into a Basque autonomous region, and moderate regionalists accepted that this was politically impossible for the foreseeable future. As a gesture to their feelings, the possibility of eventual incorporation was recognised in the fourth Transitional Disposition [1.1.2].

Even before the Constitution was approved, moves were under way to implement Transitional Disposition 2. In the three regions affected, bodies were set up to prepare for devolution (*órganos preautonómicos*) – specifically, to negotiate with the central government over the exact contents of the regions' Statutes. By the autumn of 1979 drafts had been agreed in the crucial Basque and Catalan cases; all that remained was for them to be submitted to regional referendums.

On 25 October 1979 the Basque and Catalan Statutes received overwhelming popular approval. The less pressing nature of Galician demands was reflected in rather slower progress towards an agreed draft Statute, the lower degree of autonomy it conferred and also in low turnout at the subsequent referendum. Held on 21 December 1980, this none the less resulted in acceptance of the devolution proposals.

3.1.2 Fast and slow routes to autonomy

In constitutional terms the devolution process could perfectly well have stopped at that point. Indeed, it may well have been that those who framed the Constitution expected it to do so, or at most to extend only to a few clearly distinctive areas, such as Andalusia. That devolution went much further was principally due to the course of events in Spain's largest and poorest region. They, in turn, were the direct result of the Constitution's complex attempts to keep autonomy to a minimum outside the historic nationalities.

Under these provisions, two 'routes' to self-rule were defined. Article 143 specified a procedure by which regions might accede to the range of powers set out in Article 148 [3.1.1]. It was relatively simple, involving merely approval by sufficient of the region's municipalities. A region which adopted this approach had to wait five years before taking on any further powers, up to the limit set by Article 149. Moreover, it would then have to get parliamentary approval for amending its Statute of Autonomy, a potentially difficult process since Statutes have entrenched status [1.3.3]. Because of this time lapse, the relatively simple route to autonomy set out in Article 143 is known, rather confusingly, as the 'slow route' (*vía lenta*).

In order immediately to acquire a Statute with powers beyond the level of Article 148, regions were required to satisfy much more complex and demanding conditions, set out in Article 151. These included holding a referendum, in which the proposed Statute must be approved not just in the region as a whole but also in each of its provinces. Transitional Disposition 2 [3.1.1] effectively gave the historic nationalities a head start on this 'fast route' (*vía rápida*).

Andalusia's leading politicians were determined that their own region should join the three frontrunners in obtaining extensive autonomy immediately. A Statute along these lines was drawn up, and agreed with representatives of the central authorities. On 28 February 1980 the text was submitted to a referendum, obtaining a clear majority in the region as a whole. However, it failed narrowly to do so in the single province of Almería. Whatever the Constitution might say, this result was politically intolerable. Recognising as much, the government defied explicit constitutional restrictions and allowed a second referendum on a slightly revised text. Held on 20 October 1981, it resulted in a favourable majority in all of Andalusia's eight provinces. The region accordingly joined the three historic nationalities on the devolution fast track.

3.1.3 Devolution all round

Throughout Spain these convoluted and highly publicised developments triggered off 'devolution fever' (*fiebre autonómica*). Even in regions where there was little sense of a distinct identity, and where self-rule had never previously been an issue, demands grew loud for a measure of autonomy – for 'coffee all round' (*café para todos*) in the phrase of the day. They were viewed with alarm by the centrist government and the main opposition party, the Socialists. Especially after the 1981 attempted coup, both were concerned that the army might use Spain's 'disintegration' as an excuse for further interventions. In the summer of 1981 they therefore reached a 'pact on the regions' (*pacto autonómico*) intended to keep devolution within bounds. Specifically they agreed that they would block any attempts by other regions to follow Andalusia down the 'fast route' [3.1.2].

They also agreed on a Devolution Standardisation Act (*Ley Orgánica del Armonización del Proceso Autonómico – LOAPA*), bulldozed through Parliament with their joint support. The LOAPA laid down that, in the numerous policy areas where both the Madrid government and the regions enjoyed legislative powers, central laws would always take precedence. It also asserted Madrid's right to pass 'coordinating' laws to constrain regional legislation, even in fields where regions' Statutes had given them exclusive legislative powers.

The LOAPA triggered off a furious reaction in Catalonia and, especially, the Basque Country, where regionalists saw it as an attempt to take back much of the autonomy they had only recently been granted. They challenged its provisions in the Constitutional Court [1.1.3] which, to the government's considerable embarrassment, found almost entirely in their favour. In 1983 all the LOAPA's key provisions were struck from the statute book.

The other main point of the 1981 pact proved largely irrelevant. No more regions made any real attempt to follow the 'fast route'. On the other hand, devolution itself proved unstoppable; the question was no longer whether it would extend to the whole of Spain but how the country would be divided up. The main problems in this regard arose in and around the two Castiles, Old and New.

One was how to deal with the province of Madrid, historically part of New Castile but now totally distinct from the remainder of an overwhelmingly rural region. This was solved by creating a separate Madrid autonomous region. The other difficulty was posed by various provinces on the edges of Old Castile. In this case, the claims to separate status of Cantabria and, rather more dubiously, the Rioja were recognised, while those of Segovia were rejected. The remainder of Old Castile was amalgamated with the historically separate region of Leon, creating the European Union's largest regional entity in terms of area, and one of its most thinly populated.

Overall, these decisions served to increase markedly the disparities between the new autonomous regions in terms of population and resources, and in doing so stored up certain problems for the future [3.5.3]. But in the short term they enabled much more speedy and complete devolution than had seemed likely in 1978. By the end of 1983 only the two North African enclaves of Ceuta and Melilla had not received Statutes of Autonomy – indeed, they still have not, 13 years later. All the rest of the country was divided into autonomous regions, 17 in total.

3.1.4 Institutions and powers

The maps which soon appeared showing Spain neatly divided into regions gave the impression that these constituted a homogeneous tier of government. Another Spanish neologism, '*autonómico*', was coined to refer to it, once again to avoid hurting Basque and Catalan sensibilities through the use of 'regional'. The impression of homogeneity was reinforced by the remarkable similarity in the institutional structures of the new regions. In effect, all of them adopted the model prescribed by the Constitution for those following the 'fast route', itself largely a copy of that applying at national level.

Thus, each of the regions has a High Court of Justice [9.1.3]. A regional prime minister (*presidente*) – known in the Basque Country as the *lehendakari* – leads the regional government (*consejo de gobierno*), the official designation of which often reflects historical or linguistic factors (*see* Table 3.1). It is made up of regional ministers (*consejeros*) who head the various departments (*consejerías)* into which the regional administration is divided.

Regions also have a single-chamber parliament elected for a four-year term, using electoral systems which, with minor differences, are copies of the national one [1.3.1]. In most, the provinces serve as constituencies and are represented roughly in proportion to their population. All three which make up the Basque autonomous community, however, have equal representation in the regional parliament, despite their widely differing populations.

The four 'fast route' regions [3.1.2] have their own electoral calendars, both because their initial polls were held on individual dates and because in all four the government has exercised its power to call an early election. In the remaining 13 regions elections are held on a single day, coinciding with the nation-wide municipal elections. These polling days have acquired importance as indicators of the national political situation.

Table 3.1 Autonomous regions and their governments

Official region name	English form	Government designation
Andalucía	Andalusia	Junta
Aragón	Aragon	Diputación General
Asturias	Asturias	Principado
Baleares	Balearic Islands	Gobierno
Canarias	Canary Islands	Gobierno
Cantabria	Cantabria	Diputación
Castilla-La Mancha	Castile-La Mancha	Junta de Comunidades
Castilla y León	Castile-Leon	Junta
Catalunya	Catalonia	Generalitat
Comunidad Valenciana	Valencia	Generalitat
Extremadura	Extremadura	Junta
Galicia	Galicia	Xunta
Comunidad Autónoma de Madrid (CAM)	Madrid	Gobierno
Región de Murcia	Murcia	Gobierno
Comunidad Foral de Navarra	Navarre	Diputación Foral
Comunidad Autónoma Vasca (CAV)	Basque Country	Gobierno Vasco/Eusko Jauralitza
La Rioja	The Rioja	Gobierno

However, by far the most significant differences among the regions at the end of the initial devolution process lay in the extent of their powers (*competencias*) or, more precisely, of the fields in which they could legislate independently. In the case of the 'fast route' regions these were wide, and in many fields virtually untrammelled once the central government's right to impose 'coordinating' legislation had been limited by the Constitutional Court [3.1.3]. The precise extent of these regions' autonomy varied according to provisions of their Statutes. All had education powers, for instance, whereas only the Basques and Catalans had the capacity to establish their own police forces [9.2.2].

The powers of the 'slow route' regions were limited to the fields specified in the Constitution's Article 148 [3.1.1]. These exclude all major economic functions, as well as education and policing. In other fields the 'slow route' regions had powers to legislate only if authorised to do so by the Madrid *Cortes*, and then only within the guidelines of framework laws passed by it [1.3.3]. Otherwise they were restricted to carrying out administrative tasks delegated by the central government.

In all cases, the speed with which powers were assumed in practice was inevitably conditioned by logistical considerations, such as the availability of suitable premises in the regional capitals, as well as by the enthusiasm and competence of the new regional administrations. Clearly these could not assume all powers accorded to them overnight. Instead there was a gradual process of handing over individual areas of responsibility (*transferencias*), the course of which was negotiated between the central authorities and those of the region concerned in joint committees.

The situation was further complicated by the arrangements made in three regions. In Navarre, Valencia and the Canary Islands regional feeling was relatively strong; the Canaries were also exceptional for obvious geographic reasons. There, and in Valencia, the government made use of the constitutional provision to devolve legislative responsibility by decree in a number of fields excluded from the minimum list [3.1.1].

Navarre represented a very special case. Like the three provinces of the Basque autonomous region it had traditionally enjoyed certain historic rights (*fueros*), to which allusion is made in the Constitution's first Additional Disposition [1.1.2]. Along with Alava, Navarre had retained these rights largely intact under the Franco regime, a reward for the province's support of the 1936 uprising [0.1.1]. As a result, uniquely of all the 17 autonomous regions, Navarre already enjoyed a degree of self-rule.

Its representatives insisted that it accede to autonomy through an adaptation of these existing privileges. Their object was achieved by the 1982 Act reaffirming the region's historic rights (*Ley Orgánica de Reintegración y Amejoramiento del Régimen Foral de Navarra*). Known usually as the *Amejoramiento Foral*, it is effectively Navarre's Statute of Autonomy. The extensive powers it granted 'promoted' Navarre, along with Valencia and the Canary Islands, out of the group of regions with only minimal legislative powers.

3.1.5 Funding

A further area in which differences were apparent between the various regions was in the manner of their funding (*financiación*). Most of the regions were covered by a common scheme, the basis of which was set out in the Autonomous Regions' Funding Act (*Ley Orgánica de Financiación de las Comunidades Autónomas – LOFCA*). Under this measure regions received a block grant, dependent on the cost of carrying out the responsibilities transferred to them. They were also allowed to retain the revenues from certain specified taxes and other sources, such as fines, once authorised to do so by the central government.

In practice, this system meant that much depended on political negotiations. Officially they took place in a body established by the LOFCA, the Joint Fiscal and Funding Council (*Consejo de Política Fiscal y Financiera de las Comunidades Autónomas*). This Council was made up of the central government Ministers of Finance and Public Administration, and the various regional finance ministers (*consejeros de Hacienda*). Unofficially, deals were inevitably struck behind the scenes, between and within parties. That gave a double advantage to the regions with the greatest autonomy – and therefore the largest block grants – which were almost by definition those with most political clout. Moreover, in a number of cases, specifically that of Catalonia, they were also already among the wealthiest. The system thus tended to widen the already considerable economic disparities between regions [5.3.5].

This effect acquired particular significance once the Socialist Party (PSOE) came to dominate Spanish politics in the mid-1980s [2.3.2], since it relied heavily on support from the country's three poorest regions (Andalusia, Castile-La Mancha and Extremadura). In 1985 the PSOE introduced various reforms, designed to reduce the system's imbalances. The most important was to activate an instrument provided for in the Constitution but previously unutilised; the Inter-regional Compensation Fund (*Fondo de Compensación Interterritorial – FCI*). Drawn from central resources, the FCI is distributed on the basis of regions' needs and so provides a mechanism, albeit relatively limited, for redressing the disparities between them.

The first exception to the standard funding scheme (*régimen común*) was provided by the Canary Islands. They, like Ceuta and Melilla, were subject to special arrangements because of their geographical distinctiveness. The second applied to two mainland regions, the Basque Country and Navarre, which were among the country's richest. Since their funding arrangements were perceived as advantageous they served to complicate further the question of whether devolution was aggravating regional differences.

Like other features of their autonomy, the funding mechanism for the two regions stemmed from their historic rights. Essentially these had meant that, up to the nineteenth century, Navarre and the three Basque provinces lay outside the Spanish economy. When the rights were suppressed in 1876 they were replaced by a system of financial agreements (*conciertos económicos* in the Basque case, *convenio económico* in that of Navarre). Under them the provinces were responsible for collecting taxes. They then paid an agreed amount, a reverse block grant (*cupo* or *aportación*), to the central government in respect of the services it provided to the regions. This system was enshrined in both the Basque Statute of Autonomy and the reaffirmation of Navarre's historic rights [3.1.4].

This traditional funding system (*régimen foral*) also placed considerable importance on political negotiation, in this case over the precise amount of the reverse grant. However, in their discussions, which take place every five years, the Basques and Navarrese are clearly better placed than their counterparts in the general talks held in the Joint Council. First, they negotiate directly with the central government and do not have to face up to the competing demands of other regions. Second, their tax collecting role means that any delay in reaching a decision prejudices not them but the central government – and so any pressure to reach a rapid agreement falls on Madrid.

3.2 CATALAN REGIONALISM

Of the two regionalist movements to which devolution was in large measure a response, historically much the stronger was the Catalan one. Under the Second Republic it enjoyed support right across the political spectrum, and the backing of the region's powerful industrial elite. Catalan regionalism was also noted for the moderation of its aims and means; its desire for only limited self-government and willingness to negotiate with the Madrid authorities. Since the return of democracy, however, changing economic circumstances and the attainment of autonomy have led to significant changes in the nature of Catalan regionalism.

3.2.1 Regionalism before 1980

Regionalism first appeared in Catalonia in the late nineteenth century, in parallel with a revival of the Catalan language and its rich literary culture. Yet its emergence was above all the result of economic factors, specifically the existence in the region of an important textile industry. The first party set up to pursue self-rule was the Regionalist League (*Lliga Regionalista*), set up and dominated by the textile magnates.

Essentially they wished to retain Catalan tax revenue for use within the region but they also wanted access to the Spanish market for their manufactures. The League's views on self-rule reflected these pragmatic aims; it demanded autonomy within a federal Spain. Convinced that Catalonia's prosperity depended on modernisation of the whole country's economy, the League and its sponsors were concerned with Spanish as much as purely Catalan politics.

In the 1930s the League lost its importance, unable to muster mass electoral support. Under the Second Republic the dominant force in the region's politics was Catalan Republican Left (*Esquerra Republicana de Catalunya – ERC*). Unconnected with the industrial elite, ERC differed from the League also in its left-wing nature. However, in other ways it resembled the older party; it too favoured federalism and showed the same willingness to reach compromise agreements with Spanish parties and institutions that the League had previously used with considerable success.

Crucially, in Catalonia regionalist sentiment (*catalanismo*) was not limited to these two parties and their supporters, but pervaded most of society. No political force of any significance in the region opposed the creation of a regional government under the Republic. The establishment of a specifically Catalan Communist Party (*Partit Socialist Unificat de Catalunya – PSUC*), separate from the Spanish one, indicated how the workers' movement in particular was broadly sympathetic to regionalist goals.

Under the Franco regime, Catalan autonomy was suppressed and expressions of regional distinctiveness, whether cultural or political, were banned. This attempt to stamp out Catalan regionalism backfired spectacularly. The Catalan language, still very widely used, and the culture based on it became the focus of a flourishing underground opposition. After Franco's death, not only was there overwhelming popular backing for some form of self-rule, but Catalan autonomy was seen as an integral part of the transition to democracy by political leaders both in the region and in the rest of Spain.

Moreover, these two groups overlapped. Catalans were prominent in the main Spanish parties. The largest Catalan one was represented on the committee charged with drafting the Constitution [1.1.1], and played an important part in designing its provisions, especially those relating to devolution. On the other hand, at the general elections of 1977 and 1979 the most successful parties in Catalonia were the regional wings of the three largest Spanish formations. As a result they, above all the Socialists and Communists, played the leading role in the relatively smooth process of negotiating a Catalan Statute of Autonomy [3.1.1].

3.2.2 CiU and its challengers

In March 1980 the first election was held for seats in the newly established regional parliament. Victory went to a new force on the Catalan political scene, Convergence and Union (*Convergència i Unió – CiU*). CiU was an alliance of two parties: the Christian Democrat Catalan Democratic Union (*Unió Democràtica de Catalunya – UDC*) and Catalan Democratic Convergence (*Convergència Democràtica de Catalunya – CDC*). CDC had no clear ideology other than regionalism. It was and is much the more important partner in CiU, and since 1980 its leader, Jordi Pujol, has been regional prime minister (*president de la Generalitat*).

CiU's 1980 victory was far from conclusive and left it well short of an overall majority in the regional parliament (*see* Table 3.2). Yet Pujol had no need to form a coalition. There was broad consensus on the desirability of autonomy, and on the fundamental features of Catalan autonomy: the symbols of the new regional authorities (flag, anthem, etc.), and their institutional structure. In any case, the opposition was fragmented and disunited, and CiU could always achieve the necessary support for specific measures.

Once installed in government CiU exploited the position to great effect. It set about a busy legislative programme, and acquired a reputation as an effective defender of Catalonia's interests. Pujol, in particular, enhanced his already considerable personal standing, gained in underground activity before 1975, through his high-profile role as regional premier. In 1984 CiU won an overall majority in the regional parliament which it eventually lost only narrowly in 1995. Since 1980 it has formed the regional government, without recourse to coalition partners, a record even more successful than that of the Socialist Party (PSOE) at Spanish level.

The effects of office on the party were similar to those experienced by the PSOE [2.3.2]. Like it, CiU became very much a party of government, heavily concerned at all levels with retaining office and with a tendency to shady activities if not downright corruption. In CiU's case the effect was in some ways more pronounced; as a new party it had no existing organisation and an even smaller membership base than the PSOE. It too became a highly centralised party, over which the regional government, and Pujol personally, exercised a high degree of control. Like the PSOE, CiU cultivated links

Table 3.2 General and regional election results in Catalonia, 1977–96

		General elections								Regional elections (total seats = 135)				
		1977	1979	1982	1986	1989	1993	1996		1980	1984	1988	1992	1995
Convergence & Union (CiU)	P	17	16	22	32	33	32	30	P	28	47	46	46	41
									S	43	72	69	70	60
Catalan Republican Left (ERC)	P	5	4	4	3	3	5	4	P	9	4	4	8	10
									S	14	5	6	11	13
Catalan Socialists (PSC-PSOE)	P	28	29	45	41	36	35	39	P	22	30	30	28	25
									S	33	41	42	40	34
Catalan Communist Party (PSUC)[1]	P	18	17	5	4	7	7	8	P	19	6	8	7	10
									S	25	6	9	7	11
Spanish centre-right[2]	P	26	23	16	16	15	18	18	P	13	8	9	7	15
									S	18	11	9	7	17

Notes: [1] From 1986 Initiative for Catalonia (IC); in 1996 allied with Catalan Greens (IC-EV).
[2] Democratic Centre Union (UCD), Social and Democratic Centre (CDS), People's Alliance (AP),
People's Coalition (CP), People's Party (PP).
P = per cent poll; S = seats.

to the powerful banking sector, in its case by promoting the establishment of a new bank, *Banca Catalana* [5.3.3].

As in the PSOE, too, the leader worked in close partnership with his second-in-command, in CiU's case, Miquel Roca. Here, however, there were differences. Unlike the PSOE's Alfonso Guerra [2.3.3], Roca was less a party manager than the CiU's 'man in Madrid'. He represented CiU among the 'fathers of the Constitution' [1.1.1]; later he headed CiU's group of MPs in the Madrid Parliament. This latter was an important role, as CiU became a key player not just in Catalan but in Spanish politics [2.3.4, 2.4.3].

Roca was a particularly strong advocate of the traditional Catalan strategy of engaging fully in Spanish politics. It was at his initiative that in the mid-1980s an attempt was made to set up a Spain-wide party linked to CiU [2.2.3]. The project's failure provoked one in a succession of disputes with Pujol, always much more cautious about involvement at Spanish level. Whether or not in response to these, Roca retired from party politics in 1995.

The only other strictly Catalan party of any significance is ERC [3.2.1], which re-emerged after the Franco period but has failed to attain anything like its former importance. In the late 1970s it was unable to make an impact as a left-wing force because of the strength of the PSOE. Subsequently its role as defender of Catalan interests was usurped by CiU, along with much of what electoral support it enjoyed. In the late 1980s ERC acquired a new leader, Angel Colom. He abandoned the party's traditional moderate stance on self-rule and began to advocate outright independence. Yet, although this shift yielded some electoral dividends, ERC remains an essentially marginal player in Catalan politics. In 1996 Colom and his closest supporters left the party to form a new, pro-independence grouping.

Today, as in the past, some of the Spanish parties operating in Catalonia also reflect regionalist sentiment. Thus the traditional association of the Catalan Communist Party (PSUC) with such ideas [3.2.1] is maintained by Initiative for Catalonia (*Iniciativa per Catalunya* – IC), the alliance of parties formed in 1986 around the PSUC. Although formally linked to United Left (IU), IC enjoys semi-independent status within it. The friction between IC and IU does not merely reflect differing views on political strategy [2.5.2], but also a continuing commitment on IC's part to the notion of Catalan nationhood.

More importantly, since it is by far CiU's largest opponent, the same is also true of the PSOE's Catalan wing, the Catalan Socialist Party (*Partit dels Socialistes de Catalunya* – PSC). The PSC is a relatively recent creation; indeed, prior to the Franco era socialism had virtually no roots in Catalonia. It was formed in 1978 when several socialist groupings in the region merged, of which the PSOE's existing Catalan section was only one and by no means the largest. The PSC enjoys considerable autonomy within the highly centralised PSOE [2.3.3], whose leadership it has not hesitated to defy. Most notably, it has consistently advocated Spain's transformation into a federal state. Its electoral fortunes have been mixed. At general elections it consistently tops the poll in Catalonia, and it controls a number of the largest local authorities, including Barcelona. On the other hand, it has failed to mount a real challenge to CiU's hold on regional government.

3.2.3 *Pujolismo*

In some respects assumption by CiU of control over the new institutions of self-rule has accentuated the traditional features of Catalan regionalism. In particular it has led to close links between the party and the regional business community. However, the development of a regional political system, and CiU's central role within it, have brought about substantial changes in the nature of the movement as a whole.

First, Catalan regionalism has become much more closely identified with a single political party. This is partly due to the marginalisation of ERC. The key factor, however, has been the creation of a Catalan focus for politics. Previously, Catalonia's interests had to be defended by negotiation and manoeuvre in Madrid. Now there is a body, the regional government, whose job that is, and which a purely Catalan party can hope to control.

In recent years, CiU has used its exclusive hold on the regional government to portray itself as the only true and effective defender of Catalan interests, as the 'party of Catalonia'. As part of the same strategy it has tried to undermine the Catalan credentials of its Spanish opponents, and especially those of the largest, the PSC [3.2.2]. Thus CiU exploited the PSOE's lengthy control of central government to brand the PSC a mere 'subsidiary', under the orders of its Madrid masters – a tactic it used even while maintaining a Socialist central government in power between 1993 and 1995 [2.3.4].

That is not the only way in which CiU has deliberately increased tensions in Catalan politics and society. In the mid-1980s especially, the regional government seemed anxious to seek confrontation with the central one during the inevitably fraught process of handing over administrative responsibilities [3.1.4]. The result was a succession of cases referred to the Constitutional Court [1.1.3].

CiU's language policy has also been confrontational. It has attempted to make Catalan indisputably the region's main language, in particular by giving it privileged status in administration and the education system. Such 'normalisation' has antagonised some parents, concerned at the downgrading of Castilian Spanish in schools. It has also effectively raised barriers to employment in the public service for those not well versed in the language.

Within the PSC these developments caused some discontent, but the party has by and large supported normalisation. The conservative People's Party, by contrast, saw it as an invitation to establish the electoral foothold in the region it had previously lacked. Particularly in the early 1990s it attempted to project an image as defender of the region's essentially Spanish identity. This in turn served to accentuate a second feature of contemporary Catalan regionalism; its tendency to see Catalonia as involved in a conflict with Spain, rather than as an integral part of the country.

This is closely linked to a further change; CiU's hints of a desire for Catalan independence. Admittedly these are regularly followed by public avowals of Catalonia's fundamental links with Spain – but that has not prevented their repetition. Flirting with independence reflects the demands of electoral politics. Having achieved autonomy, the 'party of Catalonia' has inevitably had to look for more ambitious goals. But it also reflects economic reality. With Spain now in the EU, it is the European not the Spanish market which matters to CiU's business backers.

Furthermore, Catalonia's geographical position means that it, unlike most of Spain, is relatively well placed to profit from the EU's future development. Significantly both Pujol, and Catalonia's second most popular politician Pasqual Maragall, the Socialist Mayor of Barcelona, have been active in various European organisations. Catalonia has joined with economically powerful regions in France, Germany and Italy to form a group known as the Four Motors. The message is clear; whether or not Spain can live without Catalonia the reverse is certainly true.

References to possible independence are in fact fundamental to the new form of Catalan regionalism embodied in CiU. In essence it is a strategy of pressurising the central government into political and economic concessions to Catalan interests, no longer seen as indivisible from Spanish ones. Indissolubly linked with its leading protagonist, Jordi Pujol, this new regionalism is often called *pujolismo*.

3.3 Basque Regionalism

Apart from the fact that it also emerged in Spain in the late nineteenth century, Basque regionalism has virtually nothing in common with its Catalan counterpart. By 1900 the Basque language (*euskera*) had disappeared from most of the region without giving rise to any significant literature; Spanish was the native language of most Basques, including early regionalists. The movement they created was long politically weak, with limited popular support and very little from the region's economic elite. It was the emergence of ETA during the Franco era which transformed Basque regionalism into an important factor in Spanish politics. And since 1975, ETA's refusal to desist from violence, together with the granting of devolution, have brought about major changes in the regionalist movement.

3.3.1 PNV and ETA

Early Basque regionalists, including their leader Sabino Arana, came from the traditional middle class of Bilbao. In stark contrast to their Catalan counterparts [3.2.1], they felt threatened by industrialisation in general and the immigrant workers it brought from the rest of Spain in particular. As a result they were relatively little concerned with the constitutional relationship between the Basque Country and the Spanish state. Their real anxiety was to maintain a division between natives and immigrants inside the region itself. That was the real purpose of the party they created and which was effectively the sole representative of regionalism up to the 1950s. The Basque Nationalist Party (*Partido Nacionalista Vasco – PNV*) was founded in 1895. Its local branches (*batzokis*) became the focus of a tightly knit nationalist community. Long before the Franco era it was a truly mass party in a way no Spanish party could claim to be [2.1.1].

In other respects the PNV was much less successful prior to the Franco era. Electorally it was never the region's major force, and outside its Vizcaya heartland only a minor one. Lacking the industrial clout of the Catalans' Regionalist League [3.2.1], it also enjoyed little success in winning government concessions; only once the Civil War had broken out was a short-lived Basque regional government created. But to a large extent that mattered little to the PNV's leaders, whose calls for 'independence' were not a political programme but a means of reinforcing their followers' sense of nationhood.

Under the Franco regime the PNV leadership went into exile. Within the Basque Country the party organised little opposition activity, lacking as it did the strong cultural focus provided by the language in Catalonia. It was frustration among younger nationalists with the PNV's inaction that in 1959 led to the formation of the group known as Basque Homeland and Freedom (*Euskadi ta Askatasuna – ETA*). In 1968 ETA carried out its first killing.

From then until 1975 it represented the main source of resistance to the dictatorship, not just in the Basque Country but in Spain as a whole. As a result, ETA acquired considerable prestige that went beyond the region. The readiness of Spanish politicians to grant the Basque Country autonomy after 1975 reflected, at least in part, a general acceptance that Basque demands for self-rule were valid, an acceptance which owed more to ETA than to the older PNV.

Neither of these organisations took any direct part in the process of democratisation, which ETA explicitly denounced. When the text of the 1978 Constitution was put to the vote, the PNV's representatives abstained, on the grounds that the recognition given to Basques' historic rights in the first Additional Disposition was inadequate [1.1.2]. In the subsequent referendum the party advised voters to do the same, an attitude which contributed to the ambiguous result in the region [1.1.1].

Meanwhile, the PNV's deep roots in Basque society enabled it to emerge as the region's largest party in the general elections of 1977 and 1979. It accordingly had the biggest representation in the body set up to prepare the ground for devolution there [3.1.1], and in effect negotiated directly with the central government the terms of the Basque Statute of Autonomy, known as the Statute of Guernica. It then won the inaugural regional election held in February 1980 with a majority large enough to form a single-party regional government.

3.3.2 Upheaval in the 1980s

For the next six years the PNV exercised a growing dominance of Basque politics. Not only did it strengthen its parliamentary majority in 1984; it also took control of the vast bulk of local authorities in the region. However, in 1986 the PNV was hit by a crisis which forced it to call an early regional election, at which it suffered severe losses (*see* Table 3.3). This setback reflected a number of internal problems. In essence, they came down to the fact that the PNV had always been a party of opposition and was quite unprepared for government office. Indeed, it arrived in power without a formal programme and made little attempt to use the wide-ranging autonomy the region had acquired [3.1.4].

Almost the only legislation passed by the Basque parliament in the early 1980s related to the symbols and institutional structure of the new autonomous region. On these issues the PNV made no attempt to seek compromise but forced through its own proposals despite virtually unanimous opposition. At the same time the PNV complained constantly and bitterly about hitches in the process of devolution, and above all about the attempt by the main Spanish parties to place strict limits on autonomy [3.1.3]. This strategy left the PNV isolated from all but ETA and its supporters, whose continuing violence the party seemed happy to use as a means of putting pressure on Madrid. Admittedly the PNV never supported violence. Yet it repeatedly questioned the new Spanish state's right to rule Basques, not least by suggesting that Basques 'had rejected the Constitution' in 1978 [1.1.1]. Wittingly or not, in so doing it helped ETA's attempts to justify the use of violence against the state.

By the mid-1980s this ambivalent attitude was becoming electorally damaging to the PNV. For not only had ETA stepped up its 'armed struggle', its violence was now directed at civilians and at the new Basque authorities, including the regional police force which was increasingly deployed in an anti-terrorist role. Progressively, Basque opinion, including moderate supporters of self-rule, turned against ETA.

These external problems for the PNV became bound up with a complex dispute between the party's leader, Xabier Arzalluz, and the regional prime minister, Carlos Garaikoetxea. In late 1984 Garaikoetxea was forced to resign by the party apparatus. Eventually he and his supporters left to form a new party, a split which cost the PNV its parliamentary majority and so effectively forced the 1986 regional election. From it Basque regionalism emerged stronger than ever, in the sense that purely Basque parties increased their combined share of the votes. Yet instead of being dominated by the PNV that share was now split between four parties.

Apart from the PNV, the largest of these was People's Unity (*Herri Batasuna – HB*), which since its foundation in 1978 has acted as ETA's political wing (*brazo político*). Like ETA, HB demands outright independence for the Basque Country and purports to regard the regional institutions set up since 1979 as merely an adjunct of the illegitimate Spanish state. These attitudes

Table 3.3 General and regional election results in the Basque Country, 1977–96

	General elections								Regional elections Total seats: 60 (1980), 75 (1984–)				
	1977	1979	1982	1986	1989	1993	1996		1980	1984	1986	1990	1994
Basque Nationalist Party (PNV)	29	28	32	28	23	24	25	P	38	42	24	29	29
								S	25	32	17	22	22
Basque Left (EE)	6	8	8	9	9			P	10	8	11	8	8
								S	6	6	9	6	6
People's Unity (HB)		15	15	18	17	15	12	P	17	15	18	18	16
								S	11	11	13	13	11
Basque Solidarity (EA)					11	10	8	P			16	11	10
								S			13	9	8
Alavese Unity (UA)								P				1	3
								S				3	5
PSOE Basque section (PSE-PSOE)[1]	28	19	29	26	21	24	23	P	14	23	22	20	17
								S	9	19	19	16	12
PCE Basque section[2]	5	5	2	1	3	6	9	P	4	1	1	1	9
								S	1	0	0	0	6
Spanish centre right[3]	20	20	13	16	13	15	18	P	13	9	8	9	14
								S	8	7	4	6	11

Notes: [1] From 1993 PSE-EE.

[2] From 1986 Basque United Left (IU-UB).

[3] Democratic Centre Union (UCD), Social and Democratic Centre (CDS), People's Alliance (AP), People's Coalition (CP), People's Party (PP).

P = per cent poll; S = seats.

had led HB to boycott not just the Spanish Parliament but also the Basque one. Even despite growing disillusion with the polarisation it perpetuated, this uncompromising stance brought HB nearly one-fifth of Basque votes in 1986.

Like HB, Basque Left (*Euskadiko Ezkerra* – *EE*) was also an offshoot of ETA, set up in 1977. However, it developed very differently. Convinced that violence was no longer necessary or justifiable once democracy and autonomy had been established, it persuaded that wing of ETA with which it was linked to abandon violence in 1981. The following year it absorbed the majority faction of the PCE's Basque section, the PCE-EPK. Thereafter EE became an outspoken opponent of ETA, and in 1986 took votes from the PNV as a result.

The PNV's biggest losses, however, were to Basque Solidarity (*Eusko Alkartasuna* – *EA*), the party formed by ex-regional premier Garaikoetxea after leaving the PNV in 1986. Following the 1986 elections it was involved in negotiations to form a new regional government. Even though they failed, for some time it appeared likely that EA would supplant the PNV as the main representative of mainstream regionalism.

The 1986 election meant that the largest force in the regional parliament was the Basque section of the Socialist PSOE. The Socialists were the PNV's historic arch-foe, their main support drawn from workers in the region's heavy industries. Many of these were either descendants of the immigrants despised by early nationalists [3.3.1], or had arrived during the more recent industrialisation of the Franco era. Although traditionally bitterly opposed to Basque self-rule, the PSOE had supported Basque devolution in 1979, and its regional organisation adopted the official title of Basque Socialist Party (*Partido Socialista de Euskadi* – *PSE*). Yet the PSE remained deeply suspicious of the new regional institutions and of the PNV itself. It was thus a major surprise when, in early 1987, a PNV-PSE coalition was formed. This unlikely alliance proved to be the PNV's springboard for recovery. Gradually improving its electoral performance, albeit without reaching the dominance of the early 1980s, by the mid-1990s it again controlled much of the region's local government. Although unable to dispense with coalition partners, it was once again clearly in command of regional government.

3.3.3 Regionalism in the 1990s

Despite the PNV's return to a position of relative dominance, the nature of Basque politics has altered radically since 1986. So too has that of Basque regionalism. Crucial to these changes was a 1988 inter-party agreement to condemn violence unreservedly, and to marginalise those who refused to do so. Known as the Pact of *Ajuria Enea*, after the official residence of the Basque prime minister, it was signed by all the significant players in Basque politics apart from ETA's political wing, HB [3.3.2].

Along with its decision to enter a coalition with the Socialists, accepting this Pact forced the PNV to tone down its anti-Spanish rhetoric and talk of independence. Only occasionally in recent years have party leaders reverted to those themes, reflecting the fact that the region is in a much weaker economic position than Catalonia [5.3.5]. This new moderation has greatly reduced tensions in the region, as well as friction between the Basque and central governments.

The process has been made easier by the relatively non-conflictual nature of the language issue in the Basque Country. It is true that the regional government has made strenuous efforts to revive the Basque language (*euskera*), building on the network of community-based Basque language schools (*ikastolas*) which grew up in defiance of the former regime. And non-Basque speakers do suffer a degree of discrimination in public sector employment. However, the fact that so many Basques, even nationalists, still cannot speak *euskera* makes unthinkable aggressive attempts at 'normalisation' on Catalan lines [3.2.3].

From the PNV's point of view the 1988 Pact was advantageous in clearly distancing the party from ETA. It also helped make Garaikoetxea's replacement as regional premier, José Antonio Ardanza, the region's most popular politician and a considerable electoral asset. But his party's recovery from the disaster of 1986 had other causes too.

Thus, in complete contrast to its previous inaction [3.3.2], the regional government set about a busy programme of legislative and other activity. The PNV was quick to claim the credit, and so establish itself as an effective defender of the region's interests. In that sense it became a party of government, and so more like the PSOE and the Catalan CiU [2.3.2, 3.2.2]. Like them, too, it has undoubtedly been guilty of abusing its strong hold on power, above all in giving preference to its own supporters in public employment.

However, in other ways the PNV remains distinctive. Proportionally, it continues to have a much larger individual membership than other parties in Spain. Partly in consequence, although Xabier Arzalluz has been its undisputed leader since the mid-1970s, power in the PNV is much less concentrated than in most Spanish parties [2.1.2]. The posts of party and government leader remain separate, and, in general, simultaneous holding of posts in both organisations is barred. As a result, the PNV has not developed a leader cult along the lines of *pujolismo* [3.2.3].

Nor can the PNV now claim, as it did in the past and as CiU now attempts to do [3.2.3], to be the sole representative of regionalism, far less of the Basque people. Admittedly, it has seen off one of the unquestionably Basque rivals which emerged in the 1980s [3.3.2]. Basque Left (EE) played an important role in drawing up the 1988 anti-violence Pact; it even entered regional government as a minor partner from 1990 to 1993. In the 1990s, however, it fell into decline, split and eventually disappeared as a party in its own right.

Yet the PNV's two remaining home-grown challengers continue to attract over a fifth of the votes in Basque elections. Indeed, EA [3.3.2] was a partner in regional government 1990/91, and has been again from 1994.

Although failing to achieve the breakthrough it once threatened, and identified more with its charismatic leader, Garaikoetxea, than with any particular policy, it still enjoys considerable backing, above all in Guipúzcoa.

Like EA, HB has suffered a steady erosion of its support which reflects ETA's political marginalisation. That is apparent also in another way. It has become clear that, to a significant extent, support for HB is unconnected with regionalist sentiment. Instead, it comes largely from disoriented and disillusioned young people in a society particularly hard hit by social problems, who sympathise primarily with ETA's anti-state violence [8.4.2].

Regionalism has thus been divorced from violence in a variety of senses; at the same time it has become more diverse. It has also extended into new parts of the political spectrum. Since 1986 the Basque Socialists [3.3.2] have undergone considerable changes. Apart from a brief interlude in 1990/91, they have collaborated with the PNV in a series of coalitions, not only at regional but also local level. Under a younger generation of leaders, the most prominent of them Ramón Jáuregui, they are now actively enthusiastic about autonomy. The new attitude has been especially marked since 1993, when the PSE absorbed the majority faction of EE, whose former secretary general Mario Onaindía is now a leading member of the merged party. Officially known as the PSE-EE (*Partido Socialista de Euskadi-Euskadiko Ezkerra*), this enjoys a degree of independence within the PSOE, although less than that enjoyed by the Catalan PSC [3.2.2].

3.4 NEW REGIONALIST MOVEMENTS

Outside the Basque Country and Catalonia there was little evidence of regionalist feelings prior to 1975. That situation changed dramatically as a result of devolution in the 1980s. For that process not only reinforced and reoriented such feelings where they already existed, but it also encouraged them where they did not. The reason lay in the focus of popular identity and political activity provided by the new regional institutions. At the most basic level, every region now has its own flag, prominent in all its public places. Interest groups of all types organise on a regional basis. Above all, regional politics and election campaigns tend to promote the idea that the inhabitants of a particular region have certain common interests distinct from those of other parts of Spain. Now there is barely a region without one or more parties which exist to defend regional interests (*see* Table 3.4).

3.4.1 Galicia

Of all Spain's regions Galicia is arguably the most distinctive in cultural terms. The indigenous language has consistently been more widely used there even than in Catalonia and a Celtic folk culture has flourished. Yet until the 1960s, and then only marginally, Galicia never experienced the factor which triggered off regionalism in both Catalonia and the Basque

Table 3.4 Principal regionalist parties, 1996 (represented in regional or national parliament)

Region	Political party	Name in Spanish
Andalusia	Andalusian Regionalist Party	*Partido Andalucista (PA)*
Aragon	Aragonese Regionalist Committee	*Chunta Aragonesista (Cha)*
	Aragonese Regionalist Party	*Partido Aragonés Regionalista (Par)*
Asturias	Asturian Regionalist Party	*Partiú Asturianista (PAS)*
Balearics	Majorcan Socialist Party- Nationalists of the Isles	*Partit Socialist Mallorquín-Nacionalistes de les Illes (PSM-NI)*
	Majorcan Union	*Unió Mallorquín (UM)*
	Formentera Progressive Independents	*Agrupació d'Independents Progrés de Formentera (AIPF)*
Basque Country	Alavese Unity	*Unidad Alavesa (UA)*
	Basque Nationalist Party	*Partido Nacionalista Vasco (PNV-EAJ)*
	Basque Solidarity	*Eusko Alkartasuna (EA)*
	People's Unity	*Herri Batasuna (HB)*
Canaries	Canary Islands Coalition	*Coalición Canaria (CC)*
	El Hierro Independents	*Agrupación Herreña Independiente (AHI)*
	Canaries Nationalist Platform	*Plataforma Canaria Nacionalista (PCN)*
	incl. Lanzarote Independents	*Plataforma de Independientes de Lanzarote (PIL)*
	and Fuerteventura Independents	*Independientes de Fuerteventura (IF)*
Cantabria	Cantabrian Progress Union	*Unión para el Progreso de Cantabria (UPC)*
	Cantabrian Regionalist Party	*Partido Regionalista de Cantabria (PRC)*
Castile and Leon	Leonese People's Union	*Unión del Pueblo Leonés (UPL)*
Catalonia	Catalan Republican Left	*Esquerra Republicana de Catalunya (ERC)*
	Convergence and Union	*Convergència i Unió (CiU)*
Extremadura	Extremadura Coalition	*Coalición Extremeña (CE)*
Galicia	Galician National Alliance	*Bloque Nacional Gallego (BNG)*
Navarre	Navarrese Democratic Convergence	*Convergencia de Demócratas de Navarra (CDN)*
	Navarrese People's Union	*Unión del Pueblo Navarro (UPN)*
Rioja	Party of the Rioja	*Partido Riojano (PR)*
Valencia	Valencian Union	*Unión Valenciana (UV)*

Country; industrialisation. Politically it remained stuck in the nineteenth century, the most notorious fief of local party bosses controlled by their Madrid masters [2.1.1].

Galicia's privileged treatment in the constitutional provisions for devolution thus bore no relation to demands from the region itself. Rather, it derived from the desire to find a formula which would allow the Basques and Catalans priority treatment without conceding that that was a response to political pressure [3.1.1]. In the referendum on Galicia's Statute of Autonomy a mere 30 per cent of its electorate turned out to vote.

Before and after autonomy was granted, however, various small parties – and a tiny terrorist group [9.4.2] – took up the banner of Galician interests. The most successful was the short-lived Galician Coalition (*Coalición Gallega* – *CG*), a breakaway from the party which formed the first regional government in 1981, the conservative People's Alliance (AP) [2.4.1]. In 1986 CG took part in the attempt to set up a new nation-wide centrist grouping [2.2.3]. When this failed, it joined with the Socialists to oust AP from the regional government. CG, however, was less a political party than a vehicle for the personal ambitions of its leader, Joxe Manuel Barreiro, deputy to both AP and PSOE regional premiers. With his disgrace due to corruption charges, CG faded away.

In the 1990s conservative Galician regionalism has found another, unexpected champion. Manuel Fraga was until 1989 leader of the largest party of the Spanish right [2.4.1], and an arch-centralist. That year he returned to his native region to head the lists of the renamed People's Party at the third election to the Galician parliament, leading it to a convincing victory. Four years later he repeated the feat.

Since his return, Fraga has displayed an unexpected enthusiasm for Galician distinctiveness and for the idea of devolution in general. In particular, he has pursued a policy of language 'normalisation' along Catalan lines, provoking some of the same tensions [3.2.3]. More generally, he has shown open sympathy with the aspirations of Catalan regionalists and their leader, Jordi Pujol.

At the same time, a specifically Galician party of the left has made significant advances. The Galician National Alliance (BNG) won 13 seats at the 1993 regional election, and over 13 per cent of Galician votes at the general election three years later. Far from channelling reawakened regionalist sentiment through the Spanish party system, Fraga's term of office appears to have had precisely the opposite effect.

3.4.2 Andalusia

As in Galicia, in Andalusia economic backwardness hampered political development of all types, including the emergence of a significant regionalist movement. Yet even though it has no language of its own, the region's moorish legacy undoubtedly makes it culturally distinct in a number of ways. Awareness of that legacy, along with resentment at long-standing economic neglect, seem to have formed the basis of the surprising groundswell of opinion in favour of extensive autonomy in 1980 [3.1.2].

As part of that groundswell an Andalusian Socialist Party (*Partido Socialista Andaluz – PSA*) was created. Despite its name, the PSA was quite separate from the PSOE; it subsequently adopted the title of Andalusian Regionalist Party (PA). In both guises it has enjoyed some success, winning seats in the national and regional parliaments and, in 1980, even the Catalan one. Its leader, Alejandro Rojas Marcos, was mayor of Seville from 1991 to 1995 with Socialist support. However, the PA has been racked by internal disputes, especially between Rojas Marcos and the long-time mayor of Jerez, Pedro Pacheco. In general it has attracted support only in specific areas, for prominent local leaders.

Arguably one reason for the PA's lack of real success was that during the long Socialist tenure of power in Madrid Andalusia had little need of other representation. A number of the PSOE's leaders, including both Felipe González and Alfonso Guerra, are themselves from Seville, and the governments they headed poured considerable resources into the region, provoking allegations from other regions of bias. The PSOE's defeat at the 1996 general election has removed this safety valve for Andalusian resentment, which may have to seek new outlets in the future.

3.4.3 Other regions

During the 1980s regionalist parties emerged in a number of regions which, although distinct in some sense, had never previously shown such tendencies. In general these parties were clearly right-wing in outlook, and their appearance reflected frustration on the right at inability to mount an effective challenge to the PSOE at Spanish level [2.4.2]. Under those conditions, espousal of regional interests represented an alternative means of ousting Socialist regional governments.

The most successful example is the Aragonese Regionalist Party (Par), whose rise has gone hand-in-hand with a sharp increase in popular support for extensive autonomy in Aragon [3.5.2]. Since 1987 the Par has participated in, and even headed, successive regional governments. In 1995 its strength enabled it to extract concessions from the People's Party (PP) in return for not contesting the forthcoming general election. That same year it was joined in the regional parliament by a second, smaller Aragonese grouping.

In two other regions, the emergence of right-wing regionalism was linked with a conservative reaction against the country's oldest and most successful regionalist movements. In the case of Valencia, this is overtly at least a linguistic issue. There the regional language, which was accorded official status under devolution, is considered by most linguists to be a dialect of Catalan. Rejection of that notion is a major concern for Valencian Union (UV), which like the Par is now a partner in regional government.

In fact, however, the language issue is part of a wider one; possible incorporation of Valencia in a 'Greater Catalonia' (*Països Catalans*). Even though mainstream Catalan regionalists have shown no interest in such a project, it provides a useful bogeyman for UV's conservative promoters. They appear to be concerned above all at what they see as excessive government concessions to Catalonia, both in political and economic terms. In a sense, UV is really an anti-Catalan, or even Spanish nationalist party.

A broadly similar situation exists in Navarre except that there it is Basque regionalism which is seen by some as a threat. Navarre is indeed regarded by all Basque regionalists as an integral part of the Basque homeland, a sentiment implicitly acknowledged in the Constitution [3.1.1]. However, while the northern part of the province is unmistakably Basque in cultural terms, and consistently provides support for Basque parties, especially HB and EA [3.3.2], the remainder bears little trace of such influences. Its most significant political tradition is reactionary carlism [0.1.1], of which Navarre was the heartland.

It was against this background that the Navarrese People's Union (UPN) was set up in 1979. UPN's creation was prompted by opposition to Navarre's possible inclusion in the new Basque autonomous region, a possibility explicitly envisaged in the Constitution's fourth Transitional Disposition [1.1.2]. UPN enjoyed considerable success in the 1980s, running the region for some years and forcing the PP to recognise its position as the right's principal local representative.

In the 1990s, however, UPN fell victim to the complexities of Navarrese politics. In 1994, faced with the PP's recovery at national level [2.4.3], it decided effectively to merge its organisation with that of the country's main conservative party. However, some in the party saw this as a betrayal of Navarre's own distinctive interests. They broke away and set up a new party, Navarrese Democratic Convergence. Since the 1995 regional election this has formed an unlikely ruling coalition with the PSOE and EA.

In geographical terms Spain's most distinctive region is the Canary Islands. There a number of regionalist parties emerged in the 1980s, later coming together in the Canary Islands Coalition (CC). CC is currently the largest party in the regional parliament and has been involved in successive coalition governments. Indeed, its four Madrid MPs are enough to make CC a factor in national politics, given the results of the 1996 election [2.4.3].

Culturally the Balearic Islands are more distinctive than the Canaries, the local form of Catalan being both officially recognised and virtually universally used. They are, however, also much less remote and considerably more prosperous. Perhaps as a result, regionalist groupings have made less impact. Even so, no fewer than three won seats at the 1995 regional elections.

Those polls also saw regionalist parties gain parliamentary representation in a further five mainland regions with no history of such activity; Cantabria, the Rioja, Castile-Leon, Extremadura and Asturias. In the first two cases they have at times formed part of the regional government. Even the Madrid regional parliament has included regionalist representatives. By 1995, however, Madrid had joined Castile-La Mancha and Murcia as the only regions lacking such a presence.

Yet another recent development is linked to resentment against the centralising tendencies of regional governments [3.5.3]. Where it has come together with older loyalties this reaction has sometimes found political expression. Thus Leon, which as an entity is older than Castile itself, was denied separate autonomous status in the 1980s [3.1.3]. A decade later the Leonese People's Union, which seeks to reverse that decision, won two seats in the Castile-Leon regional parliament.

In the Basque Country it is the provinces which provide a focus of traditional loyalties [1.6.2]. Of them, Alava is culturally much less Basque than the other two, and has a long history of rivalry with Vizcaya in particular. The new regional institutions were sited in the Alavese capital, Vitoria, precisely to counter such feelings. Yet that could not prevent the emergence in the early 1990s of Alavese Unity, whose success was based on exploitation of grievances against the new Basque authorities.

Finally, the nineteenth-century phenomenon of 'cantonalism' has resurfaced in political form. Historically the best-known example was the claim of the Cartagena area of Murcia province to separate provincial status. In the 1990s a party was formed to pursue the same aspiration for the Bierzo district of Leon province. Its 900 votes in the 1995 regional election suggest that it is unlikely to provoke the military hostilities which resulted in the case of Cartagena.

3.5 THE SECOND DEVOLUTION ROUND AND ITS EFFECTS

The initial round of devolution between 1978 and 1983 was both consequence and cause of regionalist pressures. Essentially a response to those already apparent in the Basque Country and Catalonia, it triggered off new ones both there and elsewhere. They, in turn, were a major reason why in the 1990s a new round of devolution got underway. And, inevitably, the institutional changes it brought about have once again fed back into regionalist politics. Where this iterative process will end remains unclear.

3.5.1 Second pact on the regions

During the 1980s there was little question of altering the *Estado de las Autonomías* that had emerged from the first round of regionalisation. Having 'solved' one of the great problems of the transition, Spain's leaders were reluctant to touch the complex edifice they had created. At the same time, the regions themselves were fully engaged in creating their own institutional and administrative structures, and in assuming the powers gradually handed over from the centre [3.1.4].

In the Basque Country and Catalonia this process caused tensions with the central government, and, indeed, was exploited for that very purpose [3.2.3, 3.3.2]. However, even there developments led to a steady decline in friction from 1985. In the first half of 1994 not a single dispute between Madrid and the regions was referred to the Constitutional Court. When it came, the second round of regionalisation was not triggered by pressures from Basque and Catalan regionalists, who actually opposed some of the changes involved. Instead, they were the product of factors introduced by the first round of devolution. Some of the so-called 'slow route regions' [3.1.2], especially poorer ones run by the PSOE, were concerned at the advantages enjoyed by others, above all the Basque Country and Catalonia. The PP, anxious to counter the electoral threat of the conservative groupings which had emerged in some regions [3.4.3], sought to align itself with the regionalist feelings they reflected. And the Madrid leaderships of both main Spanish parties, concerned at the cost implications of devolution as it had developed so far [3.5.3], were keen for greater uniformity in administration.

The outcome of these various factors was a second 'pact on the regions' *pacto antonómico* reached in 1992. Like the first [3.1.3], it involved the two leading parties of the day, excluding the smaller national parties and all the regional ones, even the Catalan CiU and Basque PNV. Under it, the PSOE and PP agreed to hand over more powers to the ten regions which had received only minimum autonomy in the first round – all of which they governed, either alone or in coalition.

The mechanism for the handover was to be delegation of the powers as allowed by the Constitution [3.1.1], followed by subsequent amendment of the relevant Statutes of Autonomy. This latter the PSOE and PP could guarantee, since together they held a comfortable majority in the *Cortes*. The necessary amendments were duly approved in March 1994.

By far the most important powers transferred to regional control under the 1992 pact related to education, but others affecting social services and a number of other fields were also handed over. Deliberately excluded was the health service, responsibility for which most of the regions rejected as being too complex and expensive. The result was to leave responsibility for health as the principal difference between the ten 'slow route' regions and the remainder. In addition, the Basque Country and Catalonia were distinguished only by their own police forces.

3.5.2 Reform of regional funding

It was not long before the changes agreed in the pact themselves brought about new tensions. In Aragon, one of the regions whose autonomy was to be upgraded, they triggered off calls for an even more far-reaching reform of the region's Statute than that envisaged. Mass demonstrations were seen on the streets of Saragossa, prominent local figures in both the PP and PSOE publicly defied their own Madrid leaderships, and the 1993 general election saw a doubling in support for the Aragonese Regionalist Party [3.4.3].

The 1992 pact also provoked a reaction from the four regions who had followed the 'fast route' to autonomy [3.1.2]. During 1993 and early 1994 all their governments, but especially the Basque and Catalan ones, issued a series of demands for powers in the grey areas which the Constitution did not reserve to the central government [3.1.1]. These claims acquired extra weight from the unexpected backing of Galician premier Manuel Fraga [3.4.1]. However, what brought them to top of the political agenda was the 1993 general election. Its results made the new Socialist government dependent on regionalist and, above all, Catalan backing [2.3.4]. The price of this support was apparent in Felipe González's investiture speech, where he spoke of giving new momentum to the process of devolution (*impulso autonómico*). His government began efforts to agree exactly which areas of responsibility could, under the Constitution, be devolved to regional control (*competencias transferibles*). In parallel, discussions were opened on the handover of specific powers, even in the previously taboo area of social security administration.

However, it was in another sphere that concrete steps were first taken. For some time there had been concern in Madrid that, financially, the regions were having their cake and eating it. On the one hand, the regions now enjoyed a high profile as providers of public infrastructure and services. On the other, under the block grant arrangements that applied to most of them [3.1.5], they reaped none of the opprobrium attached to raising the corresponding taxes. The central authorities were anxious to end this situation by introducing a measure of shared fiscal responsibility (*corresponsabilidad fiscal*).

At the same time, Catalan premier Jordi Pujol had been eyeing with increasing interest the alternative arrangements operated by the Basques and Navarrese [3.1.5]. In 1992 he began to push the idea of a mixed scheme; tax raising would remain a central government responsibility, but regions would have an automatic right to 15 per cent of the income tax receipts within their territory. His proposal formed the basis of the new funding scheme that was introduced on a trial basis in 1994.

Pujol's enthusiasm for a scheme that was also attractive to the Spanish parties reflected the material concerns traditionally characteristic of Catalan regionalism [3.2.1]. As was immediately obvious, it greatly favoured the richer regions – among them Catalonia – at the expense of the poorer ones. Consequently, debate over his proposal did not result in division along party lines but along those of economic geography. The most vociferous opposition came from the Socialist Juan Carlos Rodríguez Ibarra, premier of Extremadura, but he was backed by the heads of government of other poor regions, irrespective of party allegiance. Conversely, their counterparts in better-off parts of Spain tended to support Pujol, as did the PSOE's own Catalan section.

The scheme eventually piloted in 1994 contained various provisions to cushion the effects on the poorest regions. Even so, three of them – Castile-Leon, Extremadura and Galicia – refused to join it and remain covered by the old block grant arrangements. Galicia's refusal was particularly interesting. Evidently Fraga's awareness of his region's economic weakness remained stronger than his enthusiasm for wider autonomy.

Over the next two years the political balance changed radically. In 1995 the PP took power in most of the regions; the following year it did so at national level also [2.4.3]. However, the narrow margin of its general election victory left the new government even more dependent than its predecessor on the support of regionalists, especially the Catalan CiU.

To secure the CiU's support José María Aznar, the new Prime Minister, was forced to make a further concession, increasing the proportion of income tax revenue retained by the regions to 30 per cent. Once again the loudest protests came from Galicia and Extremadura. And, despite their governments having passed from PSOE to PP control, the Mediterranean regions of Murcia and Valencia continued to back the Catalan stance.

3.5.3 Towards federalism?

As well as reshaping the *Estado de las Autonomías* in practice, the events of the early 1990s reopened the theoretical debate over its ultimate form. In several respects – increased uniformity, a measure of shared fiscal responsibility – they brought Spain closer to genuine federalism. This was a step which had been broached by a number of interested parties, most notably the Catalan Socialists, the PSC [3.2.2]. Now it began to interest the PSOE's central leadership, and that of the PP, who had previously feared that federalism would mean increased leakage of powers from Madrid.

By the early 1990s, however, that fear had become irrelevant; Spain's regions already enjoyed greater autonomy than those in the most-quoted example of federalism, Germany. On the other hand, genuine federalism would mean the creation of instruments through which the regions jointly cooperated in running the state. Specifically it would mean that the politically and economically stronger regions – including the Basque Country and Catalonia – would have to negotiate with their fellows, rather than forcing concessions from the government and leaving it to pacify those who felt aggrieved.

Those considerations had already led the PSOE government, backed by the PP, to introduce one mechanism for centre–region cooperation (*cooperación autonómica*). That was the system of joint sectoral working groups (*conferencias sectoriales*), each of which deals with a single subject area and brings together representatives of all the regions and of the central government. Unsurprisingly in view of their purpose, operation of the working groups has repeatedly run up against resistance from the main Catalan and Basque parties, CiU and the PNV.

Debate about possible federalism has also focused attention on the role of the Senate. Defined by the Constitution as a 'chamber of territorial [by implication, regional] representation', the Upper House's current composition renders this notion meaningless [1.3.1]. In recent years there has been general acceptance of the need to end the anomaly. The problem has been deciding how to do so.

In 1993 the Socialist government reached agreement with the PP and CiU on setting up within the Senate a General Committee on the Regions (*Comisión General de las CC AA*). In September the following year a three-day debate was held in the House as a whole, devoted to the further development of the *Estado de las Autonomías*. It was attended by the Prime Minister and 16 of his regional counterparts. A motion was adopted, with the lone opposition of Canary Islands Coalition [3.4.3], that the Senate be converted into a genuinely regional chamber, possibly along the line of the German *Bundesrat*. Such a move would take Spain very close indeed to federalism.

The sole absentee from the 1994 debate was the Basque premier, José Antonio Ardanza, whose party also opposed the General Committee's establishment. It clearly felt politically threatened by a move that would, in effect, leave the Basque Country as just another Spanish region. Similarly, Catalonia's premier Pujol has criticised suggestions of a move to federalism, traditionally favoured by Catalan regionalists [3.2.1].

Full-blown federalism would also pose practical problems. In particular it is hard to envisage the smaller regions taking on the extra responsibilities that it would entail. The Rioja, the smallest of all, has barely a quarter of a million inhabitants. On the other hand, the system as it currently exists is imposing considerable costs of its own. For devolution has brought a seemingly unstoppable increase in the number of public servants required to run the various levels of Spain's administration, a rise that far outstrips the undoubted increase in the range of government responsibilities. It has been concentrated in the new regional administrations, most of whose governments do not have to raise the taxes to foot the resultant wages bill [3.5.2].

Most of the new regional employees work in areas of responsibility handed over in the 1980s [3.1.4]. In theory, at least, they should be replacements for central government public servants. In numerous cases, however, the corresponding posts have been retained in Madrid, or in its outlying administration [1.5.3]. At the same time, the new regions have shown a tendency to their own form of centralisation, taking on functions already carried out by the municipalities and provinces [1.6]. The result has been to aggravate further the problems of administrative overlap, not to mention the accompanying financial costs.

Although the problems are easily identified, solving them is another matter, especially in a country with a massive unemployment problem [5.2.4]. The Socialist government re-elected in 1993 drew up plans for structural reform, but before agreement on them could be reached it was defeated at the 1996 election. Included in the manifesto of the victorious People's Party (PP) were alternative proposals to deal with the problems of overlap. They were based on an idea floated by the PP's founder, Manuel Fraga, since 1989 regional premier of Galicia [3.4.1]. Fraga's suggestion is that the regions take over responsibility for all administrative tasks within their territories, irrespective of where legislative responsibility lies.

Like the proposed Senate reform, this concept of a single administrative structure (*administración única*) is based on a German model. It would involve a considerable loss of administrative responsibilities, and accompanying status, for the central government, and it remains to be seen whether the PP will implement Fraga's proposal now it holds office. Even if it does, there will still be potential for friction and confusion due to the Constitution's failure to define clearly the division of responsibilities between regions and Madrid [3.1.1]. Outright federalism would provide one possible solution to that technical dilemma. Its political feasibility is much less certain, given opposition from the very forces devolution was originally intended to placate; Basque and Catalan regionalism.

3.5.4 European dimension

Since the initial round of devolution completed in 1983, Spanish politics as a whole has been considerably affected by an important change in the country's international position; its 1986 accession to the European Community (now Union) [0.2.1]. The impact of accession was first and foremost economic, and varied from region to region. One result was an increase in the bargaining power of some regions, notably Catalonia, and a reduction in that of others, among them the Basque Country [5.3.5]. But accession has also had a number of other implications for the complex relationship between regions and central government in Spain.

Throughout the EU moves towards greater political integration have led to speculation about an enhanced future role for regions, as a means of reducing the remoteness of government. Indeed, in the later 1980s it briefly seemed likely that the EU might evolve towards a 'Europe of the Regions', in which regions replaced existing states as the principal tier of government. This possibility was a crucial factor in the moderation of Basque regionalism, since it offered a less confrontational alternative to 'independence' as the movement's goal [3.3.3].

In the 1990s the prospect has receded. Yet, even so, EU membership has given new importance to the regions in other ways, not least since they play an important role in allocation and distribution of resources provided by the EU's Structural Funds [5.1.2]. Given the importance for them of EU decisions, the regions have understandably clamoured for an input into EU decision-making. In 1994 the central government attempted to meet their demands through the system of joint sectoral working groups [3.5.3]. This, however, did not satisfy some regions, especially the Basques and Catalans, who have both set up their own lobbying offices in Brussels.

Finally, in so far as Spain has ceded powers to the EU, it has meant the introduction of a new layer of government and so accentuated the problems of overlap already apparent [3.5.3]. At the same time, Spain's anxiety to meet the criteria for European Monetary Union [5.1.3] has implied strenuous efforts to cut the country's budget deficit, to which the regions are now a massive contributor. As a result, pressure to rationalise the structure of administration has increased further.

3.6 GLOSSARY

abertzale mf	(militant) supporter of Basque regionalism; Basque nationalist
administración única f	(system of) single administrative structure
Ajuria Enea	residence of Basque PM
Amejoramiento Foral m	Restoration of Navarre's Historic Rights
aportación f	reverse block grant (paid by Navarre to central govt)
autonomía f	autonomy; autonomous region
batzoki m	PNV local branch premises
brazo político m	political wing
cacique m	(corrupt) local party boss
café para todos m	(see *fiebre autonómica*)
cantonalismo m	cantonalism, demands for local self-rule
catalanismo m	Catalan regionalism
comisión mixta f	joint committee
competencias fpl	powers, responsibilities (of govt)
competencias transferibles fpl	areas of responsibility susceptible to being handed over to the regions under the 1978 Constitution
Comunidad Autónoma f	autonomous region
concierto económico m	financial agreement (between Basque Provinces and central govt)
conferencias sectoriales fpl	joint sectoral working groups
consejería f	regional ministry
consejero m	regional minister
consejo de gobierno m	(regional) cabinet
Consejo de Política Fiscal y Financiera de las CC AA m	Joint Fiscal and Funding Council
convenio económico m	financial agreement (between Navarre and central govt)
cooperación autonómica f	centre–region cooperation
corresponsabilidad fiscal f	shared fiscal responsibility
cupo m	reverse block grant (paid by Basque Provinces to central govt)
elecciones autonómicas fpl	regional election(s)
Ertzaintza f	Basque police force
Estado de las Autonomías m	present regionalised form of Spanish state
Estatuto de Autonomía m	Statute of Autonomy
Euskadi m	Basque homeland; Basque Country
euskera m	Basque language
fiebre autonómica f	'devolution fever', outbreak of demands for devolution in 1980–82
financiación autonómica f	regional funding
Fondo de Compensación Interterritorial m	Inter-regional Compensation Fund
fueros mpl	historic rights (esp. of Basque Provinces and Navarre)
Generalitat f	Catalan regional govt/Valencian regional govt
gobierno autonómico m	regional government

ikastola f	Basque-language school
impulso autonómico m	fresh momentum given to process of devolution
Junta f	name of govt of various regions, esp. Andalusia
lehendakari m	Basque prime minister
mapa autonómico m	division of Spain into regions
Mossos d'Esquadre m	Catalan police force
nacionalidad histórica f	'historic nationality', region granted autonomy under 2nd Republic
órganos preautonómicos mpl	bodies set up specifically to prepare for devolution
pactisme m	(Catalan) traditional readiness to reach negotiated agreements
pacto autonómico m	pact on the regions (1981; 1992)
Països Catalans mpl	Greater Catalonia (incl. Valencia and Balearics)
parlamento autonómico m	regional parliament
parlamento unicameral m	single-chamber parliament
presidente autonómico m	regional prime minister
proceso autonómico m	(process of) devolution
pujolismo m	contemporary Catalan regionalism, associated with J. Pujol
régimen común m	funding scheme applicable to most regions
régimen foral m	traditional system (esp. of funding) applicable to Basque Provinces and Navarre
sucursal f	branch party, regional party subordinate to Madrid leadership
transferencias fpl	handover of powers to regional govts
vasquismo m	Basque regionalism
vía lenta f	slow route (to autonomy)
vía rápida f	fast route (to autonomy)
Xunta f	Galician regional govt

4

INTERESTS AND LOBBIES

Modern democratic societies are characterised by a complex relationship between the apparatus of government and the rest of society. The interests of civil society, that is, those areas of national life outside the state's ambit, are channelled not just by political parties but a host of other organisations. In doing so they attempt to influence public policy but, like parties, they can act also as reverse channels, assisting the state to manipulate civil society. In Spain the nature of the Franco regime meant that certain of these organisations acquired a particular importance, and this chapter will begin by examining them. It will then go on to consider the representatives in Spain of the main interests and lobbies in contemporary Western societies: economic interest groups, the media and non-institutional pressure groups.

4.1 FRANCOISM'S 'DE FACTO AUTHORITIES'

Under the Franco regime, so powerful was the influence of certain interests outside what would normally be understood as the structure of the state that it was habitual to speak of them as the country's 'de facto authorities' (*poderes fácticos*). By its very nature the term is a vague one, and deliberately so. Yet there was never any doubt about the identity of the two main 'powers behind the throne' of the Franco era. Although retaining a degree of influence since 1975, both have seen their role greatly diminished, especially since the end of the transition.

4.1.1 The military

During the transition it was common to regard the greatest problem facing Spain as that posed by the military. Even into the late 1980s the question of how to ensure that the three armed forces (*fuerzas armadas – FF AA*) were kept out of politics continued to exercise the country's rulers. In fact, their concern was focused almost exclusively on the army (*Ejército de Tierra*). Not only was it by far the largest of the three services (*ejércitos*); in 1975 it numbered 220 000 men, the navy (*Marina*) only 46 000 and the air force (*Ejército del Aire*) a mere 35 000. It was also the army that had been particularly closely involved in the former regime and was most heavily impregnated with francoist beliefs.

4.1.1.1 Transition and the army

It is well known that the Spanish army has a long tradition of intervening in civil politics. In a sense, Franco's 1936 rising was merely the latest in a string of coups dating back to the 1820s [0.1.1]. However, his regime was unique in the extent to which the army subsequently became involved in running the country. Serving officers habitually held ministerial posts unconnected with military affairs; they exercised administrative responsibilities of many types and at various levels; they helped run the economy's huge public sector; they were even involved in private business, being invited on to the boards of a number of important companies.

These activities were clearly different from those normally expected of the army in a democracy. The same was true of its operational role during the Franco era. Rather than defending Spain against external threats, the army acted essentially as an internal occupation force, defending the regime against its own people. It was accordingly deployed on a territorial basis, in military regions each under the command of a captain-general. In each province a military authority (*Gobierno Militar*) worked alongside the civilian one [1.5.3], and the army was frequently called in to maintain public order.

Finally, the army had an important ideological role, exercised through the system of compulsory military service. As well as providing the army with the necessary manpower, this was seen by many officers as a means of inculcating into the country's young men the fundamental principles of the regime; unquestioning respect for authority, represented above all in the person of Franco, fervent Spanish nationalism and contempt for any vaguely socialist, or even liberal ideas.

Against this background it is scarcely surprising that, after the death of its former leader, the army should have been the main centre of extreme reactionary thinking and activity (*involucionismo*). Between 1976 and 1981 a succession of coup plots was uncovered, the most serious being the Galaxia affair named after the Madrid café where it was planned. The wholly negative reaction evoked by the 1981 failed coup attempt [0.1.3.3], which ranged from the monarch to the mass of ordinary Spaniards, was a salutary lesson for the reactionaries. But as recently as 1985 it would seem that a plot to assassinate King Juan Carlos, involving senior army officers, reached an advanced stage of planning before it was thwarted.

The centrist governments of 1976–82 were keenly aware of the dangers posed by the army's predisposition to plotting coups (*golpismo*). After the inaugural 1977 election a senior army figure convinced of the need for change, Lieutenant-General Manuel Gutiérrez Mellado, was brought into the cabinet as deputy to Prime Minister Adolfo Suárez. Given special responsibility for defence matters, his task was to ensure that the army's opportunities to intervene in politics were removed.

The 1977 cabinet changes also ended the practice of according ministerial rank to the heads of the three armed forces. Instead, a Ministry of Defence was set up, to whose political authority the service chiefs were subordinate. Military direction was placed in the hands of a new Joint Chiefs of Staff Council (*Junta de Jefes de Estado Mayor- JUJEM*). The following year the Constitution distinguished the role of the armed forces in defending Spain against external threats from that of the civilian security forces (*cuerpos de seguridad*) [9.2].

The Constitution's characteristic ambiguity was evident in other key aspects of the military's role. Its mission to defend Spain's sovereignty and territorial unity was given the status of a fundamental principle by inclusion in the Introductory Title [1.1.2]. Much less prominence was given to a specification that all the military's actions, including any related to national unity, are carried out under the supreme command of the monarch, itself subject to endorsement by democratically elected authorities [1.2]. It has sometimes been argued that this left the door dangerously open for the army to take unilateral action 'in the national interest'. Yet any such action would have been aimed against the constitutional order itself. In practice what mattered was not the Constitution's wording but the army's readiness and effective capacity to act unconstitutionally.

Sensibly, the government moved to limit both these factors. Before standing down as Defence Minister in 1979 to make way for a civilian, Gutiérrez Mellado took steps to reform pay scales and so reduce the risk of discontent. Under Suárez's successor, Leopoldo Calvo Sotelo, legislation was introduced to allow the dismissal of officers for 'incompetence'. This second measure was, in effect, a recognition that the government's real control over the army remained dangerously limited. Indeed, that had been demonstrated by the 1981 coup attempt, a number of whose instigators had already been found guilty of involvement in the Galaxia plot but had received only laughable sentences. Gutiérrez Mellado had been publicly insulted on several occasions by officers opposed to his reforms. It was only with the arrival in office of a government with a massive popular mandate that this situation was to change.

4.1.1.2 Modernisation and reform

Just as reform of the military during the transition is associated above all with the name of Gutiérrez Mellado, so the further changes undertaken thereafter are linked with that of Narcís Serra. Defence Minister from 1982 to 1991, Serra was himself a civilian. Under his tutelage, the military was for the first time brought clearly under the control of the civil authorities. Unlike its predecessor the new government invariably took quick and decisive action against recalcitrant officers.

Crucially the Socialist governments of the 1980s also recognised that the Spanish army's tendency to intervene in politics was not solely due to political conviction. As in the past it was partly the result of officers' grievances, over pay, conditions of service and professional satisfaction. Serra's initial reforms, carried out in 1983/84, set out to address these complaints, which in some respects had been aggravated under the former regime.

Franco's maintenance of a large officer corps constantly replenished from the military academies had left the country with a top-heavy army – of the 1975 strength of 220 000, over 24 000 were officers (*oficiales*). The result was that, even though individual officers' pay was poor, the overall wages bill was high and represented a major constraint on purchase of modern equipment. At the same time, promotion remained strictly based on length of service (*ascenso por antigüedad*). This ensured that mediocre officers reached senior positions while more able colleagues languished lower down the scale, with ample time to channel their frustration into political plotting.

Calvo Sotelo had attempted to address this problem by introducing merit bars to promotion at the level of major and brigadier. Inevitably these measures would take time to produce effects. Serra opted to tackle the traditionally sensitive issue of promotion indirectly. Merit criteria became general, but applied only to active commands, the number of which was greatly reduced. Those who failed to meet them continued to receive pay and even promotion, just as they would have done under the old system, but were transferred to a bizarrely named 'active reserve'. These measures improved officer quality and provided a means of sidelining potential troublemakers. In the longer term they also cut the real wages bill: more immediately they allowed financial juggling to free up funds for spending on hardware. That in turn was essential for the second front of Serra's strategy; involving the army in new, strictly defence tasks. It was a route on which Calvo Sotelo had already embarked by taking Spain into NATO [0.2.3].

The PSOE had opposed that move when in opposition, but reversed its position once in office [2.3.2]. This U-turn allowed the government to press ahead with ever-closer integration of the Spanish army's activities with those of forces from the country's democratically run neighbours. More recently, participation in UN peace-keeping missions has provided another such outlet. In 1989, in Angola, seven Spanish officers became the first to take part in such a mission. Within three years Spain had become the largest single contributor to UN forces.

At home the PSOE governments redeployed the army along lines more in accord with an external defence role, a process begun by the plan known as META (*Modernización del Ejército de Tierra*). The posts of captain-general and, later, provincial military governor were abolished. In 1984 the JUJEM [4.1.1.1] was reorganised and its head renamed Chief of the Defence Staff (*Jefe del Estado Mayor de la Defensa*). A second major plan approved in 1994, and known as Norte (*Nueva Organización del Ejército de Tierra*), provided for closure of many installations no longer needed and a slimmer, restructured army.

Once the forces' new role had had time to take root in military thinking, Serra returned to the attack on the promotions issue. In 1989 he introduced fast and slow tracks for promotion as low down the scale as major. The measure proved controversial at the time, but did not give rise to any lasting problems. Instead, debate about and within the military now centres on ensuring that the services can effectively carry out their external defence role. That has given rise, even inside the army itself, to voices advocating moves to a fully professional army, with the consequent scrapping of military service. The Socialist governments in power up to 1996 showed great caution in responding to such suggestions, despite the potential electoral benefits of scrapping the highly unpopular *'mili'* [8.4.2]. Plans drawn up in 1993 envisaged only 50 per cent professionalisation by the year 2000.

One reason was sensitivity to the feelings of army officers. Opinion polls in the late 1980s suggested that officers were still highly suspicious of democracy, with only a narrow majority preferring it to an authoritarian regime. However, the PSOE's reluctance to act also reflected the high potential cost of abandoning conscription altogether.

Defence spending in Spain is very low, at 1.26 per cent of GDP proportionately the lowest in NATO outside Luxembourg. As a direct result severe logistic problems have been apparent for some time in the operation of all the services. The conservative government elected in 1996 might be expected to be responsive to such problems. Yet it arrived in office committed to cut public spending, and also to more rapid professionalisation. It is unclear how it intends to square this circle.

Under these circumstances there is understandable concern in the forces over their ability to carry out satisfactorily the new role they have been allotted. Resultant discontent now probably represents the main threat of a return to traditional interventionist thinking. However, the changes of the last two decades mean that the military is in no position to take over the reins of government. Since 1975 government and business have become far too complex for it to control. Moreover, the military has lost its former links to other powerful interests in the country's business and political elite. Nor have potential plotters been able to forge alternative ones. Parties linked to reactionary elements in the military have enjoyed negligible success [2.6] and their only significant media mouthpiece proved unable to survive under democratic conditions [4.3.1].

4.1.2 The Church

Like that of the military, the position of the Roman Catholic Church in Spanish society has been a major issue for a century and a half. From the time of the Napoleonic Wars opposition to Church privileges and influence was a major feature of all the country's progressive forces. When they finally reached power, the anticlerical provisions they included in the Constitution of the Second Republic contributed directly to the Republic's downfall. Under the Franco regime which succeeded it, however, Church influence was not just restored but massively increased.

4.1.2.1 Transition and the Church

Like the military, the Church was a pillar of the Franco regime. School education was largely under its control, as well as most of what passed for a health and welfare system; it played a major part in censorship of the arts and media; its youth organisations helped to inculcate the regime's values. Its political importance to the regime was clear in the determination with which Franco defended his hard-won right, enshrined in the 1953 Concordat with the Vatican, to appoint Spain's bishops. In return the Church received extremely generous funding that effectively met the costs not only of its social service provision but also of its own ministry.

As a result of these various factors, the Church's position promised to be a major concern during the transition to democracy. Yet this proved not to be the case. The reason was to be found in the changes which had occurred in the Spanish Church itself during the latter part of Franco's dictatorship, changes encouraged by the Second Vatican Council (*Concilio Vaticano II*) held between 1962 and 1965. They were particularly apparent after 1971, when Cardinal Enrique y Tarancón became chairman of the Conference of Spanish Bishops (*Conferencia Episcopal Española – CEE*).

Under Tarancón support for liberalisation of the regime was increasingly apparent within the Church. At the same time, priests and bishops in the Basque Country and Catalonia became more vociferous in their backing, never completely hidden, for regionalist feeling in the two regions. Such attitudes were by no means universal in the Church, large parts of which remained deeply conservative in their social and political views. But they were sufficiently widespread to prevent the Church providing anything like unified opposition to democracy.

Certainly it tended to back the most conservative of the new, legalised political parties – in 1979 Church leaders explicitly called on the faithful to vote for People's Alliance [2.4.1]. Aware of the danger of reopening old wounds, however, they refrained from backing the formation of a specifically Christian Democrat party. They also urged voters to support the 1976 Political Reform Act, which effectively destroyed the political structure of the old regime [0.1.3.2], and the 1978 Constitution which defined the new democratic one.

The Constitution implicitly acknowledged the Church as an objective feature of Spanish society (*hecho sociológico*) – Catholicism remains Spain's largest faith, indeed virtually its only one since membership even of other Christian Churches is negligible. Yet the acknowledgement was minor and grudging. It required a parliamentary amendment to the draft text to insert the only specific reference to the Catholic Church. Even that was bracketed with mention of the 'remaining confessions', with whom the state must also 'maintain cooperative relations'. In general, although not going as far as that of 1933 by explicitly barring the Church from fields such as the education system, the Constitution made virtually no concessions to it. Article 14 establishes equality of all religions and outlaws discrimination against any, and Article 16 declares that the state shall have no official religion.

4.1.2.2 Church and state under democracy

Church–state relations since 1978 have proved less problematic than might have been expected, not least because of Catholic involvement in opposition to the Franco regime [4.1.2.1]. The extent of reconciliation between old opponents was symbolised by the presence of practising Catholics and even ex-seminarists in successive governments formed by the Socialist PSOE, traditionally a deeply anticlerical party. And it was the PSOE which made a concession to the Church widely regarded as infringing the Constitution's provisions on religious equality [4.1.2.1]. It concerned state funding for the Church's own ministry, which had continued unchanged up to 1982. Given that Spanish Catholics had no recent tradition of donation, its removal was potentially disastrous for the Church. Rather than force the issue, the government introduced a measure allowing individual tax-payers to designate a small percentage (around 0.5 per cent) of their income tax payments for the Church's use. What is more, instead of being a transitional one, to be phased out over a six-year period, this arrangement remains in force.

The payment was immediately labelled a 'Church tax' (*impuesto religioso*). In fact that was not strictly accurate; the government had also agreed that, whatever the sum raised in this way, it would continue to maintain the Church's overall subsidy in real terms. In other words, all tax-payers continued to support the Church whether they opted to or not.

The generous settlement of its financial situation did not prevent the Church from opposing other government measures in the 1980s, especially once the conservative Angel Suquía was elected to succeed Tarancón as chairman of the Bishops' Conference in 1987. Limited legalisation of abortion in that year met with even greater Church opposition than that of divorce six years before. However, the main area of contention was education.

Both the PSOE's major pieces of schools legislation trod on Catholic sensibilities [7.2.2, 7.2.3]. Both were bitterly opposed by the Church, which organised opposition to them. The first campaign, in particular, showed the strength of the Church's hold on important sections of public opinion. Yet ultimately both measures were passed, just as divorce and abortion were legalised. Although traditional Catholic opinion was vociferous on occasion, it was very definitely in the minority.

Moreover, attempting to use its influence to affect public policy may well have been damaging for the Church. For it was clear that the great majority of Spaniards, Catholics or not, did not favour that sort of intervention. The Church itself tacitly admitted as much when the time came to replace Suquía as its effective leader. In 1993 the CEE elected as its new chairman Bishop Elías Yanes, noted for his more liberal and conciliatory attitudes.

Not only is there widespread suspicion of Church influence; in practice its presence in society is declining. Although the percentage of Spaniards who claim to be Catholics has remained fairly static, the number of practising ones (*practicantes*) is falling steadily; it is now widely estimated to stand at between 30 and 40 per cent of adults. The number of persons entering

Holy Orders (*vocaciones*) has dropped more rapidly. As with church-going there are marked regional variations, but in some regions the result is a severe shortage of personnel to carry out the Church's social functions and even its own ministry.

Nevertheless, one-sixth of Spain's schools are still run by the Church, albeit under much tighter government control than before; while in some the level of education is extremely poor, in others it is sufficiently good to persuade even non-Catholic parents to opt for them. Unlike the military [4.1.1.2], the Church has also been able to establish some links with other power centres in the new democracy. The 1989 transformation of the main conservative party into the People's Party (PP), a name explicitly indicative of Christian Democrat tendencies [2.4.2], acknowledged the Church's continuing importance as a pillar of the political right. And, despite the failure of its own press organ, it also has a continuing strong presence in the media through its radio interests [4.3.1].

A number of these links are through the agency of the Catholic lay organisation Opus Dei, which exercised great influence during the latter stages of the Franco era. Many of the regime's expert advisers were Opus Dei members [0.1.2]. It was the dictator who permitted the 'Opus', as it is widely known, to set up the University of Navarre, in Pamplona, and its business school offshoot, the Barcelona-based IESE, both of which have reputations for producing high-quality graduates. Opus Dei members also control one of Spain's largest banks, the Banco Popular [4.2.1].

As a result, despite the regime's disappearance the group has continued to extend its influence in the business world and into other areas such as the media. Several leading figures in the PP, in power since 1996, are alleged to be Opus members, thus providing a direct channel for Church influence on government. Given the order's francoist links, however, this may prove a double-edged sword for the Church – and for its political allies [2.4.3].

4.2 ECONOMIC INTERESTS

In modern capitalist democracies typically the most prominent of the lobbies which attempt to sway government policy are economically based. Specifically, they relate to the interests of the main factors of production, on the one hand, labour or the workforce, or on the other, capital and its owners, the employers. In recent years, with the emergence of the financial sector not just as an instrument of the owners of capital but as a major driving force of economic events, it has become an important interest in its own right. In Spain, perhaps surprisingly, it already had that status prior to 1975.

4.2.1 The banks

The Franco regime's extensive intervention in the country's economy [5.1.1] made control over the sources of credit vital. To a certain extent it was achieved by direct intervention. The country's central bank, the Bank of Spain, was nationalised in 1962 and the government was a major supplier of business credit. By and large, however, Franco left the large private banks (*banca privada*) untouched. They were controlled by deeply conservative individuals and families whose support for the regime was never in doubt and who, like the Church and the military, exercised considerable influence under it. Indeed, the big banks (*gran banca*) were often regarded as among the 'de facto authorities' behind the regime [4.1].

During the delicate process of transition which followed Franco's death, a functioning banking system was essential if economic collapse were to be avoided. All the leading political players, including the Socialists who might have been expected to attempt to curtail the banks' influence, were at pains not to alienate the sector. As a result the banks continued to control large swathes of Spanish industry through their shareholdings and their role as credit-provider. When large-scale investment funds appeared in the country they too did so largely under the banks' aegis. Moreover, the coming of democracy allowed them to extend their influence in several ways.

Thus with the opening up of the media to private capital, the banks inevitably acquired a considerable degree of control in that vital sector. At the same time, they acquired a new, formalised role in the formulation of government economic policy. Since government control over the Bank of Spain was loosened in 1980, the larger banks have been assured representation on its supervisory Board (*Consejo General*). Similarly, they are represented on the National Banking Authority (*Consejo Superior Bancario*), which has a statutory right to be consulted on interest-rate policy decisions.

The banks also have an important role in financing the political parties [2.1.3]; hardly surprising, then, that on coming to power in 1982 the Socialists made an obvious priority of cultivating contacts with the banks. The key intermediary was Finance Minister Miguel Boyer, who himself later returned to a senior post in the sector. Whether as a result of his efforts, or because the Socialists' economic policies earned the banks' trust, there was little or no evidence that they attempted to use their control over credit against the party while it was in office.

On one occasion, however, the banks did make a clear attempt to influence party fortunes. In 1986 they tried to torpedo Adolfo Suárez's new centrist party [2.2.3]. The outcome was interesting in two respects. First, the attempt was a spectacular failure. And second, Suárez's own outspoken attacks on the big banks evidently did him no electoral harm. That points to one way in which the post-Franco transition has limited the banks' power as well as consolidating it; their exercise of it is more open to the public gaze under democratic conditions.

However, it is not democracy as such that has most affected the banks' political influence, but rather the altered business environment it has brought about. Under the Franco regime the private banking sector operated in a way that had very little to do with modern business practice. Internally, decisions were taken by a bank's chairman, often a virtually hereditary post, with little regard for the opinions of other shareholders. The 'big seven' banks operated as a cartel, preferring cooperation to competition in business as well as in lobbying government.

Since 1975 this situation has been radically altered, as Spain's economy has been opened up to the forces of free-market capitalism and international competition. One result was a succession of mergers which reduced the number of leading banks to around four [5.3.3]. This process of concentration may have increased the commercial power of its individual survivors, but did not necessarily do the same for their collective political influence. For one thing, the Spanish banking system is now subject to a considerable degree of foreign control. By 1995 almost 30 per cent of its shares were held by foreign investors, mainly themselves banks. Neither these nor their Spanish counterparts now play the game by the same rules as their predecessors. An early illustration came when the *Banco Central*'s attempt to take over *Banesto* was thwarted by two major shareholders opposed to the chairman's plans. More recently, the sector witnessed the rise and fall of the controversial businessman Mario Conde [9.4.1] which, in its own way, also demonstrated how even the largest Spanish banks are now subject to purely market forces.

These changes do not mean that the banks can no longer significantly influence government policy. Quite the contrary; as elsewhere in the West their interests are of considerable importance in that regard, and the Association of Spanish Banks (*Asociación Española de Banca Privada – AEB*) remains one of the country's most powerful lobbies. However, those interests are now more purely economic than in the past. In so far as they are political, they are essentially those of international finance capital, not of a particular social group within Spain itself.

4.2.2 Employers

Just as in the case of the political right [2.1.1], Spain's employers (*patronal*) have only begun to organise effectively since 1975. Once again the principal reason lies in the country's late economic development. Significantly in Catalonia, the region which industrialised earliest and most intensely, the situation was different. The Catalan Development Association (*Fomento de Trabajo Nacional – FTN*) was already a powerful force before the end of the last century and indeed provided the impetus for political regionalism (3.2.1). Elsewhere, however, business interests were much less influential than those of the traditional agricultural elite.

Only after 1960 did Spain experience widespread industrialisation, and then under very special circumstances. The Franco regime's authoritarian policies ensured that, with occasional exceptions, the labour force remained docile and wage demands muted. At the same time the country's economic isolation effectively protected its businesses from outside competition. It is understandable that employers saw little need to organise, even if they had been permitted to do so.

On the other hand, Franco's belief in strict state control led him to impose on the country's developing industries an extraordinary mass of regulations, only partially dismantled after the change in economic policy in 1959/60 [0.1.2]. They covered virtually all aspects of business activity, including prices as well as the labour market. Their effect was to stifle business initiative. As a result, the more enterprising of Spain's employers latterly supported moves to bring Spain's business environment in line with the much less restricted conditions of its democratic neighbours.

Such deregulation has been the most consistent demand of the body that now represents the interests of employers at national level. The Spanish Employers' Confederation (*Confederación Española de Organizaciones Empresariales – CEOE*) was founded in 1977. As its title suggests, the CEOE is in fact a relatively loose alliance of organisations which have retained considerable independence. Some 130 of them represent employers in particular industries. Others, over 50 in total, are regional and provincial groupings among which the Catalan FTN continues to be prominent.

Individual firms typically belong to several of these affiliated organisations. They have acquired renewed importance since the mid-1980s, due both to the growing importance of regional government, and to the abandonment of the national-level 'social contracts' of the previous decade [4.2.4]. In any case, the stress placed by the CEOE's national leadership on deregulation has not always been well received by the small and medium-sized enterprises, which form such a large part of the Spanish corporate sector (*sector empresarial*) [5.4.2]. For the protected conditions of the Franco era left many SMEs technically ill-equipped and psychologically ill-prepared for the increased competition implied by deregulation.

These particular interests were reflected during the transition in the creation of a distinct Spanish Confederation of SMEs (*Confederación Española de Pequeñas y Medianas Empresas – CEPYME*). In 1980 CEPYME affiliated to the CEOE, which thus cemented its claim to represent all employers. However, a number of significant employers' organisations remain outside the CEOE, especially in the agricultural sector. CEPYME also continues to exist and to operate with considerable independence on behalf of SMEs. Moreover, these frequently regard yet another type of organisation as the most effective channel for their interests.

Spain's Chambers of Commerce, Industry and Navigation (*Cámaras de Comercio, Industria y Navegación*) date from 1911 and are organised on a provincial basis. Like those in most continental countries, the Chambers of Commerce have considerably greater practical importance than their British counterparts. They exercise statutory responsibilities relating to the general economic well-being of their area and are funded by the fees all local employers are required to pay. This compulsory affiliation naturally provokes some employer resentment. But the tensions frequently evident between the Chambers and the CEOE also reflect the fact that the Chambers represent interests specific to the CEOE's smaller members which sometimes seem to be neglected by its national leaders.

At the same time, larger firms also sometimes feel the need for alternative means of lobbying. In some cases this is done through the appropriate industry-specific organisation, of which the most powerful is that representing the banks [4.2.1]. To represent interests common to all bigger firms, a number have banded together in the Business Circle (*Círculo de Empresarios*), which in some ways resembles the UK Institute of Directors. The management education it provides is in Spain promoted by a separate organisation, the Association for Progress in Business (*Asociación para el Progreso Empresarial – APE*).

As well as in this variety of organisations, the differing interests of Spanish employers have been reflected in apparent uncertainty on the CEOE's part about how best to influence public policy. Its first chairman was Carlos Ferrer Salat, of the Catalan FNT. Under his leadership the CEOE entered a series of broad agreements on economic and social policy with unions and government [4.2.4], an approach maintained after the Socialists came to power in 1982. It was radically changed, however, once Ferrer was replaced as chairman by José María Cuevas. Before his election in 1984 Cuevas had been involved in attempts to bring together all the forces of the right and centre-right in a party capable of challenging the Socialist government [2.4.1]. After it, he took a more confrontational attitude both to the PSOE and to the unions, with whom the CEOE signed no new agreements after 1984.

Instead, the CEOE concentrated on building up influence over the conservative opposition party, People's Alliance (AP), to which it gave considerable financial backing. When in 1987 AP switched to a policy line less acceptable to employers Cuevas abruptly withdrew this support [2.4.2]. The move was instrumental in AP's transformation into the People's Party (PP), and a switch back to more employer-friendly policies. Thereafter CEOE's renewed support, public and financial, was an important factor in the PP's rise to power in 1996.

This close link with the new party of government obviously gives the CEOE greatly increased influence, yet it remains limited by other pressures on the PP. During the 1996 general election campaign, Cuevas set out publicly a 'shopping list' of CEOE's expectations of a conservative administration. The PP's leader, José María Aznar, was quick to deny that the CEOE's demands were his party's policy.

Aznar's reaction reflected his party's anxiety to portray itself as 'centrist' in its push to gain power [2.4.3]. For electoral reasons the PP cannot afford to appear to be in the employers' pocket. Recognising this, the CEOE has displayed renewed interest in agreement with unions in the 1990s [4.2.4], as an alternative means of influencing events.

4.2.3 Trade unions

Unlike the country's employers' representatives, the Spanish trade union movement (*sindicalismo*) has a long history, dating from the late nineteenth century. Like parties of the left, however, unions were long held back by the country's failure to industrialise on a large scale and, latterly, by francoist repression.

4.2.3.1 Development and legal status

The relative weakness of left-wing parties reinforced a key feature of Spanish unions – their overtly political nature. From the outset unions were concerned as much or more with furthering the general interests of workers as with workplace issues. In line with this philosophy they recruited members right across the industrial spectrum and not, as in the UK, from particular trades or industries.

Strictly speaking, the largest Spanish unions were, and are, confederations of individual 'trade' unions. Rather than in their field of recruitment they differ in their political orientation. Historically the two largest were the anarchist National Labour Confederation (*Confederación Nacional de Trabajo – CNT*) and the General Workers' Union (*Unión General de Trabajadores – UGT*), closely linked to the Socialist PSOE.

Under the Second Republic both the CNT and UGT attained considerable influence. Subsequently they were banned by the Franco regime, which permitted only its own system of government-controlled unions [0.1.2]. However, in the late 1950s the extreme economic conditions suffered by many workers led them to organise outside these, initially at the level of individual firms. The first such Workers' Commission was formed in 1958, at the La Camocha mine in Asturias.

Soon, however, the individual organisations banded together in an underground union movement, known as Workers' Commissions (*Comisiones Obreras – CCOO*). Before long CCOO came to be effectively controlled by the Communist Party (PCE). Under the PCE's direction, CCOO played a leading role in what organised opposition there was to the Franco regime. As a result, it and its leader, Marcelino Camacho, enjoyed considerable standing when the transition began. The same applied – essentially for historical reasons, as it had been only marginally involved in underground opposition – to UGT and its general secretary, Nicolás Redondo.

With the coming of democracy this popular prestige was matched by a radical change in trade unions' legal status. Included among the fundamental principles set out in the 1978 Constitution's Introductory Title [1.1.2] was the unions' right to defend their members' legitimate interests. This and other constitutional provisions were given concrete form in the 1980 Workers' Charter (*Estatuto de los Trabajadores*) and the 1984 Trade Union Freedom Act (*Ley Orgánica de Libertad Sindical – LOLS*).

In particular, the LOLS consolidated the system of workplace elections (*elecciones sindicales*) established by the Charter. They operate on a list system similar to that used for parliamentary contests [1.3.1], the lists being presented by unions or other groupings of workers. In companies with over 50 employees the elected representatives (*delegados*) make up a workforce committee (*comité de empresa*) with the statutory right to be informed and consulted by the employer. These committees differ from true works' councils in the sense that they are representatives of the workforce, not forums for debate with the employer.

4.2.3.2 Weakness and division

Acknowledgement of unions' importance in the Constitution and subsequent legislation reflected a real phenomenon during the early stages of the transition. At that time the workplace-based unions found it easier to organise quickly than the parties, like them newly legalised. Indeed, for a brief period unions' membership soared, as they seemed to represent the main channel through which ordinary Spaniards could press for far-reaching change.

Yet, when the crucial Moncloa Pacts were reached [0.1.3.3], it was the parties of the left that negotiated with the government. The unions were left with the task of persuading their members to accept the agreements, often unpalatable for them. Much the same was true of the series of pacts in which unions joined with government and employers between 1979 and 1985 [4.2.4]. Participation in them indicated not strength but weakness, traceable in part to Spain's persistent unemployment problem but also to certain features of the trade union movement itself.

First, after the brief surge experienced during the transition, the density of union membership – that is, the proportion of the workforce which is affiliated to a union – has sunk steadily. By the mid-1990s it was among the lowest in Europe, standing at around 15 per cent according to most estimates. This, in turn, is attributable to a number of causes.

One is the dominance of small and medium-sized firms in Spain's industrial structure [5.4.2], since the level of union membership is typically lower in such companies. Another is the system of workplace elections for, as employees do not have to be a union member to vote, one major incentive to join is removed. Unions themselves have relatively little incentive to seek new members, since under the 1985 Trade Union Freedom Act [4.2.3.1] nonmembers must pay a contribution towards union funds (*canon sindical*). Finally, like parties, unions receive public funding (*financiación estatal*) and that is based on the results of workplace elections, not membership figures.

Second, the union movement is fragmented. Admittedly, UGT and CCOO are by far the largest unions, regularly filling between 70 and 80 per cent of places on workforce committees. No other union can match their nation- and economy-wide strength; the CNT was fatally weakened by Franco's repression, the Workers' Trade Union (*Unión Sindical Obrera – USO*) by a split in the early 1980s that saw many of its most able leaders leave to join UGT. None the less, a number of other unions are strong in particular regions and industries.

The most important regional union is Basque Workers' Solidarity (*Eusko Langileak Alkartasuna – ELA-STV*); indeed, in the Basque Country it is the largest employees' organisation. Also significant are Basque Workers' Commissions (*Langile Abertzale Batzordeak – LAB*), which despite its name is linked to ETA rather than CCOO, and the Galician Interunion Confederation (*Confederación Intersindical Gallega – CIG*).

Sectoral unions include a number of highly disparate groups. Some represent workers in the expanding white collar occupations, the best established being the Confederation of Independent Public Servants' Unions (*Confederación de Sindicatos Independientes de Funcionarios – CSIF*). At the opposite end of the occupational spectrum is the Landworkers' Union (*Sindicato de Obreros del Campo – SOC*). Inheritor of the Andalusian tradition of rural anarchism, during the 1980s the SOC organised direct action in favour of land reform [5.3.1]. Finally, mention should be made of the company-sponsored unions to be found in some large firms, particularly in the retail sector. These are regarded with distrust by the remainder of the movement which regards them as 'bosses' unions' (*sindicatos amarillos*).

The wide differences between these smaller employees' representatives have inevitably led to disagreement on aims and strategy. However, the third – and perhaps the most critical – cause of union weakness has been disunity between its two dominant members. Thus well into the 1980s CCOO saw itself as an instrument to win both political and economic concessions from government as well as employers, and in order to achieve them it adopted militant methods. It was thus the prime mover behind the high level of industrial unrest (*conflictividad laboral*) during the early part of the transition, frequently backing strikes in individual firms or calling them to support wider political demands. Meanwhile UGT tended to take a more cautious line. It concentrated on workplace issues, specifically pay and conditions, and was much more disposed to pursue demands through negotiation, either with individual employers or with the government.

4.2.3.3 From militancy to moderation

In practice UGT's moderate approach proved more successful than CCOO's militancy in winning concrete concessions. By 1982 it had overtaken CCOO in terms of support in workplace elections [4.2.3.1]. Its leaders expected to consolidate this success by exploiting links with the union's sister party (*partido hermano*), the Socialist PSOE, which came to power that year.

As regards its own interests as an organisation, these hopes were largely fulfilled. In particular, the Trade Union Freedom Act [4.2.3.1] contained two provisions for which UGT had lobbied. It increased the period between union elections from two years to four, and gave the main role in collective negotiations not to the company committees, but to union sections representing a whole industry (*sección sindical*). In both cases these measures favoured UGT at the expense of CCOO, which tended to be better established at workplace level.

However, UGT's expectations on behalf of its members were disappointed; from an early stage the Socialist government pursued economic and social policies which hit them hard [5.1.2]. In 1985 reform of the pension system, to the actual or potential disbenefit of many union members, led UGT leader Redondo to threaten resignation as a Socialist MP; two years later he carried out his threat in response to proposals for further cuts in social spending. Thereafter relations between the industrial and political wings of the socialist movement (*familia socialista*) deteriorated progressively.

UGT increasingly joined Workers' Commissions in demanding that the government pay less attention to purely economic considerations and more to social ones. It also adopted the more militant methods favoured by CCOO. On three occasions between 1988 and 1994 the two largest unions jointly organised general strikes against government policy. The biggest of these stoppages was the first, called on 14 December 1988 (*14-D*) against government plans for special low-wage contracts for the young. The enormous turnout brought virtually the whole country to a standstill. Some four years later a government decree cutting unemployment benefit provoked a second general strike. This stoppage, held on 27 May 1992 (*27-M*), commanded less popular support. The downward trend continued when UGT and CCOO issued their third joint strike call, in January 1994, directed as in 1988 against proposed labour market reforms [5.2.4].

Declining public support for such militancy, despite considerable sympathy with its motives, both mirrored the unions' relative impotence and further aggravated it. Although the youth employment plan was withdrawn in 1988 and minor concessions made in 1992, in neither case did the unions' show of strength force a change in the general direction of government policy. Admittedly, unions' lobbying bore some fruit in the relatively favourable provisions of the 1994 Strikes Act (*Ley de Huelga*). But in general their influence remained low in the later years of Socialist rule. It is hardly likely to be increased with the 1996 election of a right-wing government closely linked to employers [4.2.2].

This low level of influence is partly due to international developments. Throughout the West unions have had little success in preventing deregulation of economies which in turn has further weakened their position. However, in Spain their position was particularly difficult in the 1980s. Time and again unions were effectively in the position of defending measures introduced by the Franco regime against the liberalising measures carried out by a government of the left.

In recent years, there have been signs that the big unions are aware of the need to escape from the legacy of their past. In both cases this has involved a change of leader, UGT's Redondo being replaced by Cándido Méndez, and CCOO's Camacho by Antonio Gutiérrez. It has also meant moves away from militant tactics aimed at changing government social and economic policy, towards a more moderate approach centred on workplace issues.

For CCOO, which remains the principal employee representative in most of Spain's larger firms, this change of line has brought problems. It implies a radical break with the union's past; Gutiérrez, its chief supporter, has attempted to distance CCOO from the Communist Party (PCE) to which, although always close, the union was never formally linked. His moves have produced a strong reaction both from the PCE leadership and from dissidents within the CCOO itself (*sector crítico*). Yet, even so, CCOO as well as UGT has markedly become more moderate under Gutiérrez's leadership.

4.2.4 Limited corporatism

Corporatist is a term used to describe societies in which key decisions are taken by the government in conjunction with organised interest groups, in particular employers and employees. The Franco regime, with its government-run trade unions [0.1.2], shared some features of this model, albeit in an authoritarian form. Equally importantly, the nature of Spain's transition to democracy after Franco's death favoured the growth of corporatism, with the leaderships of all major political forces anxious to prevent events slipping out of control [0.1.3.3].

The most visible example of corporatism during the first decade of democracy was the government's practice of negotiating major policy issues with the national representatives of employers and workers (*concertación social*). It resulted in a series of agreements between these 'social partners' (*interlocutores sociales*). Some were tripartite, the government being a third signatory; on other occasions it promoted the pacts without actually joining them.

The 1977 Moncloa Pacts between the political parties [0.1.3.3] represented a forerunner of these agreements, four of which were signed between 1980 and 1984. The subject matter varied, but invariably included a national benchmark for wage increases, along with a number of other economic, industrial relations and social issues (*see* Table 4.1). The last such pact, the 1984 Economic and Social Agreement, was twice renewed after its initial one-year term, but finally lapsed in 1987.

Since then, the practice of national tripartite negotiation has not been revived. Although there has been frequent reference to the desirability of a further 'social contract' (*pacto social*), there have been few real attempts to conclude one. Those that were made ended in failure; neither the 1990 Competitiveness Pact (*Pacto para la Competitividad*) nor the 1991 Social Contract for Progress (*Pacto Social para el Progreso*) were ultimately signed. Unions were disillusioned at repeated failure to bring down unemployment levels [5.2.4], while employers and government seemed content to allow market forces to determine wage levels and other economic variables.

Another retreat from corporatism was the failure to implement fully an injunction set out in the Constitution. This required the government to establish a body, to include representatives of the social partners, charged with ensuring that economic policy reflect certain social objectives including income redistribution. After lengthy discussion a National Social and Economic Policy Forum (*Consejo Económico y Social – CES*) was finally established in 1992, with equal representation of unions, employers' organisations

Table 4.1 Social contracts, 1977–87

Title	Year signed	Signatories	Main issues covered
Moncloa Pacts (*Pactos de la Moncloa*)	1977	Political parties	Wages Taxes and public spending Public security
Union–Employer Framework Agreement (*Acuerdo Marco Interconfederal – AMI*)	1980	CEOE; UGT, USO	Wages and conditions Job creation Industrial relations
National Employment Agreement (*Acuerdo Nacional de Empleo – ANE*)	1981	Government; CEOE; UGT, CCOO	Wages Social security Industrial relations
National Union–Employer Agreement (*Acuerdo Interconfederal – AI*)	1983	CEOE, CEPYME; UGT, CCOO	Wages and conditions Industrial relations

National Economic and Social
   Agreement
(*Acuerdo Económico y Social – AES*)
	1984	Government;
		CEOE,
		CEPYME; UGT
			Wages
			Job creation and
			   investment
			Public spending
			Social security
			Industrial relations

and consumer groups. However, the CES is purely advisory, and is generally regarded as a mere talking shop.

Nevertheless, a considerable degree of corporatism continues to exist in Spain. Unions and employers enjoy statutory representation on the governing bodies of many administrative entities. Perhaps the most important are the Agencies responsible for the Health Service (INSALUD), Social Security (INSS) and Social Services (INSERSO), as well as the National Employment Agency (INEM). In addition, as union attitudes moderated in the 1990s [4.2.3.3], some union–employer national agreements have once again been reached. Unlike the general pacts of the 1980s, however, they have related to specific issues, such as vocational training [7.3.3].

One important result has been a renewed effort to improve Spain's poor industrial relations (*relaciones laborales*). This had already been attempted during the first round of post-Franco corporatism, in 1979, through the establishment of a government-run Mediation, Arbitration and Conciliation Agency (*Instituto de Mediación, Arbitraje y Conciliación – IMAC*). However, the IMAC, whose approach was based on time-consuming and expensive recourse to the courts, proved ineffectual and was wound up in 1985. The 1996 Agreement on Out-of-Court Settlement of Industrial Disputes (*Acuerdo sobre Solución Extrajudicial de Conflictos Laborales – ASEC*) aims to avoid such problems. Thus, although it commits employers and unions to submit disputes to mediation, under the ASEC conciliation services will be entrusted to independent individuals appointed by a Joint Union–Employer Mediation and Arbitration Service (*Servicio Interconfederal de Mediación y Arbitraje – SIMA*). The government's role will be limited to funding the SIMA.

Finally, union federations and employers' organisations are represented on a host of administrative bodies at the regional tier of government established in the 1980s. Andalusia is a particular stronghold of regional corporatism. On the other hand, as at national level, participation remains restricted essentially to employers and unions. Beyond the social partners, Spanish interest groups are too weak to sustain a more broad-based type of corporatism [4.4].

4.3 THE MEDIA

Nowadays the mass media (*medios de comunicación de masas*) play an important part in the power structure of all developed societies. The news media (*medios informativos*), traditionally the press but now also its audiovisual cousins radio and television, have come to represent a fourth estate (*cuarto poder*), to rank alongside parliament, government and the judiciary. In some countries that has given rise to concern about the influence of privately controlled media interests on public policy. In Spain, however, concern has until recently centred on the opposite problem; excessive state control over the media.

4.3.1 Media and the state

The Spanish media, like so many of the country's institutions, are heavily influenced by the experience of the Franco era. Not only was media output subject to censorship even after the more liberal legislation introduced in 1966 by Manuel Fraga [2.4.1], and commonly known as the 'Fraga Act' (*Ley Fraga*). In addition, the regime and its closest supporters controlled vast swathes of the media, including the government news agency Efe, a chain of newspapers and the entire radio and television networks.

Indeed, television in Spain was a creation of the Franco regime. The Spanish Television Authority (*Televisión Española – TVE*) was set up as a state monopoly in 1952 and a single channel (*canal*) began broadcasting four years later. In 1963 a second channel went on the air. In 1973 TVE was merged with the state's radio stations (*emisoras*), principally Spanish National Radio (*Radio Nacional de España – RNE*). The resultant public corporation (*ente público*) is known as the Spanish Broadcasting Authority (*Radiotelevisión Española – RTVE*).

With the coming of democracy, this concentration of media power was diluted. From 1977 elected governments reduced their direct control over the media. In the late 1970s and again a decade later hundreds of new radio broadcasting licences were issued. By 1984 the last of the state's own chain of newspapers had been sold off.

Another factor in francoist control of the media was ownership of media organs by powerful institutions closely linked to the regime [4.1]. Particularly significant in that regard was the Church, which owned a number of newspapers – most notably the national daily *Ya* – and the chain of radio stations known as COPE (*Cadena de Ondas Populares Españolas*). COPE continues under Church control to the present, and, indeed, has a very considerable audience. However, the influential Catholic lay group Opus Dei [4.1.2.2] was forced to sell its controlling interest in Spain's oldest radio station *Cadena Ser*. And *Ya* suffered a dramatic fall in readership before being sold off in 1989.

The military was even less successful in maintaining the foothold in the post-1975 press spectrum provided by the daily *El Alcázar*. It openly backed a return to authoritarianism and was closely linked to various military plots including the failed 1981 coup. In 1988, however, falling sales forced it to cease publication.

Despite these various changes, state influence over the media remained considerable into the 1980s. In part this influence was indirect. Thus governments of both UCD and the PSOE issued radio broadcasting licences to sympathetic business interests and, in the latter case, local authorities controlled by the government party. In addition, however, a degree of direct state control over Spain's media continues to exist. The central government still controls Efe, by far the largest Spanish-language news agency and among the world's biggest. This is a position unique among Western democracies; it is of particular importance in Spain given the dependence on agency reports for national and international news of the country's many regional newspapers [4.3.4].

4.3.2 Television pluralism

During the 1980s the main focus of mounting public concern over government control of the media and its abuse was the state television monopoly. In its origins this was quite unlike any other public broadcaster in the contemporary Western world, since it had been conceived as an instrument of regime propaganda. The attitudes and practices engendered by such a role could not be changed overnight.

As in public administration and the security forces, the existence of valuable technical expertise within the organisation did not allow for a complete purge of personnel in RTVE. There, however, continuity of personnel was not the decisive factor; the bulk of journalistic staff were actively in favour of change. Crucially, in the case of television, the actions of the country's new leaders reinforced old values rather than undermining them.

Not the least of Adolfo Suárez's qualifications for the task of moving Spain seamlessly from dictatorship to democracy was his period in charge of the francoist state television service. During his time as premier he drew on that experience to considerable effect. He used the powerful influence of television news programmes (*espacios informativos*), and not just to help implant democratic attitudes among Spaniards. It was also a key element in the 1977 and 1979 election campaigns of Suárez's own party, UCD, which was given massively better coverage than all its opponents combined.

Understandably, these protested vociferously and demanded that democratisation be extended to RTVE [4.3.1]. In 1980 the corporation was given a charter (*estatuto*). This set up a Board of Governors (*Consejo de Administración*) whose twelve members are appointed by Parliament. It is on the Board's advice that the government appoints RTVE's executive head, the director general, whose independence is theoretically protected in that he or she may be dismissed only on professional grounds.

Like a number of aspects of Spain's new democracy, these arrangements depended heavily for their effectiveness in limiting government control on its lack of an overall parliamentary majority [1.4.1]. Even without one, UCD was able to persuade the Governors three times in two years of successive director generals' 'incompetence'. The PSOE's sweeping 1982 election victory allowed it unbridled control over the appointment of Governors and the director general, and the party conveniently lost sight of its previous support for increasing pluralism in television by permitting private stations. Indeed, once in power, the Socialists began to trumpet the potential dangers of such a step and the virtues of public broadcasting.

Instead, the first move to increase the range of TV channels came through establishment of TV stations run by the country's new regional authorities. The first of these, Basque Television (*Euskal Telebista – ETB*) began broadcasting at the end of 1983; the following year *TV-3*, run by the Catalan Broadcasting Corporation (*Corporació Catalana de Ràdio i Televisió – CC/RTV*), came on the air. In both cases the original justification was promotion of the respective regional languages, as it was later to be in Galicia.

Yet before long ETB, in defiance of previous agreements and legislation, opened a purely Spanish language channel. In 1989 the PSOE government granted licences to three regions, two of whom had no regional language but all of which were under its political control. By 1995 a total of eight regional channels were in operation in the Basque Country (*ETB-1, ETB-2*), Catalonia (*TV-3, Canal 33*), Galicia (*TVG*), Andalusia (*Canal Sur*), Valencia (*Canal 9*) and Madrid (*Telemadrid* or *TM-3*). All are run on lines similar to those of RTVE, and so subject to a considerable degree of control from the respective regional governments.

By 1995 the issue of private television had long since been settled, forced by events in 1986. In that year bias in TVE's news coverage reached new heights, first for the NATO referendum and later for the general election, during which the government created a special team within TVE to 'coordinate' coverage of the campaign. In 1989 it was finally obliged to bring in legislation, providing for creation of three private TV stations (*televisiones privadas*) and setting conditions for the concession of licences and their sub-sequent operation.

The following year the three successful bidders – *Antena 3*, *Canal Plus* and *Tele 5* – went on the air. They brought about a revolution in the habits of Spain's viewers (*televidentes*). *Antena 3* and *Tele 5* both now argue over the largest audience share (*audiencia*) with the first public channel, *TVE-1*. *Canal Plus*, reception of which requires the viewer to buy a decoder (*descodificador*), has a somewhat lower share, but still higher than that of the second public channel, renamed *La2*. In some areas at least the regional channels also claim a significant, albeit minority audience share.

4.3.3 Media groups

The advent of private television was instrumental in the most significant recent development on the Spanish media scene; the establishment of powerful media interests outside state control. The best known of these is the group known as PRISA (*Promotor de Informaciones SA*), whose chairman is Jesús de Polanco. It was set up originally to run the newspaper *El País*, which first appeared in 1976 and rapidly established itself as the country's best-selling daily. An initial venture into radio under the same name proved a failure; however, in 1985 PRISA acquired control over the financially troubled *Cadena Ser*, Spain's oldest radio station [4.3.1]. It also controls *Canal Plus* television [4.3.2].

These various holdings give PRISA considerable potential influence. By and large it has been exercised in line with the objectives of its founders, a collection of individuals united by the desire to provide an independent information source and forum for public debate, and so promote Spain's democratisation and also modernisation. Perhaps inevitably, that led *El País* in particular to offer fairly consistent support to the Socialist Party, even once the various 'affairs' of the late 1980s and 1990s revealed a distinctly undemocratic side to the party's behaviour in power [2.3.4]. More recently the paper has returned to the more balanced editorial line typical of PRISA's organs in general.

In the 1980s, PRISA had two main domestic rivals for the title of Spain's premier media group. *Grupo16* was based on the weekly news magazine *Cambio16*, which established a justified reputation during the transition. Later it acquired a daily stablemate, *Diario16*. Aimed at a less highbrow market than *El País*, it became Spain's fifth most popular paper in the 1980s. At the end of the decade both publications became savage critics of the government, with a distinct drop in the quality of coverage linked to the loss of leading journalists. Since then *Grupo16* has lost a lot of readers and money, and is no longer a significant media force.

In that and virtually all other respects *Grupo16* differs from the Godó group, controlled by the family of the same name. Its basis was and remains the venerable Barcelona-based daily *La Vanguardia*. Founded in 1881 and sufficiently conservative to survive independently under Franco, it also proved adaptable enough to become Spain's biggest seller for a brief period after his demise. The success of *El País* subsequently hit its sales outside Catalonia but *La Vanguardia* is still the country's fourth largest daily newspaper. Essentially it remains the quality paper of the Catalan middle classes, providing coverage of events that is relatively balanced as well as wide.

When the first FM radio licences were issued in 1979, the Godo group moved to expand its activities by setting up the station *Antena 3*. A decade later it became the main shareholder in the private television station of the same name [4.3.2]. However, in 1992 the group's owner was ousted as chairman of *Antena 3* television, from which it has subsequently withdrawn altogether. This 1992 'coup' signalled the emergence of the group which has now overtaken both *Grupo16* and Godo to become Spain's second largest.

Like both PRISA and Godo, the Zeta group has its origins in the press, but in a section very different from that inhabited by *El País* and *La Vanguardia*. The weekly magazine *Interviú*, like *Cambio16*, made its name during the transition. However, its approach to news reporting was personalised and liberally dashed with soft pornography. In recent years this has proved a less popular mix, but it was the early success of *Interviú* which allowed Zeta's head, Antonio Asensio, to extend the Barcelona-based group's interests.

As well as other, less sensationalist weeklies – the best-known is *Tiempo* – these include the daily *El Periódico*. Its target readership is, in socio-economic terms, similar to that of *Diario16*, which *El Periódico* now comfortably outsells; geographically, however, it is confined largely to Catalonia. Most importantly, since 1992 Zeta has had an important stake in *Antena 3* television, of which Asensio is the chairman.

Zeta differs from PRISA, and Godo, in that it is fundamentally a business operation; the political line taken by its organs is heavily determined by market concerns. Thus *Antena 3* television, which competes with the first public channel, *TVE-1*, was highly critical of the Socialist government in the early 1990s. Yet at the same time Zeta was anxious to break the domination of the Catalan daily market enjoyed by *La Vanguardia*, which is close to the regionalist party CiU [3.2.2]. In order to do so *El Periódico* backed the Socialists, albeit not uncritically.

Zeta's main partner in *Antena 3* is Rupert Murdoch's News International, which in turn owns a quarter of Zeta. The other major international player to have entered the Spanish media market is the Italian magnate – and briefly right-wing Prime Minister – Silvio Berlusconi, a leading shareholder in the third private television station, *Tele 5* [4.3.2]. It, in turn, was for a time part-owned by the most surprising power in the market, an organisation which straddles the line between public and private sectors. This is the ONCE, Spain's blind association [8.4.4]. Use of its considerable financial resources during the 1980s to set up a successful radio station, *Onda Cero*, seemed a logical extension of the ONCE's welfare activities. Its move into television, however, must presumably be regarded as a purely commercial venture. It took place under the leadership of the ambitious and forceful

Miguel Durán who, with Berlusconi's support, became *Tele 5* chairman in 1990.

Since at the time the ONCE was more or less closely controlled by the Socialist Party, this gave rise to suspicions that the government was intent on securing a supporter among the three private stations. They proved unfounded. *Tele 5*, although more restrained than *Antena 3*, became a government critic; in any case, its schedules (*programación*) contain significantly less news coverage than those of its rivals. Moreover, the ONCE later sold its holding in *Tele 5* [4.3.4].

4.3.4 Radio and the press

Outside television the degree of control exercised by the major groups is much less. Indeed, the overall concentration of media power in Spain is low compared with most Western countries. In the case of radio this can be ascribed to the extremely competitive nature of the market. Proportionately Spain has a very high number of radio listeners (*oyentes*), and an equally high number of channels. Issue of new licences at the end of the 1970s and again a decade later gave rise to a 'battle of the airwaves', with not only the broadcasters but also the government showing scant regard for national and international regulations limiting the number of stations.

The press, on the other hand, is in exactly the opposite position, with a notoriously low level of sales (*difusión*). Spain's biggest-selling daily, by some way, is *El País* [4.3.3]. Yet even it has a circulation (*tirada*) of only around 400 000 copies, although as with other papers this doubles in the case of the weekend edition (*dominical*), bought usually on a Saturday. The second most popular daily is *Abc*, like *La Vanguardia* [4.3.3] a long-established publication which survived the dictatorship. *Abc* is deeply conservative, in layout as well as editorial line; its publisher, *Editorial Española*, is mainly owned by the big banks.

The third largest sale belongs to *El Mundo*, founded only in 1989. The paper was a product of friction within *Grupo16* [4.3.3]. Its editor, Pedro J. Ramírez, formerly held the same post on *Diario16*, and the company set up to run it is controlled by the brother of the *Grupo16* chairman. *El Mundo*'s rapid rise was based on the strategy Ramírez had already employed successfully in his previous job. Virulent editorial attacks on the Socialist government were backed up by aggressive investigation that uncovered a succession of 'affairs'. That in itself was clearly legitimate, and positive. More worrying were the financial involvement of Mario Conde [9.4.1], and the fact that on occasions investigative journalism stepped over into manipulation, most notoriously when a story about alleged nepotism by Prime Minister Felipe González proved to be based on falsified documents.

On the whole, however, journalistic standards in Spain are high. Sales are low partly because of the absence of sensationalist equivalents to Britain's tabloids. An attempt to fill this market gap was launched in 1989, by *Editorial Española* and the German Springer group, publisher of Europe's best-selling sensationalist daily, *Bild*. However, their product, entitled *Claro*, survived for only three months. It was squeezed out by the high-selling sports dailies *As* and *Marca* and the weekly gossip magazines (*prensa del corazón*), of which the best-known is *Hola*. These, in their very different ways, appear to cover *Claro*'s target readership.

Sales of the quality national dailies are also kept down by competition from another source – the regional and local press which remains strong in Spain. As with television, only a small part of the appeal of regional papers can be attributed to language differences [4.3.2]. *Avui*, with *El País* the first new paper to appear after Franco's death, is also the most popular daily printed wholly in a language other than Spanish; published in Catalan, it sells a little over 30 000 copies. *Egin*'s readership is higher, at around 50 000, but only part of its copy appears in Basque. To an even greater extent than the similar but less successful *Deia*, closely linked to the Basque Nationalist Party, *Egin* is more a propaganda sheet than a newspaper, in its case for ETA's political wing, HB [3.3.2].

Nearly all the remaining local and regional dailies are published wholly in Spanish. They continue to attract up to half the daily readership, despite the growing trend for the big Madrid and Barcelona papers to publish regional editions. Another recent phenomenon has been the growth of chains of regional papers, the largest headed by the Bilbao-based *El Correo Español-El Pueblo Vasco*. The *Correo* group has also recently moved into another area of the media by acquiring the share in *Tele 5* formerly held by the blind organisation ONCE [4.3.3].

In general, control over the Spanish press remains in Spanish hands. Low readership has largely discouraged outside newspaper interests from entering the market, especially after the failure of *Claro*. In the other direction some investment has been carried out. In particular, *El País* has an important holding in the London daily, *The Independent*.

4.4 PRESSURE GROUPS

In Spain pressure groups (*grupos de presión*), other than those connected with either the state or any of the major economic or media interests, are of only minimal importance. Such groups are a phenomenon of developed societies, and up to 1936 Spain provided barren ground for their development. Under the Franco regime any attempt to mobilise outside the regime's own aegis was, of course, strictly prohibited.

It is true that the Franco era did see the emergence of neighbourhood associations (*asociaciones de vecinos*). In some areas these were an important local focus of opposition during the regime's latter stages. However, like the much more powerful trade unions, the associations were marginalised during the transition period. Today Spaniards remain statistically much less likely than most of their Western counterparts to be members of voluntary associations of any sort, in particular so-called non-governmental organisations (*Organizaciones No Gubernamentales – ONGs*). The most influential pressure groups are professional bodies, such as the Medical and Lawyers Associations (*Colegio de Médicos, Colegio de Abogados*).

Opinion polls consistently show that Spaniards overwhelmingly look to the state to solve social problems. Their attitude was reflected in the 1978 Constitution, which is pervaded by the ethos that social problems are best addressed communally. In practice, that essentially altruistic approach has allowed government and the parties to channel pressure through organisations they themselves control. Thus to a considerable extent development of a genuine Spanish women's movement was pre-empted by the creation of an official National Women's Bureau (*Instituto de la Mujer*) [8.4.3]. Similarly, the country's various voluntary consumer groups have been sidelined by the government's own National Consumer Bureau (*Instituto Nacional de Consumo*).

In one part of Spain the picture is very different. The Basque Country has a considerable and very active network of pressure groups. In recent years it has witnessed the most impressive example of such activity in Spain; the growth of genuinely popular protest against the violent activities of ETA [9.4.2]. This movement, whose members display not just commitment but often considerable courage in the face of intimidation, is centred on the group Gesture for Peace (*Gesto por la Paz*).

Other aspects of pressure group activity in the Basque Country are less positively connected with violence. In effect most are controlled by ETA itself, either directly or through the groups of its sympathisers who campaign for the release of convicted ETA members (*Gestoras Pro-Amnistía*). Examples were the supposedly environmentalist campaigns against the proposed Lemoniz nuclear power plant and, more recently, the new motorway link between Navarre and the French border. Neither campaign, in reality, had much to do with the environment; both were backed by ETA intimidation and, in the first case, murder.

The motorway episode also had another strange aspect. It later transpired that opposition to the original route through the Leizarán valley was also linked to corruption in the Socialist-run Navarre regional government. The revelations provided bizarre confirmation of the extent to which pressure group activity in Spain is manipulated by other powerful interests linked to the state.

4.5 GLOSSARY

The military

ascenso m	promotion
ascenso por antigüedad m	promotion based on length of service
búnker m	diehard (military) supporters of francoism
cascos azules mpl	blue helmets/berets, UN peace-keeping forces
cuerpos de seguridad mpl	(civilian) security forces

Ejército del Aire m	Air Force
Ejército de Tierra m	Army
ejércitos mpl	armed forces
fuerzas armadas fpl	armed forces
golpe m	(military) coup
golpismo m	predisposition of military to stage coups
intentona (golpista) f	(failed) coup attempt (esp. that of 23 Feb. 1981)
involucionismo m	extreme reactionary beliefs and activity
Jefe del Estado Mayor de la Defensa m	Chief of the Defence Staff
Junta de Jefes de Estado Mayor (JUJEM) f	Joint Chiefs of Staff Council
Marina f	Navy
mili f	(see *servicio militar*)
nostálgico m	reactionary
oficial m	(military) officer
problema militar m	problem of the military
pronunciamiento m	(nineteenth-century) military coup
reserva activa f	'active reserve', status of promoted officers denied an active command on grounds of merit
servicio militar (obligatorio) m	(compulsory) military service

The Church

aconfesionalidad f	absence of an official religion/Church
(Concilio) Vaticano II m	Second Vatican Council
hecho sociológico m	objective feature of society
impuesto religioso m	Church tax
practicante mf	practising Catholic
Santa Sede f	Holy See, Vatican
vocación f	entry into Holy Orders

Economic interests

14-D m	14 December 1988 (first post-1978 general strike)
27-M m	27 May 1992 (second post-1978 general strike)
agentes sociales mpl	(see *interlocutores sociales*)
banca privada f	the private banks
Cámara de Comercio f	Chamber of Commerce
canon sindical m	compulsory union levy
central (sindical) f	trade union (confederation)
comité de empresa m	workforce committee
concertación social f	system of national agreements between (government,) employers and unions
conflictividad laboral f	industrial unrest
conflicto laboral m	industrial dispute
Consejo Económico y Social m	National Economic and Social Policy Forum
Consejo General m	Supervisory Board (of Bank of Spain)
Consejo Superior Bancario m	National Banking Authority

delegado m	(workforce) representative
desregulación f	deregulation
elecciones sindicales fpl	workplace elections
familia socialista f	socialist movement
financiación estatal f	public funding
frentes sociales mpl	(see *interlocutores sociales* – now outdated)
gran banca f	the big banks
interlocutores sociales mpl	social partners, employers and unions
liberalización f	deregulation
pacto social m	'social contract', national agreements between (government,) employers and unions
partido hermano m	sister party
patronal f	employers
pymes fpl	SMEs (small and medium-sized enterprises)
relaciones laborales fpl	industrial relations
sección sindical f	industry section (of trade union confederation)
sector crítico m	dissident faction (of union)
siete grandes mpl	'big seven', seven largest banks during 1980s
sindicalismo m	trade union movement
sindicato m	trade union
sindicato amarillo m	bosses' union (i.e. controlled by employer)
sindicato vertical m	government-controlled union

The media

audiencia f	audience share/quota
canal m	(TV) channel/station
Consejo de Administración m	Board of Governors (of Spanish Television Authority)
cuarto poder m	'fourth estate', press/media
difusión f	(newspaper) readership, sales
dominical m	weekend supplement/edition
emisora f	(radio) broadcasting station
ente público m	public corporation
espacio informativo m	news programme
estatuto m	charter (of public corporation)
guerra de las ondas f	'battle of the airwaves' (proliferation of competing radio stations)
medios (de comunicación de masas) mpl	(mass) media
medios informativos mpl	news media
oferta radiofónica/televisiva f	range/choice of radio/TV stations
oyentes mpl	(radio) listeners
prensa amarilla f	(see *prensa sensacionalista*)
prensa del corazón f	gossip magazines
prensa sensacionalista f	sensationalist press (cf. UK tabloids)
presencia f	degree of control (over firm/market sector)
programación f	TV/radio schedule
público m	audience; readership
revista f	magazine; journal

semanal m	weekly (magazine, etc.)
telediario m	TV news programme
televidentes mfpl	(television) viewers
televisiones autonómicas fpl	TV stations run by regional governments
televisiones privadas fpl	private TV stations
tirada f	circulation (of paper)

Pressure groups

asociación de vecinos f	neighbourhood association
colegio m	professional association
grupo de presión m	pressure group
lobby m	lobby, interest group
organización no gubernamental (ONG) f	non-governmental organisation (NGO)

5

THE SPANISH ECONOMY

For all the enormous political transformation Spain has undergone since Franco died, perhaps the greatest changes to affect the country in recent decades have been economic. Even in the 1950s it was still regarded by the United Nations as part of the developing world: now it has the planet's seventh largest GDP. The first section of this chapter traces the course of economic change since 1975, highlighting two themes that constantly recur within that process. Yet despite Spain's rapid advance, important imbalances are apparent in four areas of its economy; they form the subject of the second section. The third then describes briefly the major sectors of economic activity in Spain, and its distribution between regions. The fourth and last section looks at the main features of Spanish companies.

5.1 *APERTURA* AND *AJUSTE*

In 1975 the Spanish economy remained largely isolated from the outside world. By far the most important factor in its development since then has been a gradual process of exposure to international, and especially European, markets (*apertura*). That process has been fundamental in promoting the country's development; almost universally it is seen as positive. Yet, especially coming at a time of unprecedented economic change in the world as a whole, it has given Spain enormous problems. Even more than its neighbours the country has repeatedly been obliged by economic circumstances to make painful adjustments (*ajustes*).

5.1.1 Boom and inflation

To a considerable degree Spain's belated economic modernisation under the Franco regime depended on isolation. Rapid growth during the 1960s and early 1970s was based largely on heavy industries such as mining, shipbuilding, metalworking of various sorts, and basic chemicals. The firms involved were severely lacking in modern equipment. Instead they relied on relatively primitive technology and an abundant supply of poorly paid human labour. Many, whether or not state-owned, received substantial government subsidies. Virtually none were in a position to compete with their better-equipped counterparts in other countries.

Consequently Spanish industrial exports were minimal, while the country's manufacturing firms relied heavily on the protection of their own domestic market from foreign imports. Most obviously Spain imposed unusually high tariffs on many incoming goods. It also operated an elaborate system of quotas (*contingentes*) on particular products, as well as other forms of non-tariff barriers. By these various means the availability and prices of imported goods were regulated in such a way as to prevent them forcing Spanish ones off the market.

Ironically, restrictions on foreign trade could not prevent Spain from falling prey to the development which brought growth in Western Europe to an abrupt end. Lacking significant energy reserves of its own, Spain had become even more highly dependent than other Western countries on cheap oil imports, above all from the Middle East. It was thus especially hard hit when, in 1973, the Organisation of Petroleum Exporting Countries (OPEC) imposed a massive rise in oil prices. The effects on the economy were devastating. Unemployment soared [5.2.4], and the balance of payments suffered severely [5.2.1]. Above all, as elsewhere in the West, inflation rose sharply. Prices throughout the economy were pushed up by the increase in transport and energy costs, even though the government ill-advisedly kept these artificially low by subsidising them.

The impact was magnified further by the political situation. For almost a decade after Franco's death the attention of Spain's leaders was focused almost exclusively on the problems of building a democratic state. Economic issues were pushed into the background. Meantime many workers were understandably concerned for their living standards in the face of rising prices, and vigorously demanded wage rises to match. Even after trade union leaders agreed to moderate their claims in the 1977 Moncloa Pacts [0.1.3.3], wage rises continued to fuel price inflation for some years.

Consequently, during the early 1980s Spain's inflation rate ran consistently well above the average for the European Community. The difference was of particular significance because, after 1975, all the major political parties were convinced that the country must join the EC. Doing so would, by definition, involve free trade with other member states. Unless inflation were brought down to EC levels, the country's products would be unable to compete in the Common Market.

5.1.2 Into Europe

EC entry was a particular concern of the Socialist government elected in 1982 [2.3.2]. Its economic policies were thus, of necessity, heavily conditioned by the need to combat inflation and, in particular, rising earnings. To do so the government promoted a series of agreements with employers and unions [4.2.4], all of which set national benchmarks for wage increases designed to bring inflation down. Such wage moderation (*moderación salarial*) was one aspect of 'adjustment' in the 1980s.

However, overcoming inflation was only one of the challenges posed by EC entry. The other was to overhaul the antiquated industries bequeathed by the Franco regime, a task tackled sporadically and ineffectually up to 1982. As a result the Socialist government had little option but to undertake a massive programme of industrial restructuring (*reconversión industrial*), the second key element of 'adjustment'.

The programme involved changing the structure of Spanish manufacturing industry at two levels. First, the intention was to shift its basis from outdated industries to those with good future prospects. Second, within individual industries or branches, the government aimed to create firms of a scale large enough to compete with their European competitors. Restructuring thus implied a managed run-down of older industries which were in decline not just in Spain but throughout the developed world.

A prime example was shipbuilding. During the 1960s, Spain had become the industry's world leader, essentially because its shipyards paid lower wages than those elsewhere in the West. By the 1980s, however, it had been undercut in wage terms by new competitors, above all the Newly Industrialised Countries of SE Asia. Similar considerations applied to a range of older industries, including iron and steel manufacture and the chemical industry. In all of them there was a need to eliminate loss-making firms (*empresas deficitarias*). Previously these had been kept alive by state financial support, much of which was now phased out to prepare for conditions within the EC.

For many companies the result was closure. The healthier ones were concentrated into potentially viable units through mergers and takeovers. The survivors of this process were rationalised through measures designed to put them on a sound financial footing. In essence that meant radical reduction in costs, typically through 'adjustments to the labour-force' (*ajustes de plantilla*) – in plain English, job losses.

Many workers were required to take early retirement (*jubilación anticipada*). Their younger colleagues were offered, at least in theory, retraining in new skills (*reciclaje*) as preparation for redeployment in the second stage of restructuring – reindustrialisation, or the establishment of new industries. This policy, however, proved less easy to implement than the first. For many, 'adjustment' turned out to mean long-term unemployment.

In terms of their overall objective the policies pursued by the Socialists proved remarkably successful. Not only did Spain's economy survive entry to the EC, it actually flourished. Between 1985 and 1989 GDP grew at an annual rate only marginally short of 5 per cent, the highest in the EC and, indeed, among the major developed countries. This 'second economic miracle', as it became known, was partly due to internal factors. Restructuring had put parts of the country's economy on a much sounder footing.

Political stability seemed assured and the country had a government with the will to act and the parliamentary majority to allow it to do so [2.3.2]. However, the main cause was precisely Spain's entry into Europe [0.2.1].

As an EC member, Spain was in a position to benefit from the expansion enjoyed in the late 1980s by the Community, and the Western world as a whole. Foreign investment, the great majority now from its new partners, flowed into the country [5.2.1]. As one of the poorer members Spain was also a major recipient of grants from the Community's Structural Funds designed to reduce imbalances between different parts of the EC (*desequilibrios territoriales*). In particular, support from the European Regional Development Fund (*Fondo Europeo de Desarrollo Regional – FEDER*) helped finance a sharp increase in public spending during the later 1980s.

5.1.3 Towards convergence

The government's massive spending programme was itself a major factor in rapid growth, pouring money into the economy. In many ways, too, it was an economic necessity. Especially in education and infrastructure investment was badly needed if growth were to be sustained. Yet spending in these areas and others, such as social welfare, rose faster than Spain's economy could stand.

That was one reason why the country's 'second economic miracle' proved to be built on even shakier foundations than the first [5.1.1]. Another was the partial nature of restructuring, that is, the failure in general to establish new manufacturing industries to replace the older ones. Growth was concentrated heavily in the services sector and financed to a dangerous degree by short-term foreign capital which could easily be withdrawn when the international economic climate changed.

Throughout Western Europe the brief boom of the late 1980s was followed by the deepest recession (*crisis*) for 60 years, from which recovery proved to be slow and patchy. As a member of the EC club, Spain was no longer cushioned from these unpleasant developments. Moreover, their impact was aggravated by the Spanish government's slowness to react. By 1989 it was already clear that the economy had reached the stage of overheating (*calentamiento*). Yet the government failed for some time to take the steps necessary to produce a gradual cooling-down (*enfriamiento*). Instead, partly because of the impending events of 1992 [0.2], it continued to spend heavily well into the 1990s. The results were very severe indeed. Inflation rose again and in 1993 economic growth went into reverse, that is, the economy contracted.

Because Spain had waited too long to adjust to the changing economic climate, the necessary deflationary measures were all the more severe when they finally came. By then wage moderation by agreement was ruled out by the split between government and unions [4.2.3.2]. Instead, the emphasis fell on public spending cuts (*ajustes presupuestarios*). Infrastructure projects came to an abrupt halt, and in 1992 the government introduced a package of measures slashing entitlements to unemployment and other forms of benefit. Issued initially by a surprise decree, they became infamous under the name of '*decretazo*'.

These austerity measures eventually proved successful in getting recovery under way, albeit rather more slowly than elsewhere in the EC. However, in the meantime another development in the Community brought Spain up against yet another form of 'adjustment'. At the 1991 Maastricht Summit leaders of the European Union, as the EC now became, committed themselves to Economic and Monetary Union (EMU) by the end of the century. In order to ensure that their economies were sufficiently alike to make this feasible, they laid down a set of conditions which countries would have to meet in order to join EMU (*see* Table 5.1).

The Maastricht convergence criteria were very demanding. It was clear that meeting them would involve considerable sacrifices for a number of countries, including Spain. In recognition of this, and under pressure from Spanish Prime Minister Felipe González, the 1992 Edinburgh Summit agreed to set up a Cohesion Fund (*Fondo de Cohesión*). This was designed to help the weaker EU economies meet the Maastricht criteria and Spain would be the main beneficiary. That same year the Socialist government drew up a Convergence Plan (*Plan de Convergencia*) which brought further restrictions on government spending and monetary policy.

Within a year the forecasts on which the plan was based had to be radically altered because of the deteriorating economic situation. Nevertheless, and despite the enormous strains convergence placed on even the healthiest European economies, the government persisted with these restrictive policies up to its defeat in 1996. Nor has its conservative successor abandoned the goal of ensuring Spain is in the lead group of countries for EMU. In his plans for the 1997 budget, the new Prime Minister José María Aznar announced further spending cuts in order to achieve that aim. As for the past twenty years, the themes of *apertura* and *ajuste*, interlinked as ever, continue to dominate the Spanish economic scene.

Table 5.1 The Maastricht convergence criteria

Indicator	Condition
1. Exchange rate	Currency must remain within narrow band of European Monetary System for two years prior to adoption of single currency
2. Inflation rate	Inflation must be no more than 1.5 per cent higher than average of three member states with lowest rates
3. Interest rates	Long-term rates must be no more than 2 per cent higher than average of three member states with lowest inflation rates
4. Public debt	Total debt must be less than 60 per cent of country's GDP
5. Public sector deficit	Annual deficit must be less than 3 per cent of country's GDP

5.2 IMBALANCES

There is no doubt that over the last two decades Spain has made massive advances. Yet it is equally true that in a number of respects the economic situation continues to display major imbalances. One such area is that most obviously affected by the process of integration into the world economy – foreign trade. Two more – the value of money and the state of public finances – relate to the conditions laid down at Maastricht for entry into Economic and Monetary Union. The fourth concerns unemployment, which was omitted from the convergence criteria, but which has been gravely affected by attempts to meet them.

5.2.1 Foreign trade

Spain's foreign deficit (*déficit exterior*) has been a recurrent problem for many years. Even in the relative isolation of the 1950s the country was unable to earn sufficient foreign currency (*divisas*) in order to pay for its purchases abroad. Indeed, this inability was one of the factors that forced the Franco regime into a radical change of economic policy at the end of the decade. In fact the problem was not a serious one at that time. Spain's foreign trade (*comercio exterior*) remained very limited, so that in absolute terms the deficit was small.

Over the next 15 years it actually grew considerably, as the country's trade also grew. However, following the liberalisation measures undertaken in 1959/60 [0.1.2], the growing gap was covered by two non-trade items. One was the remittances (*remesas*) of money sent home to their families by emigrant workers. The other was revenue from the burgeoning tourist industry. As a result, Spain's overall balance of payments with the outside world was reasonably healthy; in the early 1970s it actually moved into surplus.

This success was short-lived. As well as the internal problems the oil crisis of 1973 caused [5.1.1], it sent Spain's import bill soaring and the balance of payments plunging back into the red. Over the next decade the situation gradually improved, thanks mainly to the substantial decline in real world oil prices. From 1986, however, the improvements were largely wiped out again, as a result of Spain's entry into the EC.

The country's rulers were well aware of the potential effects of this move. They knew that, despite industrial restructuring [5.1.2], Spanish firms remained ill-equipped to face the dismantling of customs barriers (*desarme arancelario*). Accordingly, in the accession negotiations, they sought to minimise the shock of entry as far as possible. They succeeded in negotiating a transitional period during which tariffs between Spain and its new partners were removed gradually. Yet, despite that, the Spanish market was almost immediately invaded by goods from other EC countries, above all France and Germany. The influx was actively encouraged by the government which was conscious that, in order to build up new industries, Spain must import capital goods (*bienes de equipo*). A further factor was the coming into force of the Single European Act (*Acta Unica Europea*) on 1 January 1993. The Act created a single market throughout the EC by removing many of the remaining non-tariff barriers to internal trade. The opening up of trade in services was of particular significance, as Spain's own service sector was small and inefficient, and the country offered a tempting new market for European firms.

At the same time, Spanish exports rose but at nothing like the same rate. The result was that the trade deficit increased fourfold between 1985 and 1989. Nor was it any longer feasible to balance it by non-trade earnings. Remittances have long ceased to play any significant role. Tourism, it is true, continues to represent a major source of income for the country. When the steady increase in its volume was reversed in the early 1990s, the foreign deficit noticeably worsened, and its subsequent improvement was aided by a recovery in tourist numbers and receipts [5.3.4]. Even so, with the trade in goods and other services having grown so much in real terms, tourism alone can never again, as in the 1970s, compensate for the trade deficit.

Since the mid-1980s the foreign deficit has also been eased by the arrival of significant amounts of foreign investment (*inversión extranjera*). That, however, is no solution to the problem, since such inward investment is always likely to be withdrawn whenever economic times get rough. More encouraging is the fact that, for the first time in the country's history, recovery from the slump of the early 1990s was export-driven; in other words, firms' export earnings were the first means by which new demand was injected into the economy. In addition, the composition of exports is shifting from traditional agricultural products to higher-value manufactured goods. Yet here, too, caution is required. Exports were boosted by a sharp fall in the value of the peseta [5.2.2], which effectively cut the price of Spanish products on foreign markets by some 30 per cent. By 1994, once the effect of devaluation had worn off, exports had ceased to rise significantly.

5.2.2 Monetary aspects

The fall in value of the peseta which boosted exports in 1992/93 had, ironically, been bitterly resisted by the Spanish government. For some years its exchange-rate policy (*política monetaria*) had been to maintain a strong peseta, in order to keep imported capital goods cheap [5.2.1]. Accordingly, when the then Finance Minister, Carlos Solchaga, took the peseta into the European Monetary System (EMS) in 1989 he did so at a rate which, in the eyes of most observers and of the international money markets, was too high for the country's weak economy to sustain.

Over the next three years the peseta repeatedly came under pressure to devalue. This the government resisted, determined to meet the Maastricht criteria which require a country's currency to show stability if it is to qualify for Monetary Union (*see* Table 5.1). The pressure proved too great, however.

Yet the Spanish government was reluctant to acknowledge the extent of the peseta's overvaluation. The result was that on 13 May 1993 Spain was forced to devalue by a full 13 per cent, far more than allowed by the criteria. The date became known as Black Thursday (*jueves negro*),

This setback was a humiliation for the government but by no means disastrous for the economy, helping in particular to improve its export performance. In any case, the impact was greatly reduced when, only a few months later, the EMS itself effectively collapsed. Yet the Spanish government continued to express both confidence in EMU and determination to ensure Spain was in a position to join. When a new, more flexible EMS was cobbled together in late 1993 the Spanish government rejoined, even though it was already clear that the peseta's fall had been insufficient to maintain export growth [5.2.1].

This enthusiasm for the enforced discipline of the EMS reflected government concern about another factor affecting the currency's value – inflation. Considerable inflationary pressures had been built up by the high-spending policies pursued right up to 1992. Renewed EMS membership was designed to curb these, and indeed to a large extent did so. Since 1993 Spanish inflation has generally remained less than 1 per cent above the EU average. Compared with the record of the previous 20 years that represents a very satisfactory performance. Yet it still leaves Spain some distance from the second Maastricht criterion.

Moreover, continuing efforts to reach this demanding target have had a considerable price, and not just in terms of drastic public spending cuts [5.1.3]. Together with the need to attract foreign funds to keep the peseta strong, they have required Spanish interest rates to remain well above the EU average. In real terms these high rates have been very damaging, holding back the investment needed to ensure recovery after the recession of the early 1990s. Ironically they also mean that Spain fails to meet the third of the convergence criteria on which the government's policy has been centred (*see* Table 5.1).

5.2.3 Public finances

One advantage of belated economic development is that Spain has not yet built up the large national or public debt (*endeudamiento público*) typically associated with that process. As a result, it comes close to meeting the fourth Maastricht condition. Since the Franco era, however, debt has been steadily rising, due to the annual public sector deficit (*déficit público*). Well before it was established as one of the convergence criteria, the deficit's size gave rise to mounting concern.

Many reasons underlie the deficit problem. One is the high cost of building a modern welfare state [8.1.1], another the state's involvement in a number of unprofitable economic activities [5.4.1]. While some were disposed of during industrial restructuring [5.1.2], that process added new burdens on the public purse in the shape of redundancy payments, early pensions and unemployment benefit [5.2.4]. Moreover, even after the massive expenditure of the 1980s, Spain continues to need costly investment in infrastructure and technology, much of which has to come from the state. A further pressure on state spending has been the high interest rates of recent years [5.2.2], which have pushed up the interest payments on government bonds or debt (*deuda del estado*).

Yet, despite all these pressures on expenditure, the main reason for Spain's public deficit lies on the income side. It is true that rates of both personal income tax (*impuesto sobre la renta de las personas físicas – IRPF*) and corporation tax (*impuesto de sociedades*) have increased substantially. In addition, Spain's entry into the EC also brought the introduction of value added tax (*impuesto sobre el valor añadido – IVA*). However, these increases in the overall tax burden (*presión fiscal*) started from a level which, by the standards of the developed world, was extraordinarily low.

Moreover, the burden was also most unusually distributed. Throughout the francoist era direct taxes (*fiscalidad directa*) were levied almost exclusively on those whose wages were easily monitored. In practice that meant employees (*trabajadores por cuenta ajena*) who figured on the payroll of a large firm. Little attempt was made even to establish the tax liability of workers in the small firms which dominate the country's economy [5.4.2], or of the self-employed (*autónomos*). More than half of all tax revenues came from indirect taxation (*fiscalidad indirecta*), the rates of which were higher on basic than luxury items.

Reform of this bizarre system began in the late 1970s. The then Finance Minister, Francisco Fernández Ordóñez, launched a series of publicity campaigns to promote public awareness of the essential nature of taxation in a democracy. He also instituted the first effective system for checking tax returns and so eliminating some tax evasion (*fraude fiscal*). Under the Socialist governments of the following years efforts to increase revenue continued. By 1989, not only had tax rates been increased, the system had also been made more progressive, in the sense that more tax income now came from direct taxes, the rates of which rise with income levels. As a result, the growing prosperity of the 1980s automatically brought proportionately more into the government's coffers (*arcas del estado*).

The state's growing demands, and its increasing effectiveness in tax collection (*recaudación*), caused considerable public resentment, especially among those unused to the roll of taxpayer (*contribuyente*). This was especially true of firms. Previously little bothered by the tax authorities (*Hacienda*) they now had to face not only a growing burden of corporation tax, but also successive rises in their social security contributions. In this situation, the acceptability of tax evasion has remained high; a senior employers' representative has gone so far as to suggest that it is 'essential for firms' survival'. Inevitably such attitudes constrain further increases in tax revenue.

They are also reflected in the growth of a large informal economy (*economía sumergida*). By that is meant all those economic activities carried on outside the state's knowledge and so omitted from official statistics. By its very nature the extent of a country's informal sector is hard to measure, but in Spain's case studies have suggested it may account for as much as 20 per cent of GDP. Industries believed to be particularly affected are construction and footwear. What is beyond doubt is that the informal economy, as well as its negative implications for workers' health, safety, social security protection and job security, also causes a substantial leakage of government revenue.

5.2.4 Labour market

Unlike the three areas of imbalance already discussed, mass unemployment is new to Spain. During the depression of the 1930s it remained a rural society. In the Franco era it exported joblessness through emigration [0.1.2]; into the early 1970s the unemployment rate remained below 3 per cent. Thereafter, however, it rose sharply and remained well above those in other EU countries. For lengthy periods, over three million Spaniards were officially recorded as out of work by the government-run National Employment Agency (*Instituto Nacional de Empleo – INEM*). Using the rather higher figures of the Official Labour-force Survey (*Encuesta de Población Activa*) introduced in 1984, and following two years of economic recovery, in 1996 the jobless figure stood at over 22 per cent.

Unemployment hits women especially hard, among whom it is generally over 10 percentage points higher than that for men. On the other hand, men are disproportionately represented among the long-term unemployed (*parados de larga duración*). The most worrying aspect is the extremely high rate of youth unemployment (*paro juvenil*), which affects both sexes. In recent years it has stood at around 40 per cent and in some areas reaches 75 per cent.

Since 1975 joblessness has consistently been the Spanish public's greatest concern. Prominent in the manifesto of the Socialist government elected in 1982 was a promise to create 800 000 jobs. Persistently high unemployment was often quoted to show that this pledge had been broken, but such accusations reflected misunderstanding of unemployment's causes. In fact, over the next decade the number of people in work rose by well over a million. The problem was that the labour force (*población activa*) – the number of Spaniards working or seeking work – grew even more.

There were several reasons for this. Few Spaniards now work outside the country, and the high birth rates of the Franco era have worked through into the numbers of working age. Most important of all, relatively more adults are now seeking jobs than before. Since 1970 Spain's participation, or economic activity rate (*tasa de actividad*) has increased steadily. The rise would have been even greater had not many men made redundant in older industries ceased to seek work. By contrast, the female participation rate – previously very low indeed – rose dramatically. The trend is set to continue, since the Spanish participation rate is still around 5 per cent below the EU average, and even more so in the case of women.

A further cause of unemployment lies in the uneven distribution of job losses and gains between regions and sectors of the economy. Since 1986 in particular, employment has been created in new, light industries and, above all, in the service sector. By contrast, traditional industries and agriculture have experienced massive job losses (*destrucción de empleo*).

The government has attempted to counteract the resultant social problems, in part by improving training provision in general [7.3.3], and providing specific retraining (*reciclaje*) for those thrown out of work. The impact of these schemes has been limited. Moreover, the pressure on public finances [5.2.3] has brought cutbacks in the level and coverage of unemployment benefit. In one particular respect, however, the Socialists greatly expanded such relief.

The Rural Employment Plan (*Plan de Empleo Rural – PER*) provides benefit for casual farm labourers, and a programme of public works designed to compensate for the chronic lack of agricultural employment in regions such as Andalusia. The PER has given rise to accusations of corruption because of the control exercised over its operation by local authorities, which in the rural south are overwhelmingly controlled by the Socialist Party. However, a more fundamental objection to the PER is that it contributes to the problems facing Spain in creating the jobs it needs to provide for a growing workforce.

According to most economists the Spanish labour market (*mercado laboral*) suffers various different forms of rigidity (*rigideces*), that is, a lack of the flexibility required to meet rapidly changing economic conditions. In large measure they result from the complex system of employment regulation instituted by the Franco regime. One aspect was the standard minimum wage (*salario mínimo interprofesional – SMI*) introduced in 1963 and set annually by the Ministry of Employment after consultation with unions and employers' organisations.

These latter have shown little concern over the SMI, as its effect on wage levels is negligible. Even in theory only 5 per cent of the workforce are affected by it: in practice, high unemployment means that workers are willing to collude with employers in working for lower rates in the informal economy [5.2.3]. Altogether more important in holding back job creation are employers' social security contributions (*cuotas empresariales*). Appreciably higher than in other EU countries, they are often called a 'jobs tax'.

The main causes of labour market rigidity relate to the legal conditions on employing workers, which were updated in the 1980 Workers' Charter (*Estatuto de los Trabajadores*). It made collective agreements (*convenios colectivos*) between unions and employer representatives binding, thus restricting individual firms' ability to respond to their circumstances. The Charter also consolidated the strict regulations on terms and conditions of service, and on the nature of employees' contracts, almost all of which were automatically permanent. Any changes to them required an official authorisation (*expediente*), and were subject to appeal to an employment court [9.1.3]. In particular, it was both difficult and costly for employers to reduce the size of their workforce.

During the 1980s this situation caused concern not only to employers but also the government, since regulation gave a significant boost to the informal economy [5.2.3]. In 1984 it introduced reforms, including legalisation of fixed-term contracts (*contratos temporales*). The aim was to encourage employers to take on new workers in the knowledge that they were not saddled with the related costs indefinitely. Although fixed-term contracts soon became the norm, their net impact on job creation was marginal. Moreover, they reduced job security, and thus the consumer confidence essential in a modern economy. Nor did the 1984 changes satisfy employers who remained subject to restrictions in various respects.

Accordingly, in 1994 the government introduced a much broader set of labour market reforms. For the first time since the 1940s employers were permitted to issue part-time contracts (*contratos a tiempo parcial*), thus regularising a situation already common in the informal economy. More significantly in terms of employment policy, two new contract types – work placements (*contratos en prácticas*) and apprenticeships (*contratos de aprendizaje*) – were introduced, allowing for greater flexibility in terms of wages and conditions.

The 1994 reforms also included several other measures. They abolished the INEM's monopoly as an employment broker by lifting the ban on private employment agencies (*agencias de contratación*). They relaxed the obligations on employers to respect national or sectoral agreements. Also significantly eased were the restrictions applying to dismissals (*despidos*). Even so, Spanish employers are still far from enjoying the unrestricted right to fire at will (*despido libre*), which remains an extremely hot political potato in Spain.

5.3 SECTORAL AND GEOGRAPHICAL STRUCTURE

The continuing existence of imbalances – and, in the case of unemployment, the appearance of new ones – reminds us that Spain's recent economic history has not been an unbridled success story. Indeed, in some senses the country's economic situation has changed remarkably little; for instance, its per capita GDP stands at around three-quarters of the EU average, a proportion very little different from that in 1975, or even 1960. Yet in other respects change has been enormous and irreversible, especially when one looks beyond the features of the economy as a whole to its constituent parts; the different sectors of economic activity and the country's various regions.

5.3.1 Primary sector

Spain's primary sector has been shrinking for decades. In 1960 it accounted for over 20 per cent of GDP; by the 1990s the figure had fallen to around 6 per cent. As in other countries it is made up of various subsectors. Of these both forestry (*sector forestal*) and the mining industry (*sector minero*), although of considerable significance in particular areas and especially in environmental terms, play purely minor roles in the economy as a whole.

The fishing industry (*sector pesquero*), by far the largest in the EU, is rather more important, although for obvious reasons its significance is also restricted to certain areas. It also faces a number of problems. Inshore fishing (*pesca costera*) has declined due to severe overfishing (*sobreexplotación*). More generally, EU conservation measures have forced reductions in the size of the fleet, especially in the main centres of Galicia and the Basque Country. Fishermen from these regions have led the way in seeking new fishing grounds (*caladeros*) on the high seas. Their often aggressive methods have led to confrontations with the authorities of several countries, including Ireland, Morocco and Canada.

By far the most important component of the primary sector is agriculture (*sector agropecuario*), which in proportional terms still accounts for considerably more employment in Spain than in the EU as a whole. Indeed, into the 1990s it provided over a fifth of jobs in 19 provinces; in two (Lugo and Ourense) over half the employed population still works in farming. Nevertheless, since 1960 Spain has experienced a massive drift of population from the land (*éxodo rural*), a process begun by the low priority placed by the Franco regime on agriculture. The results of its neglect were clearly apparent in 1975, when Spanish agriculture was extremely backward and unproductive.

One pressing issue was the structure of agricultural landholding (*estructura agraria*), which in the south was linked to the question of ownership. In much of Spain farmers, whether owners or tenants, have traditionally enjoyed reasonable security of tenure. In wide areas of Andalusia and Extremadura, however, the countryside was dominated by large estates (*latifundios*). The bulk of the rural population consisted of day-labourers (*jornaleros*), employed at low wages and on extremely poor conditions. Their parlous situation was the main motive for attempts during the Second Republic at land reform (*reforma agraria*), that is changes in the structure of land ownership. Even at the time little was achieved in terms of breaking up the estates: under the Franco regime virtually all were returned to their former owners.

The question of land ownership overlapped with another, that of the size and nature of farm units (*explotaciones*). For the large southern estates were often notoriously ill-managed. In other parts of the country, on the other hand, many holdings were uneconomically small. To make matters worse, tiny smallholdings (*minifundios*) were often split up into plots (*parcelas*), sometimes widely separated. The first attempt at combating these interconnected problems was made during the transition, when a Landholdings Rationalisation Service (*Servicio de Concentración Parcelaria*) was established to encourage the creation of larger, unified holdings through the exchange and sale of plots between smallholders. Government grants were provided to help the process along.

When the Socialists came to power in 1982 attention was extended to the question of the big estates, and the Service absorbed into a new Land Reform Agency (*Instituto de Reforma Agraria*). Working in conjunction with regional governments, and spurred on by the protests of the Landworkers Union [4.2.3.2], the Agency has enjoyed some success in transferring previously unused land to new owners. In recent years, however, the pressure to do so has relaxed, given the extension in unemployment support to landworkers [5.2.4].

Instead, the focus of attention has shifted to the more general issue of agriculture's efficiency. In that sense the small scale of most farms continues to be a problem, because it makes the use of modern machinery difficult for both technical and financial reasons. Only recently have tractors been widely introduced into some areas; Galicia is especially notorious in this regard. Small farm size also militates against the establishment of effective distribution and marketing networks. One response to this problem has been to set up co-operatives of small farmers.

Small farmers are also disproportionately affected by lack of knowledge about new techniques and alternative crops. As a result, attempts to increase productivity by these means have often created fresh problems. By and large they have involved bringing more land under irrigation (*riego*), a practice which is not only often harmful to the environment but also of doubtful utility in the longer term [6.2.2].

Provision of information on crops and techniques, and incentives to apply it, is one purpose of the EU's Agricultural Guidance and Guarantee Fund (*Fondo Europeo de Orientación y Garantía Agrícola – FEOGA*), from which Spanish farmers have benefited since 1986. Unfortunately for them, however, the bulk of its resources are devoted to the system of guaranteed prices operated under the Common Agricultural Policy (CAP). And the CAP continues to be oriented mainly towards the needs of farmers in the original, more northerly EC member states.

More generally EU membership has had effects on Spanish agriculture which vary dramatically between different types of farming. Especially hard hit has been the dairy industry (*sector lácteo*). Concentrated on small, hilly farms in the northern coastal regions, it is poorly placed to compete with the much larger and more easily worked holdings common elsewhere in Europe. Cereal farming, traditionally the backbone of the Castilian economy, has been another victim. On the other hand, new opportunities have opened up for some farmers, especially in the south and east where the climate is truly Mediterranean. There intensive techniques, using greenhouses (*invernaderos*) and extensive irrigation, have allowed profitable specialisation in fruit and vegetables (*productos hortifrutícolas*). The southerly location gives a particular advantage in early season products (*primicias*).

5.3.2 Industry

In contrast to the situation in other advanced countries, industry (*sector secundario*) was only briefly the largest and most important sector of the

Spanish economy. Dwarfed by the primary sector until the 1960s, it was overtaken by services when the economy finally modernised thereafter. The share of GDP and employment for which it accounts has changed little since the 1970s.

The main feature of industry's development over that period has been restructuring [5.1.2]. The process remains unfinished. Spanish industry still displays many of the same problems as before, albeit to a lesser degree. It lacks adequate technology and know-how. It suffers from fragmentation into a large number of small, often very small firms (*atomización*); many of the larger indigenous ones remain within a public sector of dubious efficiency [5.4.1]. These conditions are probably both cause and consequence of the continuing marked lack of a spirit of business enterprise (*mentalidad empresarial*) in Spanish society (here 'Spanish' should be read as excluding Basque and Catalan, but not Galician). This lack has been ascribed to a number of factors, including an alleged Castilian disdain for manual work and the negligible influence of Protestantism. Coming nearer to the present, entrepreneurial initiative was stifled by the Franco regime's policies of state intervention and protectionism [0.1.2]. Observers point also to the slow speed at which vocational training has adapted to changing economic circumstances [7.3.3].

The effects of this low level of entrepreneurial spirit are hard to identify precisely, but are serious none the less. They may well provide one reason for the poor results of restructuring in terms of generating new industrial activity [5.1.3]. Historically they seem to underlie Spain's reliance on export of primary products rather than higher value finished goods (*productos elaborados*); only in the 1990s has this situation, typical of the Third World rather than the First, begun to change [5.2.1].

The food and drink industry (*sector alimenticio*) – actually one of Spain's most buoyant – provides a good illustration of these sorts of problems. Domestic firms within it have been slow to grasp the opportunities offered by the country's wealth of produce, much of it high quality and well adapted to consumer tastes in the developed world. Yet rather than being processed in Spain, olives are exported to Italy. Traditional meat products, such as cured ham, have not been marketed adequately. Establishment of a promotional initiative in 1995 was, significantly, driven by public authorities, in this case the Andalusian regional government.

The need for public investment to supplement or replace private is a further indication of a lack of entrepreneurial spirit. Another has been a longstanding reliance on foreign capital. In the last century foreign firms virtually monopolised the only two industrial activities of any significance outside the Basque and Catalan regions – railways and mining. Indeed, the protectionist policies pursued by successive governments up to and including the Franco regime were in large part a reaction to this situation.

With the opening up of Spain's economy after Franco's death, and especially after EC entry in 1986 [5.1.2], penetration of foreign capital greatly increased. Such investment has brought Spain many benefits, generating industrial development where none existed and preserving firms and industries that would otherwise have disappeared. On the other hand, it has involved a damaging loss of control over decisions in many of the country's largest firms.

These various aspects can all be seen in the automobile industry (*sector automovilístico*), now one of Spain's largest. The only major Spanish car producer, SEAT (*Sociedad Española de Automóviles de Turismo*), was founded in 1950 and long produced models under licence from the Italian manufacturer Fiat. Gravely affected by the post-1973 recession [5.1.1], SEAT was baled out by a 1982 cooperation agreement with the German Volkswagen company, which now has a controlling share. Similarly, the production of Pegaso trucks, begun by the state-owned firm ENASA (*Empresa Nacional de Autocamiones SA*) is now in Italian hands.

All other vehicle production in Spain is the result of inward investment. The longest established foreign manufacturer is the French FASA-Renault which began production in 1951. Subsequently it has been joined by its compatriot Peugeot-Citroën, and by leading firms from the USA (Ford, General Motors) and Japan (Toyota, Suzuki). Many dependent component manufacturers (*industria auxiliar*) are also wholly or partly foreign-owned.

In conjunction these various operations are a major source of employment. However, it is a source which is highly vulnerable to changing business conditions. When economic times are hard the first to be hit are often subsidiaries based outside the home country of the parent company (*casa matriz*). The results can be traumatic. Thus in 1993 Suzuki announced its intention to close the Santana jeep factory on which the town of Linares was almost entirely dependent.

Their importance as job providers gives multinationals enormous bargaining power *vis-à-vis* public authorities. Also in 1993 Volkswagen invested heavily in a new hi-tech SEAT plant at Martorell in Catalonia. Yet almost immediately VW announced its intention to pull out of the existing factory in the Barcelona 'Enterprise Area' (*Zona Franca*) to which it had been lured by tax breaks and other incentives. The plans were only altered after further financial concessions from regional and national governments desperate to preserve jobs.

5.3.3 Financial sector

Lack of investment in Spanish industry is closely linked to another aspect of the country's late modernisation; the relative underdevelopment of mechanisms for the supply of business finance. Spain's stock exchanges (*bolsas*) were, until recently, minuscule operations by international standards. Even though trading on them has increased substantially in recent years, Spanish companies remain heavily dependent on credit to finance their operations.

Under the Franco regime state agencies were set up to provide this. They included an Overseas Trade Bank (*Banco Exterior de España*), as well as a number of institutions designed to channel credit to specific industries. In

1971 these were brought together as the Official Credit Agency (*Instituto de Crédito Oficial – ICO*). Nevertheless, the principal supplier of credit remained the banking system. Traditionally this was divided into two parts. The first – slightly the smaller – consisted of the savings banks (*cajas de ahorros*). Locally based and managed they served a particular city or province; many were originally pawnbrokers (*montes de piedad*). Today the savings banks remain an important source of credit for particular types of business, especially farmers. They also continue to provide much useful documentation on the economy of their area and to carry out non-lucrative tasks (*obra social*), e.g. cultural and recreational projects, even though they are no longer required by law to devote stipulated proportions of the loans they provide to such projects of public interest.

The effective elimination of this requirement, and of other measures giving the savings banks protected status, means that there is now little practical distinction between them and the remainder of the banking system. In order to compete in this new environment, most savings banks have come together in larger entities covering several provinces or even the whole country. The Barcelona-based *Caixa*, originally a mutual pension fund, is now one of Spain's largest financial institutions. Concentration has enabled the savings banks to survive, but it has also effectively prevented their conversion into semi-public regional banks on the German model, specifically charged with industrial promotion in their area.

Concentration has also been the main feature of developments among the commercial banks. A first round of mergers and takeovers was triggered off by the failure of a number of smaller banks during and immediately after the transition. It resulted in the emergence of a group of major banks, known as the 'big seven': the *Bilbao, Vizcaya, Central, Hispanoamericano, Banesto, Santander*, and *Popular*. In 1987 a second period of upheaval began. It began with the crisis experienced by *Banca Catalana*, closely linked to Catalan prime minister Jordi Pujol and his regionalist supporters [3.2.2]. Soon, however, it spread to the big banks themselves.

The causes lay in the outdated practices characteristic of Spanish banks and in the 1987 Single European Act, under which there would be open competition between banks across the EC from 1993. Faced with the prospect of competing with more efficient foreign banks, whose advantages derived partly from sheer size, the more dynamic of the 'big seven' opted to break the gentleman's agreement that had previously governed relations between them [4.2.1]. The result was an outbreak of forced mergers and takeover bids, often tacitly encouraged by the government.

The first two bids, by the *Bilbao* and then the *Central* for *Banesto*, failed. In 1989, however, the two great Basque banks came together to form the *Banco Bilbao Vizcaya* (BBV). Two years later the ailing *Hispanoamericano* was absorbed by the *Central* to form the *Banco Central Hispano* (BCH). Finally in 1994, after a severe crisis which led the government to exercise its emergency powers to intervene, *Banesto* was effectively acquired by the *Santander*, although technically the two remained separate. The 'big seven' were thus reduced to four, of which the *Banco Popular* is much the smallest. Meantime, a further major player was added by the merger and privatisation of the state's banking interests under the name of *Argentaria* [5.4.1].

Even after these changes the main Spanish banks are still too small to compete successfully on the international stage; indeed, there is a continuing question mark over their ability to defend their domestic market against foreign incursion. At the same time they are too big in terms of their number of branches, twice as high relative to population as in the EU as a whole. Inevitably this has implications for their efficiency. Moreover, concentration has also reinforced dominance of the Spanish market by a few large players, a feature which undermines competition and so is bad for consumers.

5.3.4 Services

The service or tertiary sector (*sector terciario*) has come to dominate Western economies in recent decades. The same is true of Spain, albeit to a slightly lesser degree, with services now providing around 60 per cent of employment. This situation represents a remarkable change for the country; in 1960 services accounted for little over a quarter of the economy. As in other countries it is difficult to generalise about the service sector, composed as it is of a wide range of highly diverse activities. Of these, two are especially important in terms of the employment they provide.

The first is wholesale and retail trade (*comercio mayorista y minorista*), which accounts for around a quarter of all service jobs in Spain. In recent years this share has been declining steadily as small shops (*pequeños comercios*) are driven out of business by the less labour-intensive large-scale outlets (*grandes superficies*), such as super- and hypermarkets. Their supremacy is likely to increase as a result of the deregulation brought about by the 1995 Trading Act (*Ley de Comercio*), which among other measures partially deregulates shops' permitted opening hours (*horario comercial*). Unlike the case in most EU countries, in Spain the larger outlets are mainly in foreign ownership; French chains are particularly important.

The second major subsector in employment terms is that of public administration and other services provided by public authorities (principally education, health and social services). All these activities expanded rapidly in the 1980s, at both central and regional level. Combined, they now account for almost as many jobs as wholesaling and retailing.

The most rapidly growing subsector in recent years has been that of financial services. As well as the banking system [5.3.3], this includes insurance and business services. Like the banks, they remained heavily protected up to the coming into effect of the EU's single market in 1993. Largely as a result the financial sector as a whole remained underdeveloped and inefficient by international standards, and offered a tempting target to foreign investors.

In terms of overall economic significance, a fourth service subsector stands out. Now, as for many years, Spain's ability to pay for its imports depends crucially on the tourist industry (*sector turístico*) [5.2.1]. After tailing off from the late 1980s, the tourist trade has again risen sharply in the mid-1990s. Spain's attractiveness has been increased by the troubles suffered by several of its Mediterranean competitors. The authorities have also invested heavily in campaigns designed to distribute tourism more evenly over the country and the calendar year.

A major problem continues to be the low average amount injected into the Spanish economy by each tourist who visits the country. In part this is a reflection of the continuing emphasis on mass tourism (*turismo de masas*). But it also derives from the dominant role played by foreign tour operators (*tour operadores*) in managing the trade. As in the case of industry [5.3.2], here is evidence of inability on the part of Spanish business to exploit fully the country's natural resources.

5.3.5 Regional differences

As well as the massive sectoral shifts it has undergone in recent decades the Spanish economy has also experienced another sort of structural change. The geographical distribution of economic activity and wealth is markedly different now from what it was in 1960, or even 1975. The causes of change lie in the decline of certain established economic activities – traditional agriculture, heavy industry – and the rise of new ones, whose location is determined not by the presence of raw materials but by other factors, especially proximity to markets.

Up to the 1960s the two wealthiest and most developed parts of Spain were Catalonia and the Basque Country or, more precisely, the metropolitan areas of Barcelona and Bilbao. Otherwise industrial development was limited to a few smaller outposts, mainly along the northern Atlantic coast (*Cornisa Cantábrica*). Madrid, almost entirely because of its role as centre of administration, was the single enclave of prosperity in a vast area covering both Castiles, and the entire south.

In the 1990s this pattern has been replaced by another in which wealth and development is concentrated in two connected strips. The more important extends down the Mediterranean coast from Catalonia, through Valencia and Murcia and into the easternmost Andalusian province of Almería. The other runs up the valley of the Ebro from Tarragona in Catalonia, through Saragossa, into Navarre before petering out in the inland Basque province of Alava. Together with the y-shaped area formed by these two strips, Madrid and the two island regions (Balearics and Canaries) now make up 'rich Spain'.

The reasons why these areas have prospered vary. In the case of Madrid, success is mainly attributable to the expansion of government and the growing attractiveness of capital cities in general as business locations. In the islands tourism has obviously played the leading role. It has also been vital to the rise of the Mediterranean coastal strip (*eje mediterráneo*). This last area, however, also displays a number of features common to economically successful regions in developed countries. Thus it has little heritage of industrial blight, in terms of outdated plant and environmental damage. Its workforce is young and unwedded to the skills and practices of traditional heavy industry. It has a number of medium-sized centres, which provide an attractive working and living environment for incoming executives, as well as a major financial and business centre in Barcelona. Since the 1980s it has enjoyed an excellent system of internal communications. And it is also directly linked, through Catalonia, with one of the EU's main growth areas, the Mediterranean coastal area of southern France and northern Italy.

In all these respects conditions are very different along the northern Atlantic coast, the part of Spain which has lost most ground in the last few decades. From being among the country's most prosperous regions the Basque Country and, above all, Asturias, have fallen down the regional league table. In the former case, a strong business tradition and a series of initiatives by a determined regional government have helped to alleviate the problems of industrial decline. Yet the peripheral position of the area as a whole relative to the main centre of the European economy mean that its prospects are far from rosy.

That also applies to the southern regions of Andalusia, Extremadura and Castile-La Mancha which continue to be the country's poorest. As such, they have been major recipients of EU regional aid. Rather more hopefully, there are signs that, as in the Basque Country, devolution is producing positive effects. There is some evidence that regional governments are more sensitive to the needs of regional economies, and quicker and more innovative in responding to them than Madrid. In a reversal of previous experience, the poorer regions were less badly hit by the recession of the early 1990s than the country as a whole. And, albeit slowly, the gap between them and their richer neighbours is narrowing.

5.4 Spanish companies

The basic building blocks of a country's economy are its individual companies. These can and do vary enormously in size, management structure and ownership within countries as well as between them. In Spain's case the last of these three features has been and remains of particular importance. Compared to the Anglo-Saxon countries in particular, in Spain the state's role as entrepreneur has been, and continues to be, an important one.

5.4.1 Public sector

The public sector of the economy embraces a number of activities that relate to the country's people as a whole. In most of the developed world, as well as administration itself they include responsibility for education, health and social services. In Spain too the state is a major employer in this capacity [5.3.4]. There, however, its role in the economy goes much further. For it is also the owner, in whole or in part, of a considerable number of firms operating in industries that elsewhere in the West are usually in private hands.

The Spanish state's first major venture into business was CAMPSA (*Compañía Arrendataria del Monopolio de Petróleos SA*), the oil and petrol monopoly created in 1927 by the then dictator, Primo de Rivera. However, it was under Spain's second twentieth-century dictatorship that the government became a major economic player. Partly from the same desire as Primo to prevent the penetration of foreign companies, partly because the state was the only significant source of capital after the Civil War, the Franco regime became involved in many diverse industries.

In 1941 Franco set up a state holding company, the National Industry Agency (*Instituto Nacional de Industria – INI*), to oversee the government's rapidly burgeoning interests. Some of these, however, he assigned to an expanded Directorate General of State Assets (*Dirección General del Patrimonio del Estado – DGPE*), which dated from the previous century. By his death these two bodies had a considerable presence in many sectors of the economy.

Thereafter the public sector grew further as a result of industrial restructuring in the 1980s [5.1.2]. In a number of industries acquisition by the state was the only way of preserving either jobs or a Spanish presence, or both. By 1988 the INI had become Spain's largest industrial conglomerate (*grupo*). More than 150 000 workers were employed in the widely diverse companies – over 50 in total – in which it had holdings.

In fact, along with the illogical division between the INI and DGPE, excessive diversity was one of the public sector's main problems. Another was the unproductive, loss-making character of many of the companies it had acquired. These considerations led the government to implement major changes. In 1981 the National Hydrocarbons Agency (*Instituto Nacional de Hidrocarburos – INH*) was created, bringing together the INI's various petroleum and petrochemical interests in a separate unit. In a number of other cases, companies in the same or related fields were merged in order to create more viable entities.

The Socialist governments of the 1980s also took steps to rationalise the overall structure of the public sector by clarifying the roles of the INI and DGPE. The latter, subsequently renamed as the State Assets Group (*Grupo Patrimonio*), became the holding company for a diverse range of operations, mainly related to some sort of government or monopoly service. A new holding company, the Teneo Group, was set up within the INI, to oversee companies capable of showing a profit, and hence with potential for privatisation.

The INI was left with direct responsibility for those firms which, for various reasons, were incapable of surviving unsupported in the marketplace, mainly in declining traditional industries. The division was by no means clear, however. The notoriously inefficient national airline, Iberia, was assigned to Teneo – indeed, the firms within the new group generally failed to show the desired profitability. On the other hand, the highly profitable telecommunications monopoly, Telefónica, was assigned to the State Assets Group.

From the late 1980s onwards the government has privatised a number of state-owned companies, although in the larger ones in particular it has usually retained a significant holding of its own. Some have been sold off directly to private sector firms, and several of the largest have been floated on the stock market, including Telefónica, the electricity company Endesa, and the oil firm Repsol set up within INH in 1981. In the last two, as in most of the larger companies affected, the government retained 50 per cent of the stock, and thus a decisive voice in company policy.

Also partially privatised was *Argentaria*, the state banking corporation. This was created in 1991 by bringing together in a single federated entity a number of public financial institutions, including the Post Office Savings Bank (*Caja Postal de Ahorros*) as well as the Overseas Trade Bank and the Official Credit Agency [5.3.3]. By 1996 three-quarters of Argentaria's shares had been sold through the stock market.

One of the last acts of the Socialists before their removal from power was to dissolve the INI in 1995. Its functions were assumed by two new entities: the State Industrial Holding Company (*Sociedad Estatal de Participaciones Industriales – SEPI*) and the Spanish Industry Agency (*Agencia Industrial Española – AIE*). The conservative government elected in 1996 has indicated its intention to pursue further the policy of privatisation, selling off more firms and pulling out of those in which the Socialists retained a stake. However, it is unclear how this will be possible in the case of the loss-making public companies, a number of whom remain crucial to the economy as a whole and in particular regions (e.g. Asturias).

5.4.2 Private sector

The most obvious characteristic of Spanish private sector firms is their small size. Numerically both industry and the service sector are dominated by SMEs, that is small and medium-sized enterprises (*pequeñas y medianas empresas – pymes*). Over 90 per cent of firms employ less than 100 people. In fact, the most common form of business operation in Spain continues to be the sole trader (*comerciante*).

Of course, larger firms provide a disproportionate share of both employment and output. Yet even Spain's largest companies are relatively small by international standards. Apart from the hybrid public holding company INI [5.4.1], only one figured among Europe's hundred largest in 1994 – the oil company Repsol, also previously state-owned, at position 62. Of enterprises whose entire life has been spent in the private sector, Spain's sole representatives among the world's 500 biggest companies are three banks: the *Santander, Bilbao Vizcaya* and *Central Hispano* [5.3.3]. Moreover, many of the largest firms in Spain are owned by foreign interests (*see* Table 5.2).

The problems posed by small scale have led to the formation of cooperatives in certain areas and sectors (e.g. wine production). The best-known example is the group founded in Mondragón, in the Basque province of Guipúzcoa, in the 1950s. Its activities have since expanded throughout the

Table 5.2 Spain's largest companies, 1994 (excludes financial sector)

Company	Business
Repsol (S)	Energy (hydrocarbons, gas)
Telefónica (S)	Telecommunications
El Corte Inglés	Retail distribution (department stores, hypermarkets)
CEPSA (F)	Energy (hydrocarbons, gas)
Endesa (S)	Energy (electricity)
Tabacalera (S)	Cigarettes and tobacco
Iberdrola	Energy (electricity)
Fasa Renault España (F)	Cars and components
Opel España (F)	Cars and components
Pryca (F)	Retail distribution (hypermarkets)
RENFE (S)	Railways and bus services
Ford España (F)	Cars and components
Iberia (S)	Air travel
Seat (F)	Cars and components
Centros Comerciales Continente (F)	Retail distribution (hypermarkets)
FCC	Construction and property
Dragados y Construcciones	Construction and property
Citroën Hispania (F)	Cars and components
Petronor (S)	Energy (hydrocarbons)
Unión Fenosa	Energy (electricity)
BP Oil España (F)	Energy (hydrocarbons)
Alcampo (F)	Retail distribution (hypermarkets)
Nissan Motor Ibérica (F)	Cars and components
Sevillana de Electricidad	Energy (electricity)
Fiat Ibérica (F)	Cars and components
Eroski	Retail distribution (hypermarkets)
Peugeot Talbot España (F)	Cars and components
Fecsa	Energy (electricity)
Gas Natural	Energy (gas)
IBM España (F)	Information technology

Notes: F = Foreign (non-Spanish) controlling interest. S = State holding (at least 25 per cent)

region and beyond, and now encompass a wide range of activities including a domestic appliance manufacturer (*Fagor*) and a supermarket chain (*Eroski*).

Other than cooperatives, companies are of four main types. The first corresponds roughly to the British concept of the partnership (*sociedad colectiva*); in such firms the partners (*socios*) are personally liable in the event of bankruptcy (*insolvencia*). By contrast, in a limited partnership (*sociedad comandita*) some or all of the partners have liabilities limited to their initial capital participation. Companies of these types are identified by the suffixes *y Compañía* (*y Cía*) and *Sociedad en Comandita* (SC) respectively. Neither is common in Spain.

The remaining two types of business association are forms of limited company, corresponding broadly – but not exactly – to UK private and public companies. Under the 1990 Companies Act (*Ley de Sociedades*) the conditions governing their structure and operation were substantially revised. One result has been to save from likely extinction the Spanish equivalent of the private limited company (*Sociedad de Responsabilidad Limitada – SL*). For this type of enterprise there is no longer any upper limit on the company's capital (*capital social*) as recorded in the Register of Companies (*Registro Mercantil*); the minimum required is 500 000 pesetas. The capital is held in the form of shares; as and when they are offered for sale the existing owners and the company itself have the right of first refusal. These and other stipulations ensure that the Spanish private limited company remains of the 'family-firm' type, control over it being relatively protected from the open market.

The reason why the 1990 Act resulted in a revival of the private company was that, for the first time, it set a minimum on the capital required to form a public company (*Sociedad Anónima – SA*). Currently this stands at ten million pesetas. Public companies are also distinguished from private ones by the fact that their shares can be freely traded. In some, but not all cases, trade occurs through the mechanism of a stock exchange listing (*cotización*). Changes of share ownership are not required to be recorded in the Register of Companies, as is the case for private limited companies – hence the Spanish name.

By law, a public company is required to hold an annual general meeting of shareholders (*Junta de Accionistas*), which must approve the annual report and set a dividend. Between such meetings the company's affairs are run by the board (*Consejo de Administración*), made up of directors (*consejeros*) elected by the AGM. The board has the power to appoint one of its members as managing director (*consejero delegado*), who then exercises in the board's name the powers bestowed on it by law, and by the AGM.

5.5 GLOSSARY

adquisición f	purchase; takeover
agencia de contratación f	employment agency
agricultor m	farmer
agrios mpl	citrus fruits
agro m	agriculture
ajuste m	adjustment; reduction
ajuste de plantilla m	job losses, redundancies
ajuste presupuestario m	cut in (government) spending
ajuste salarial m	wage cut
aparcero m	sharecropper
apertura f	opening-up (of economy to outside world/competition)
arcas del estado fpl	government coffers, the Treasury
arrendatorio m	leaseholder

atomización f	fragmentation (of economy), existence of many small firms
autónomo m	self-employed person
autoridad laboral f	employment authority
ayuda f	grant
banda ancha/estrecha f	broad/narrow band (of EMS)
barreras aduaneras fpl	customs barriers
barreras no tarifarias fpl	non-tariff barriers
bienes de equipo mpl	capital goods
bolsa f	stock exchange
caja de ahorros f	savings bank
caladero m	fishing ground
calentamiento m	overheating (of the economy)
casa matriz f	parent company
cierre m	(factory) closure
comerciante m	(sole) trader
comercio m	trade; shop
comercio exterior m	foreign trade
concentración parcelaria f	rationalisation of landholding structure
congelación salarial f	wage freeze
consejero m	company director
consejero delegado m	managing director
Consejo de Administración m	Board of Directors
contingente m	(import) quota
contratación f	hiring (of labour)
contrato de aprendizaje m	apprenticeship
contrato de duración indefinida m	permanent contract
contrato en prácticas m	work placement
contrato temporal m	temporary/fixed-term contract
contrato a tiempo completo/ parcial m	full/part-time contract
contribuyente mf	tax-payer
convenio colectivo m	collective agreement
cosecha f	crop; harvest
cotización f	share price; exchange rate; social security contribution
crisis f	crisis; recession
crudos mpl	(crude) oil
cuota empresarial f	employer's social security contribution
déficit exterior m	foreign deficit
déficit público m	public sector deficit
demanda laboral f	demand for labour
desarme arancelario m	removal of customs barriers
desequilibrio m	imbalance; problem
desequilibrios territoriales mpl	regional imbalances
desmantelamiento m	removal (of trade barriers)
despido m	dismissal, sacking
despido colectivo m	dismissal of a number of employees
despido libre m	employer's right to (hire and) fire
destrucción de empleo(s) f	job losses

deuda del estado f	government debt/bonds
devaluación f	devaluation; fall (in value of currency)
divisas fpl	foreign currency
economía sumergida f	informal/black economy
eje mediterráneo/atlántico m	Mediterranean/Atlantic coastal strip
empleo m	employment; job
empresa deficitaria f	loss-making firm
empresa nacional f	Spanish firm; domestic firm
Encuesta de Población Activa f	Official Labour-force Survey
endeudamiento público m	public/national debt
enfriamiento m	cooling-down
estacionalidad f	seasonal nature
estanflación f	stagflation (simultaneous stagnation and inflation)
Estatuto de los Trabajadores m	Workers' Charter
estructura agraria f	structure of land-ownership
excedente m	surplus
éxodo rural m	rural depopulation, flight from the land
expediente m	authorisation
explotación f	farm, (land)holding
extinción f	termination (of a contract)
filial f	subsidiary
fiscalidad f	taxation; tax rate
flexibilización f	making the labour market more flexible/less rigid
formación continua f	in-service training
fraude fiscal m	tax evasion/fraud
fusión f	merger
grandes superficies fpl	large-scale retail outlet
grupo m	group (of companies), conglomerate
holding m	holding company
horario comercial m	permitted shop opening hours
horario laboral m	working hours
horas extra(ordinarias) fpl	overtime
hostelería f	hotel and restaurant trade
impuesto de sociedades m	corporation tax
impuesto sobre la renta de las personas físicas (IRPF) m	income tax
impuesto sobre el trabajo m	'jobs tax'
impuesto sobre el valor añadido (IVA) m	value added tax (VAT)
indemnización f	compensation
industria f	industry; firm
industria auxiliar f	component industry/firm
insolvencia f	bankruptcy
Instituto Nacional de Empleo (INEM) m	National Employment Agency
invernadero m	greenhouse
inversión en cartera f	portfolio investment
inversión extranjera f	foreign investment

jornada laboral f	total working time/hours (usually weekly)
jornalero m	day-labourer
jubilación anticipada f	early retirement
Junta de Accionistas f	Annual General Meeting (AGM)
latifundio m	large estate
medidas deflacionistas fpl	anti-inflation measures/policies
mentalidad empresarial f	entrepreneurial spirit
mercado laboral/de trabajo m	labour/jobs market
mercado nacional m	domestic market
minifundio m	very small farm/holding
minifundismo m	predominance of excessively small farms
minifundismo empresarial m	(see *atomización*)
minorista m	retailer
moderación salarial f	wage moderation
monte de piedad m	pawnbrokers
nómina f	payroll
obra social f	non-lucrative work (of savings banks)
oferta laboral f	labour supply
oferta pública de adquisición (OPA) f	takeover bid
oferta de trabajo f	job offer
Organización de los Países Exportadores de Petróleo (OPEP) f	OPEC
parcela f	plot (of land)
paro femenino/juvenil/ masculino m	female/youth/male unemployment
paro de larga duración m	long-term unemployment
persona en edad de trabajar f	person of working age
pesca f	fishing (industry)
pesca de altura f	high-seas fishing
pesca costera f	inshore fishing
política monetaria f	monetary policy; exchange rate policy
presión fiscal f	tax burden
primicias fpl	early-season produce
productos mpl	products; (agricultural) produce
productos elaborados mpl	finished products
pyme f	SME (small/medium-sized firm)
rama f	branch; industry
recaudación f	tax receipts; tax collection
reciclaje m	retraining; recycling
reconversión (industrial) f	industrial restructuring
recuperación f	recovery
reforma agraria f	land reform
Registro Mercantil m	Register of Companies
remesas fpl	remittances
revaluación f	rise (in value of currency)
riego m	irrigation
rigidez f	(source of) rigidity (in the labour market)
salario m	wage; earnings

Salario Mínimo Interprofesional (SMI) m	standard minimum wage
saneamiento m	rationalisation; streamlining; setting on sound financial footing
sector m	sector; industry
sector agropecuario m	agriculture
sector alimenticio m	food and drink industry
sector automovilístico m	vehicle/car industry
sector hortifrutícola m	fruit and vegetable growing
sector lácteo m	dairy industry
sector naval m	ship-building industry
sector pesquero m	fishing industry
sector productivo m	manufacturing industry
sector siderúrgico m	(iron and) steel industry
sector turístico m	tourist industry
sobreexplotación f	over-exploitation; overfishing
sociedad anónima f	public limited company
sociedad colectiva f	partnership
sociedad comandita f	limited partnership
sociedad de responsabilidad limitada f	private limited company
socio m	partner
subvención f	subsidy
tasa de actividad f	participation rate, economic activity rate
tasa de desempleo/paro f	unemployment rate
tipo central m	central rate (of currency in EMS)
trabajador cualificado/sin cualificar m	skilled/unskilled worker
trabajador por cuenta ajena m	employee
trabajador por cuenta propia m	self-employed person
turno m	shift

6

THE ENVIRONMENT

Throughout the Western world, concern for the environment has grown with the realisation that economic development has negative as well as positive effects. Given that Spain long missed out on the advantages of growth, it is scarcely surprising that it has as yet paid relatively little attention to the draw-backs. The result is that a country which naturally is one of the most favoured in Europe now faces increasing environmental problems. This chapter begins by looking at those caused directly by pollution. It then goes on to examine underlying changes to the country's landscape and their effects in both eco-logical and economic terms. Finally it considers the response to these issues in terms of attempts to protect Spain's environment.

6.1 POLLUTION

Precisely because of its nature as a single system, it is hard to classify into distinct categories the impact of human activities on the environment. In Spain as elsewhere, the changes they produce in one aspect inevitably have knock-on effects in others, often apparently unrelated. Perhaps the best starting point is to examine the process known as pollution (*contaminación*), that is the changes produced in the chemical make-up of the elements essential for human, and other life; air, water and the earth itself.

6.1.1 Air pollution

One aspect of the environment in which Spain has, as yet, experienced few problems is that of air pollution (*contaminación atmosférica*). In that sense the late development of industry has been advantageous. Only in small areas of the country did economic development follow the 'classic' pattern common in the UK and northern Europe and based on heavy industry. Elsewhere in Spain development has been on the basis of more modern industrial tech-niques, or of service activity. In neither case were the environmental effects anything like as serious as those associated with classical industrialisation.

In addition, Spain's location at the Western end of the European continent brings the further advantage that the prevailing winds carry relatively few airborne pollutants.

Nevertheless, this positive picture must be severely qualified in two groups of areas. The first consists of those parts of the country which industrialised early. Particularly badly affected is the Greater Bilbao area, the country's main industrial centre up to the early 1980s, which now reputedly has the poorest air quality in the EU. On over 100 days per year the exposure level (*nivel de inmisión*) of its inhabitants to a range of airborne pollutants exceeds official health guidelines. The result is a very high incidence of respiratory illness. Similar, if less grave effects are observable in the Avilés area of Asturias.

Air pollution also reaches severe proportions in and around centres where industrial development was promoted by the Franco regime. These include Huelva on the southern Atlantic coast; the eastern Mediterranean ports of Cartagena and Tarragona; and Puertollano, in the province of Ciudad Real. The activities principally to blame are the chemical industry, oil refining and petrochemical manufacture, and the generation of electricity in fossil-fuel-fired power stations (*centrales térmicas*).

The second important exception to Spain's generally low level of air pollution comes in the country's two main metropolitan areas, centred on Madrid and Barcelona. Especially in the latter the presence of older industry is a factor here too, but only one among several. In both cities, road traffic has reached extremely high densities, to which the government has reacted only recently and as yet without great success. It was also slow to encourage the use of unleaded petrol (*gasolina sin plomo*), which only became cheaper than leaded varieties in 1990.

Emissions from domestic heating systems are a further burden on air quality, especially in Madrid. The capital's geographical position in a shallow, elevated basin, along with the climatic phenomenon of temperature inversion, gives rise in winter to the characteristic 'beret' (*boina*) of visibly polluted air hanging over the city.

Another environmental problem affecting the air in Spain's urban areas, although not strictly speaking pollution, is regarded as such in semi-technical language; noise pollution (*contaminación acústica*). It is a field where international comparisons are fraught with difficulties, due to differences in measurement techniques. So figures suggesting that Spain rivals Japan as the world's noisiest country must be treated with caution, particularly as they have been contested by Spanish official bodies. Nevertheless, even these authorities' own data make clear that noise levels in central Madrid regularly exceed international guidelines. Moreover, those figures relate to background noise levels and do not take into consideration the situation of workers involved in particularly noisy activities. In such cases, the effects on individuals depend on observance of prescribed safety precautions, often lax in Spain.

6.1.2 Water pollution and dumping of wastes

In the case of water pollution (*contaminación del agua*) any advantages accruing to Spain from its late economic development have been more than neutralised. Indeed, the problems the country faces in this area are some of the most severe of all. In part they are inherited from the very special conditions under which rapid industrial development occurred in the 1960s.

Many of the industries which grew up then used technically outdated processes which were viable partly because labour costs were low, but partly also because firms were not required to bear the costs of reprocessing harmful wastes (*residuos*). Two especially important examples of this phenomenon were the chemical industry and paper manufacture. In the Basque Country in particular emissions from paper mills (*papelerías*) produced very high levels of river pollution. The result was that by the 1970s many towns and villages depended for employment on activities which produced large quantities of wastes, with virtually no controls exercised over disposal. In this situation the further wave of industrialisation in the 1980s had catastrophic effects. Between 1983 and 1988 production of toxic wastes increased by 300 per cent; even the government ministry responsible admitted that less than a third of the total was being monitored. Inevitably a significant proportion found its way into water courses.

Moreover, industry is not the only source of pollutants entering Spain's supplies of surface and ground water (*aguas superficiales y subterráneas*). New, intensive forms of agriculture employ considerable amounts of pesticides and artificial fertilisers (*abonos químicos*). These are widely used in greenhouse production of early fruit and vegetables along the Mediterranean coast, especially in Huelva and Almería provinces. Another problematic crop is rice; it was pesticides used by rice farmers that in 1987 caused the death of 20 000 water birds in the Doñana National Park [6.3.1] when their habitat suffered contamination (*intoxicación*).

Spain's households also contribute significantly to water pollution because of low levels of sewage treatment. Despite construction of new treatment plants (*depuradoras*), significant amounts of raw sewage continue to be pumped directly into water courses; less than half of all domestic sewage is adequately treated. The problems are particularly grave in areas of rapid population growth, and in some coastal areas. Along the Mediterranean coast, for example as much as 30 per cent of sewage passes untreated into the sea.

Spain's coastal waters (*aguas litorales*) are also affected by dumping of solid wastes. Particularly important in this regard are the mining operations carried out around the bay of Portman, east of Cartagena on the Murcia coast. Lead and zinc have been mined there for centuries, but it was under the Franco regime that a massive open-cast operation got under way. One of the largest of its kind in the world, this involved 'washing' earth directly into the bay using a mixture of sea water and highly toxic chemicals, including cyanide and sulphur. The bay is now silted up and badly contaminated; a large area on the landward side has been turned into a 'moonscape'. In 1988 the EU obliged the authorities to take action as a result of which the impact of the operations was reduced, but they nevertheless continue.

Inevitably a major contributor to pollution of the seas around Spain is the oil industry. As yet the only major incident occurred in the winter of 1992/93, when the tanker *Aegean Sea* ran aground off Corunna with considerable damage to marine life, including economically important shellfish stocks. However, the typical 'spillages' from tankers occur on a regular basis.

Deliberate dumping at sea has also been practised in a number of cases with the active encouragement of the Spanish authorities. For 15 years from 1974 they allowed a chemical firm to dump titanium dioxide waste in the ocean 55 km off Cádiz, until protests from local people forced a reassessment of the situation. Up to 1983 foreign nuclear waste (*residuos nucleares*) was dumped at a site 700 km off the Galician coast, making it the world's largest off-shore deposit of such material.

More recently Spain's own mounting stocks of nuclear waste have begun to pose a major problem. By the 1990s over 500 tons of highly radioactive waste were stored at the country's power stations; by the year 2020 the figure is anticipated to rise to some 6000 tons. As in other countries the search for permanent sites has met with understandable resistance from people in the areas potentially affected. At the end of 1992 the first permanent disposal site (*cementerio nuclear*) for low and medium level waste was opened, at El Cabril in Córdoba province.

6.2 LANDSCAPE CHANGE

Environmental damage does not, of course, begin and end with the question of pollution. As well as the relatively direct effects of waste dumping and other emissions, change in the environment as the result of human actions involves also more complex and longer-term processes. Some operate at continental or world scale; thus Spain too is affected by the thinning of the ozone layer (*capa de ozono*) or the greenhouse effect (*efecto invernadero*). Other such processes, however, are more localised, in the sense that they operate exclusively or with particular intensity within individual countries. In Spain, two are especially importance.

6.2.1 Deforestation and reforestation

The story that in ancient times a squirrel could travel from Gibraltar to the Pyrenees without touching the ground may be apocryphal. What is undeniable is that Spain's once vast woods have been severely depleted over the centuries. It was not principally ecological considerations – nowhere had they reached the political agenda at that time – that led the Franco regime to attempt to reverse the process of deforestation from the 1940s on. Its massive programme of reforestation was promoted largely by economic concerns. The species planted were chosen for their rapid growth, many of them imports to Spain such as the Australian eucalyptus.

In addition to the implications in terms of habitat change [6.2.3], this policy has also had an unintended side effect which works against its original objective. For as well as growing quickly, eucalyptus and the various species of pine introduced also burn easily. And the biggest threat to Spain's woodland and scrubland (*monte*) today comes from the forest fires (*incendios forestales*) which became alarmingly frequent in the 1980s and literally flared up again in 1994. Such fires have hit the new species hard, but not exclusively. Evidently other factors are at work too, some of which are inherent to the Mediterranean climate and vegetation prevalent in much of the country. Summers are long, hot and dry, lightning a frequent occurrence; indigenous woodland also burns relatively easily, and is intermixed with highly inflammable stretches of scrubland. Yet these climatic factors do not explain the upsurge of fires in the 1980s, especially as one of the worst hit regions was Galicia, whose climate is Atlantic.

One cause there and elsewhere in the country is the declining economic value of Spain's woodland (*bosque*), most of which is privately owned. With wood no longer used significantly for heating, there is no incentive to carry out the work of selectively lopping branches, collecting fallen ones and clearing undergrowth. The resultant dense mass of live and dead timber both burns easily and makes extinction difficult; it cannot, however, explain why fires start so frequently. That can only be the result of human action, which is increasingly impacting on woodland. Population growth and changing leisure patterns are bringing more people into the Spanish countryside; many, unlike their forebears, are completely unacquainted with it. Carelessness of various types undoubtedly causes many fires. Nor are the countryside's own inhabitants blameless in this regard; careless burning of stubble (*rastrojo*) and pasture land (*pastizales*) is another significant cause.

Fires, however, are not always the result of accident. Rural resentment against afforestation is based on a number of grounds including loss of farming land and damage to it allegedly caused by woodland wildlife. Nor is it restricted to farmers; in some areas it appears to have become part of local tradition, perhaps dating back to the loss of former common lands in the nineteenth century. Sometimes, too, burning of woodland seems to be used as a means of settling private disputes. For all these reasons, some fires – no one can be sure what proportion – are undoubtedly the result of deliberate action by local people.

Finally it is widely suspected that much larger interests are also at work. In some case logging firms (*industrias madereras*) have been accused of responsibility, their alleged object being to buy up large quantities of fire-damaged, but still usable wood at knock-down prices. However, the most serious allegations have been levelled at property developers (*empresas inmobiliarias*), especially in areas close to the Mediterranean coast where there is high pressure for new holiday developments (*urbanizaciones*). There prime building land is often wooded, and subject to planning restrictions. A number of the most serious fires have removed the woodland such restrictions were designed to protect – and hence also the arguments against development, which economically may be very attractive not just for the developer but for the local economy as a whole. For that reason suspicion has occasionally been voiced against local councillors; the interests of their municipality, and also the prospect of party or personal rake-offs [2.1.3], provide possible motives for collusion with fire-raisers.

To the extent that such suspicions are justified, it is clear that more than environmental measures will be needed to remove the main contemporary threat to Spain's woodland. However, that is not to say that such measures cannot help, and indeed in a number of areas they are being taken. Both central and regional governments have undertaken campaigns designed to increase environmental awareness [6.3.2]. More directly, Galicia has had particular success with simple measures designed to stop fires spreading once started, for example through the systematic cutting of firebreaks (*cortafuegos*).

6.2.2 Desertification

Deforestation is a particularly serious problem in Spain because it, in turn, is one of the main causes of a second process of long-term landscape change – desertification. Here it is necessary to clarify a point of terminology. That used internationally distinguishes between desertification – the process by which arid land becomes effectively incapable of sustaining life, in other words a desert – and desertisation, the abandonment of an area by its human population.

This distinction is also made in official Spanish usage. In Spain, however, the latter phenomenon was already well known as 'depopulation' (*despoblación*). As a result, the less clumsy '*desertización*' is frequently used, even by experts, as a synonym for the technically correct '*desertificación*' when speaking of landscape change in areas of the country which were long since virtually uninhabited.

Desertification, most commonly associated with Africa, is a threat facing a number of countries in southern Europe. Since the early 1980s Spain, along with Italy and Greece, has participated in a joint Campaign against Desertification in the Mediterranean Region (*Lucha contra la Desertificación en el Mediterráneo – LUCDEME*). However, the scale of the problem is considerably greater in Spain than anywhere else in the continent. Already the country has Europe's only genuine desert, an area in Almería province famous – or notorious – as a Western film-set. However, desertification is also a real danger in other provinces of Andalusia, in parts of Extremadura and Valencia regions, and above all in the interior of Murcia.

Deforestation [6.2.1] is clearly an important factor in the erosion which is the prelude to desertification. In Spain this is caused less by wind (*erosión eólica*) than by the action of water (*erosión hídrica*). Here, as with deforestation, the Mediterranean climate plays a key part, with its highly irregular rainfall pattern (*pluviometría*). Lengthy dry spells are typically broken by torrential rainstorms (*trombas de agua*), which in the absence of tree cover wash away large amounts of topsoil.

Agricultural practices (*técnicas agrícolas*) have also contributed to erosion. In Castile, in particular, extensive cereal farming put a premium on bringing as much land as possible under the plough. With the advent of mechanisation more marginal land, especially on slopes, was cleared of its natural vegetation and worked with heavy tractors, becoming more vulnerable as a result. Elsewhere overgrazing (*sobrepastoreo*) or other inappropriate land-uses produced similar results. The inefficient methods and general neglect typical of the large estates of the south [5.3.1] may also have played a part.

In recent years such factors have probably become less important; in particular the EU's encouragement of land set-aside (*abandono de tierras*) has taken much marginal agricultural land back out of production. Yet the threat of desertification has not been diminished, and indeed was accentuated by the almost total absence of rainfall throughout much of southern and central Spain during the period 1990–95. The drought (*sequía*), however, may only have served to divert attention from the most serious cause of desertification which, although water-related, is not climatic but man-made in origin.

That cause is excessive use of what is becoming a scarce resource worldwide, not merely in countries like Spain where supply is uncertain. Rising water demand in Spain comes from various sources. Both domestic and industrial consumption are partly to blame; in some localities, especially on the Andalusian coast, heavy watering of golf courses is also a factor. However, the main cause is the recent large increase in the amount of agricultural land under irrigation. This technique is used both for intensive fruit and vegetable farming, concentrated along the south-eastern and southern Mediterranean coast, and for other crops, most notably rice, of which the Murcia region is now a major producer. The effect has been a significant reduction in the water table in a number of areas – on Grand Canary, where water demand comes mainly from tourism, it appears to be particularly marked. The consequence is to increase the danger of erosion and thus desertification.

In some coastal areas the drop in the water table has allowed sea water to enter the underground reserves known as aquifers, which in turn affects water used for irrigation. Thus in Almería the presence of salt in irrigation water is thought to be responsible for a reduction in crop yields. More importantly, it gives rise to excessive concentrations of salt in the earth (*salinización*), a further cause of desertification.

Even without sea water contamination it is known that irrigation can produce the same result. High salt concentrations in Extremadura are believed to have been caused in this way when local farmers were encouraged to abandon traditional crops on unirrigated land in favour of others, especially asparagus, which require irrigation. Extremadura has now joined the list of Spanish regions where desertification is a significant danger.

6.2.3 Ecological and economic impact

Both deforestation and desertification are extreme examples of a more general phenomenon. Climate and landscape change results in the loss of natural habitats and so to a decline in biodiversity, that is, of the wealth of plant and animal species. This is of especial importance in Spain, which hosts a considerable number of rare, even endangered species. The presence of Western Europe's last brown bear colonies is perhaps the best-known example, but it is only one among many, often surprising. The evergreen oakwoods of Extremadura, for instance, are the world's largest and home to the black vulture and other bird species found nowhere else in Europe.

Alongside the oakwoods themselves, Extremadura also contains large expanses of a habitat effectively unique to Spain, the thinly oak-covered parkland known as *dehesa*. The *dehesa* is, in fact a man-made landscape, produced by partial deforestation to allow various forms of extensive agriculture (wheat-farming, pig-rearing, cork collection, etc.). The uneconomic nature of such activities in conventional terms has led to pressures for more profitable uses, irrigation and so potential desertification. However, whether or not that drastic stage is reached, upsetting of the delicate balance of uses which maintains the *dehesa* in its current condition will inevitably lead to serious losses in terms of biodiversity.

Wetlands (*zonas húmedas*) are by no means unique to Spain but are important there because of the country's location on the migration routes of various species of waterfowl. As well as by direct reclamation for agricultural use, their area is being steadily reduced by increasing irrigation and the consequent fall in the water table [6.2.2]. Three of the most important wetland areas have received some protection through designation as national or regional parks [6.3.1]. Such measures, however, do little to maintain the water table; in the largest wetland area of all, the *Coto Doñana*, it is estimated to be falling at around one metre every year.

Landscape change is detrimental to Spain not just in ecological terms but also in the economic ones that dominate official thinking. Especially as the country seeks to diversify its tourist industry away from the Mediterranean coast, it is coming to be recognised that the attractiveness of landscapes – and habitats – is a key asset in maintaining Spain's market leadership. This applies not only to the conservation of hitherto unspoilt areas but also the improvement of conditions in existing tourist areas whose appearance has suffered particularly from development's visual impact (*impacto paisajístico*). This comes from a number of sources. One is the massive transport projects undertaken in the 1980s. Another is a problem common in Spain; the uncontrolled – and sometimes even controlled – dumping of rubbish on the fringe of settlements in full view of the public. Much the most important form of visual impact, however, is tourist accommodation itself, whether in the form of medium- to large-scale holiday villages or as individual second or holiday homes. For many years such developments were subject to only minimal planning controls; in any case they were frequently constructed without the requisite permission and rarely demolished thereafter. Since the 1988 Coastline Act (*Ley de Costas*) much greater control has been exercised. Unfortunately, however, its approval was preceded by a final orgy of visually intrusive building which blighted new stretches of coast and further worsened conditions on others.

6.3 PROTECTION OF THE ENVIRONMENT

When, in the early 1990s, Spain was a candidate to host the EU's future environmental authority the government was embarrassed by the revelation that none of its ministries included the word 'environment' in its title. Many of the comments passed were unfair. Few governments pay more than lip-service to ecology; in the case of the UK, the ministry which bears the title of Environment in fact has little to do with the subject. However, it is true that Spain is not well-placed to undertake the task of protecting the environment (*defensa del medio ambiente*), not least because it lacks coherent structures to do so.

6.3.1 Environmental authorities

The oldest Spanish authorities with specifically environmental responsibilities are the National Parks, which date back to 1918. In that year the first two Parks were designated. One (*Montaña de Covadonga*) is located in the *Picos de Europa* range on the borders of Asturias, Cantabria and León, the other (*Ordesa y Monte Perdido*) in the Aragonese Pyrenees.

From 1954 a further ten Parks were established (*see* Table 6.1). The most recent, designated in 1995, protect rare habitats on Spain's central plateau, the *meseta*, including some of the country's most valuable in Extremadura [6.2.3]. The remainder are either wetlands areas or located in the island regions of the Balearics and Canaries, with one exception; *Aigüestortes y Lago San Mauricio* Park in the Pyrenees. In 1988 responsibility for this last was transferred to the Catalan regional government. It retains the title National Park but does not form part of the 'national network' (*red estatal*) made up of the remaining eleven.

In addition, Spain has two Regional Parks. The first, comprising a further important wetland area in the Ebro Delta, was originally proposed for National Park status by the Catalan regional government. When it received no backing from Madrid, it took the initiative and negotiated separate arrangements with an international environment agency. The second adjoins the *Covadonga* National Park and covers a further area of the *Picos de Europa* in the region of Castile-Leon.

Table 6.1 National Parks

	Area (has)	Year set up	Province
Montaña de Covadonga	16 925	1918	Asturias/Cantabria/León
Ordesa y Monte Perdido	15 608	1918	Huesca
Teide	13 571	1954	Tenerife
Aigüestortes y Lago San Mauricio[1]	22 396	1955	Lleida
La Caldera de Taburiente	4690	1964	Tenerife (La Palma)
Doñana	50 720	1969	Huelva/Cádiz/Seville
Las Tablas de Daimiel	1928	1980	Ciudad Real
Garajonay	3984	1981	Tenerife (La Gomera)
Timanfaya	5107	1981	Gran Canaria (Lanzarote)
Archipiélago de Cabrera[2]	10 025	1991	Balearics
Cabañeros	38 500	1995	Ciudad Real
Monfragüe	17 852	1995	Cáceres

Notes: [1] Control transferred to Catalan Regional Government in 1988.
[2] Officially designated a 'land-sea park' (parque marítimo-terrestre).

Each of the National Parks has a Strategic Plan (*Plan Rector*), setting out aims and policies. Yet while they undoubtedly offer a degree of protection to sensitive areas, they also increase pressures on them by attracting visitors. Nor can the Parks offer protection against practices carried on outside their boundaries which nevertheless impact strongly within them.

As well as the National Parks, Spain has a large number of other categories of protected countryside areas (*espacios naturales protegidos* – ENP). Most owe their status essentially to being areas of natural beauty (*parajes pintorescos*), although some are nature reserves (*reservas naturales*) and others are intended to conserve stocks of game. The level of protection offered is, in practice, low.

After the original National Park authorities, the oldest public authority in Spain with environmental responsibilities is the National Nature Conservancy Agency (*Instituto Nacional para la Conservación de la Naturaleza* – ICONA). ICONA was created in 1971 under the auspices of the Ministry of Agriculture, Fisheries and Food. It has wide and rather ill-defined responsibilities covering a number of aspects of conservation, as well as for fighting forest fires [6.2.1]. It also has the task – a considerable one in Spain – of issuing shooting and angling permits.

A year after ICONA's establishment the need for environmental considerations to inform policy in various ministries was recognised, at least formally, with the creation of an Interministerial Environment Committee (*Comisión Interministerial del Medio Ambiente*). This was dissolved in 1987, since when coordination has taken place through the Under-secretaries' Committee [1.5.2] and a special cabinet committee. Meanwhile, the 1978 Constitution had included what is very close to an injunction for the government to set up an

contained major new transport projects, and proposals for further tourist development and afforestation with non-indigenous species. It was described by one commentator as a 'declaration of war on nature'.

A concern with other priorities is apparent even in plans drawn up in the environment section of the MOPTMA, such as the 1993 National Reforestation Plan (*Plan Nacional de Reforestación – PNR*). Among other provisions, the PNR attempts to reverse previous errors by offering four times more financial support for planting indigenous species than non-indigenous ones [6.2.1]. Yet under the PNR replanting depends on individual farmers' acceptance of grants; inevitably it will be small-scale and uncoordinated. Nor will it affect land outside agricultural use where erosion is already under way. Moreover, although the financial arrangements are clearly beneficial in a sense, they do nothing to ensure that the choice of species is made on the basis of appropriateness to the terrain concerned. In essence, the PNR is not an environmental measure but an agricultural one.

6.4 GLOSSARY

abandono de tierras m	set-aside
abono químico m	chemical/artificial fertiliser
aguas litorales fpl	coastal waters
aguas residuales fpl	sewage
aguas subterráneas/superficiales fpl	underground/surface water
bosque m	woodland
cabecera de cuenca f	headwaters
capa de ozono f	ozone layer
cementerio nuclear m	nuclear waste dumping facility
centrales térmicas fpl	fossil-fuel power station
conciencia (medioambiental) f	(environmental) awareness
Consejo Nacional de Aguas m	National Water Board
contaminación acústica f	noise pollution
contaminación atmosférica f	air pollution
cortafuegos m	firebreak
defensa del medio ambiente f	protection of the environment
deforestación f	deforestation
delito ecológico m	environmental offence
depuradora f	sewage treatment plant
desarrollismo m	belief in absolute priority of economic growth
desertificación f	desertification
desertización f	depopulation; desertification (*see* 6.2.2)
efecto invernadero m	greenhouse effect
empresa inmobiliaria f	property company/developer
empresa maderera f	logging company
erosión eólica/hídrica f	wind/water erosion
espacio natural m	countryside area
especie autóctona f	native/indigenous species
gasolina sin plomo f	unleaded petrol

impacto paisajístico m	visual impact
incendio forestal m	forest fire
industria maderera f	logging company
ingeniero de montes m	forester
intoxicación f	contamination
inundación f	flood
medio ambiente m	environment
medio físico m	natural environment
monte m	scrubland
nivel de inmisión m	exposure level
papelería f	paper mill
paraje pintoresco m	area of natural beauty
pastizales mpl	grazing land
pieza cinegética f	game animal or bird
pluviometría f	rainfall pattern
rastrojo m	stubble
reforestación f	reforestation
regadío m	land under irrigation
repoblación forestal f	(*see reforestación*)
reserva natural f	nature reserve
residuos mpl	waste(s)
salinización f	salinisation, excessive build-up of salt
secano m	unirrigated land
sequía f	drought
sobrepastoreo m	overgrazing
técnica agrícola f	agricultural practice
terreno inclinado m	slope
tromba de agua f	sudden, tropical downpour
urbanización f	development (i.e. group of houses)
zona húmeda f	wetland area

7

EDUCATION

Contemporary observers have tended to be impressed by the high value placed by Spaniards of all social classes on education. They point to seemingly insatiable demand for university places, as well as the popularity of various forms of continuing and community education. Yet growing demand has placed additional strains on what, by international standards, has historically been a very poorly resourced system. Nor were resource problems the only ones bequeathed by history; a number of issues of principle also remained unresolved in 1975. This chapter begins by examining these underlying issues, before going on to look at the way governments have addressed them and other, more immediate ones. The final section considers the way in which educational studies are structured as a result of these various reforms.

7.1 EDUCATIONAL PRINCIPLES

As Spain returned to democracy after 1975, three issues underlay the problems of its education system. All have affected most Western countries at some point. In Spain, however, the peculiar nature of the country's social and economic history meant that they had remained unresolved much longer than in its neighbours. The issues concerned could not be more fundamental; they related to the questions of who should receive education, who should provide it, and why.

7.1.1 Elite versus mass education

Compulsory education (*enseñanza obligatoria*) was introduced relatively early in Spain. It dates from the 1867 'Moyano Act' named after the minister responsible for its passage. The duration of education required by the Act was only four years. More importantly, no funds were made available to ensure that children received even that brief schooling. The Act, in reality, was a mere statement of aspirations. In practice education remained the preserve of an elite, geared to producing administrators for the relatively small state apparatus.

The governments of the Second Republic were the first to attempt to bring education to the mass of Spaniards. Yet their ambitious plans, including a massive programme of primary school building and corresponding teacher training, were cut short by the 1936 military uprising [0.1.1]. Thereafter, the Franco regime reverted to the traditional, elite-oriented approach. The primary sector was neglected, with the meagre funds available going to provide secondary and tertiary education for the few. Theoretically education was compulsory to age 12; in practice, the level of coverage remained well below 100 per cent even in that age group.

This step backwards, along with a similar reversion to tradition in terms of content, led to serious problems which were highlighted in a 1969 White Paper. The origins of this report lay in the regime's switch to an expansive economic policy after 1960 [0.1.2], for it had become clear that low general levels of education were holding back the country's development. A modern industrial workforce required more than the minimalist, outdated education which was all most Spaniards had received up to then.

The result of these concerns was the 1970 General Education Act (*Ley General de Educación – LGE*), again often known by the name of the responsible minister. The Villar Palasí Act implicitly shifted the emphasis onto mass education. It lengthened the period of compulsory education, to age 16 in theory. It also sought to end the division that had previously existed from the age of ten between 'academic' pupils and others. Yet, once again, provisions on paper were not fully translated into reality. Thus, little was done to ease the chronic shortage of school premises in the urban areas to which many families had moved. No adequate budget was made available to finance the LGE's ambitious plans for vocational education [7.3.3]. In large part as a result, a significant number of children continued to leave education at 14. In addition to this problem of drop-out (*abandono*), adherence to traditional methods and content led to an alarmingly high percentage of pupils failing to complete their compulsory studies successfully (*fracaso escolar*).

The return of democracy released the pent-up demand for education among the Spanish public, increasing the pressure on inadequate facilities still further. The problems were aggravated by the effects of high birth rates in the Franco era. As a result Spain's schools suffered a lengthy period of severe overcrowding (*masificación*) which began to ease only around 1987 as the year cohorts entering the school system began to shrink. By then it had struck in even more severe form at a university sector even less equipped than schools to cope with a mass clientele.

7.1.2 Church and state

The mass education systems which developed in other Western European countries were essentially a state initiative. In a number of cases, notably

France, that brought governments into conflict with the Catholic Church. In Spain, too, control of education was a focal point of the lengthy struggle between the Church and secular liberals. And liberalism's repeated defeats were reflected not just in the lack of mass education. They also meant that much of what provision there was developed under Church control.

Only the university sector remained outside the Church's hands; even there, its influence was felt in deeply traditional teaching. In any case, until recently the universities served only a tiny minority of the Spanish population. Under the Second Republic, attempts to bring education to the masses [7.1.1] were accompanied by exclusion of the Church from the whole of the education system – a constitutional provision that contributed to the Republic's downfall. Subsequently, during the Franco era, great swathes of the expanded school system were handed back, or over to the Church, which came to control the bulk of primary education as well as much of the secondary sector. In addition, Franco conceded a long-standing Church demand by granting four of its institutions the right to issue university degrees [7.2.1.3].

Since 1975 this Church presence in higher education has not proved controversial. The same cannot be said of non-state involvement in the school system, which was further increased by the actions of the centrist governments in power up to 1982, elements in which were closely linked to the Church [2.2.2]. Faced with ever-growing pressure for school places, they were unable or unwilling to find the resources to satisfy this through state provision. Instead they vastly extended the practice instituted by the Franco regime of paying grants (*subvenciones*) to private schools, most of them Church-run, to do so. As a result, much-needed changes in the school system were bound to impinge directly on the Church. What is more, the challenge of reform was taken up after 1982 by the Socialists, a party by tradition deeply suspicious of Church involvement in education.

7.1.3 The aims of education

The predominant role of the state in the mass education systems of most Western countries was not a disinterested one. It reflected more or less explicit aims on the part of countries' rulers; to forge a sense of common nationhood and to promote economic development. In a number of the most advanced countries – Germany and the UK spring to mind – this philosophy provoked a reaction, in the shape of educational movements or individual schools run on very different principles. They believed that education should centre on the interests of the individual, not on those of the state.

Just as the impulse given by the state to education in Spain was a weak one [7.1.1], so too was the individualist reaction. It was limited essentially to the Free Education Institution (*Institución Libre de Enseñanza – ILE*), set up by Francisco Giner de los Ríos in 1876. Particular initiatives between then and the 1930s, especially the students' residence it established in Madrid, meant that the ILE's ideas exerted considerable influence over several generations of Spanish intellectuals. Other than during the brief period of the Republic, however, its effects on the education system in general were strictly limited. In 1940 the ILE was dissolved by order of the Franco regime.

In a sense the ILE enjoyed a posthumous triumph with the arrival of the Socialist Party (PSOE) in power in 1982. As has frequently been pointed out, its leaders were the first representatives of the so-called 'generation of 68' to reach power. Notions of child-centred schooling – and more generally, of education centred on the needs of the individual – were prominent among their ideas. In particular, they strongly influenced the thinking of José María Maravall, Education Minister from 1982 to 1988.

At the same time, the PSOE regarded education as an instrument of social change, as a means both of anchoring democracy in Spain and, in some sense, of improving the lot of individuals. That it saw very much in material terms, as an aspect of the country's long overdue modernisation which formed the main focus of its policies [2.3.2]. And that, in turn, meant that education was seen ultimately in a third light, as the servant not just of the individual and society but also, and indeed primarily, of the economy. This idea had been presaged by the 1970 Education Act [7.1.1], which had introduced new provisions for vocational training (*formación profesional – FP*). However, within a decade it was clear that they were inadequate. FP facilities were few and mostly of poor quality. Its content was geared to the needs of the relatively primitive industrial economy of the Franco era [5.1.1]. Especially once industrial restructuring got under way in the 1980s, training was hopelessly out-of-touch with the Spanish economy's rapidly changing needs.

Spain's higher education system was perhaps even worse placed to provide a job-oriented education, above all in technical fields but also in the arts and humanities. The content of courses had typically remained unchanged for many years. Teaching methods continued to be based on learning by rote in conventional lectures. Once numbers began to increase in the 1970s the problems were multiplied still further. They were compounded by the abysmally low level of research in Spanish universities. Hopelessly neglected for many years, by the early 1980s spending in this area was minimal compared to that of Spain's counterparts – and economic competitors.

Thus, the Socialist governments of the 1980s were prompted by various conflicting views of the purpose of education. In practice, economic motives came out on top; for example, the university sector was the first to be reformed [7.2.1], even though it reached far fewer Spaniards than school education. Much lower priority was given to a type of institution which to a considerable extent embodied the ideal of education centred on the individual.

The 'people's universities' (*universidades populares*) had emerged in the 1970s as local, community-based initiatives. Their activities ranged from basic literacy training (*alfabetización*) to advanced level studies, depending on the expressed needs of their students, and the teaching resources available.

Indeed, they were a practical application of the principles of individual participation and community control. But they were of no obvious economic utility, and benefited hardly at all from the massive growth of government spending on education after 1982.

7.2 THE REFORMS OF THE 1980s

Perhaps due not least to the strong presence of university and school teachers in the ranks of the Socialist Party (PSOE), education was a major priority for the government elected in 1982. More than almost any other sector of the economy it benefited from the growth of public spending over the next decade. Between 1985 and 1991 alone the government education budget rose by some 70 per cent in real terms. By 1992 it had reached 4.7 per cent of GDP, a proportion still somewhat below the EU average, but more than two-fifths up on the 1984 figure. Increased spending reflected an overhaul of virtually the entire education system, centred on three major reforms.

7.2.1 Higher education

The universities were more affected than any other part of the system by mass access to education [7.1.1]. In the academic year 1962/63 about 60 000 students were enrolled; by 1969/70 the number had risen to some 150 000. In 1991/92 it reached over 1.1 million, and continued to rise until the middle of the decade. Nor do these figures include the number of students in other forms of higher education institution [7.3.2], which were also rising. By the mid-1990s, Spain had a proportionately larger student population than any other Western country.

These changes inevitably resulted in unsatisfactory conditions for university students and teachers alike. They also held back the already urgent modernisation of higher education in the areas of syllabus content, teaching methods and research activity, all – but particularly the last – regarded by the PSOE as crucial to the country's economic performance. Hence the speed with which the party addressed the university issue on coming to power in 1982.

7.2.1.1 The LRU

In 1983, the year after coming to power, the Socialist government passed the first of its major education laws, the Universities Reform Act (*Ley de Reforma Universitaria – LRU*). The Act focused on a long-standing problem of Spanish higher education, the strict and bureaucratic control traditionally exercised by the central government over the universities. In the 1980s it was felt that this centralist approach had stifled individual institutions' initiative and flexibility, preventing them from finding solutions to the problems they faced. The LRU's solution was to grant universities a considerable degree of freedom to manage their own affairs.

Universities' own autonomy was accompanied by transfer of responsibility for higher education to the newly autonomous regions, finally completed in the mid-1990s. It provided the frame within which the network of public universities was expanded. Institutions were founded in regions which had previously lacked one; in others where population increase or dispersal restricted access to existing universities additional ones were established (*see* Table 7.1). In some cases, these new foundations were the initiative of regional governments.

Table 7.1 Spanish universities

Region	University	Notes	Students (94/95) (in thousands)
Andalusia	U de Almería	N	11
	U de Cádiz	N	20
	U de Córdoba		19
	U de Granada		60
	U de Huelva	N	11
	U de Jaén	N	12
	U de Málaga		33
	U de Sevilla		68
Aragon	U de Zaragoza		56
Asturias	U de Oviedo		41
Balearic Islands	U de las Islas Baleares		14
Basque Country	U de Deusto	C	14
	U del País Vasco		59
Canary Islands	U de La Laguna		23
	U de Las Palmas de Gran Canaria		21
Cantabria	U de Cantabria		13
Castile-La Mancha	U de Castilla-La Mancha	N	26
Castile-Leon	U de Burgos	N	10
	U de León	N	14
	U Pontificia de Salamanca	C	6
	U de Salamanca		31
	U de Valladolid		37
Catalonia	U Autónoma de Barcelona		36
	U de Barcelona		76
	U de Girona		9
	U de Lleida		11
	U Politécnica de Cataluña		38
	U Pompeu Fabra	N	3
	U Ramón Llull	P	6
	U Rovira y Virgili, Tarragona	N	10
Extremadura	U de Extremadura		22
Galicia	U de La Coruña	N	23
	U de Santiago de Compostela		39
	U de Vigo	N	25

Table 7.1 (*continued*)

University	Notes	Students (94/95) (in thousands)
Madrid	U de Alcalá de Henares		18
	U Alfonso X el Sabio	P	3
	U Antonio de Nebrija	P	
	U Autónoma de Madrid		30
	U Carlos III de Madrid	P	8
	U CEU-San Pablo	CN	4
	U Complutense de Madrid		126
	U Europea de Madrid	P	
	U Politécnica de Madrid		50
	U Pontificia Comillas	C	8
Murcia	U de Murcia		33
Navarre	U de Navarra	C	13
	U Pública de Navarra	N	9
Rioja	U de La Rioja	N	5
Valencia	U de Alicante	N	26
	U Jaume I de Castellón	N	8
	U Politécnica de Valencia		31
	U de Valencia		65

Notes: C = Church foundation; N = Post-1975 foundation; P = Private foundation.

Within the universities, the LRU provided the basis for a much-needed reform of staffing arrangements. In 1987 it led to abolition of the problematic category of non-tenured, or temporary lecturers (*profesores no numerarios – PNNs*), who had come to represent 60 per cent of teaching staff. A distinction was established between tenured staff, made up of professors (*catedráticos*) and permanent lecturers (*profesores titulares*), and other lecturers. These latter were to make up no more then a fifth of total staff. They included junior lecturers (*ayudantes*) – mainly those completing a higher degree – and teaching associates (*asociados*), part-time teachers who were also practitioners in the relevant field.

In practice, however, these changes have not worked out as planned, in part due to the difficulty of reallocating resources. Some departments in established but less popular subjects, such as history, are top-heavy with staff. Yet others cannot appoint sufficient tenured staff to meet student demand, so that the posts of junior lecturer and teaching associate have become almost as widely abused as the former PNNs.

However, the underlying problem is that overall resources have not kept pace with rising student numbers. In that regard the large increase in student grants (*becas*), admirable in that it has widened access to higher education, has only served to make the situation worse. Repeatedly the problems have erupted in the form of student, and sometimes staff, unrest.

7.2.1.2 Autonomy in practice

Dissatisfaction with the results of the LRU in part reflects the strictly limited nature of the autonomy it granted to universities. This allowed institutions to elect their own vice-chancellors (*rectores*); the management boards (*juntas de gobierno*) they head have power to take many decisions on internal policy. Yet in significant respects the universities remain subject to outside influence.

One channel for such influence is another creation of the LRU, which required each university to establish a University Court (*Consejo Social*). 60 per cent of the Court's members are representatives of local trade unions and employers, the intention being to ensure that universities are responsive to the economic needs of their immediate catchment areas. As yet there is little evidence that this is being achieved.

Other forms of outside influence are less apparent but more effective. The election of vice-chancellors is frequently politicised, in that different candidates are closely associated with particular political parties or factions within them. As a result, educational considerations can get entangled with political ones, especially those of the regional governments which now supply much of universities' funding.

At the same time, under the complex arrangements for devolution made in the 1980s, the central government retains powers to 'coordinate' education and specifically the universities. They are exercised through the Universities' Council (*Consejo de Universidades*), attached to the Education Ministry. Despite supposed 'autonomy', many university decisions must still be referred to the Council. As a result the delays traditionally typical of Spain's centralised system continue to occur, as for example with the introduction of new undergraduate course structures [7.3.2].

Nor has such real autonomy as does exist had entirely positive results. Appointments and promotions are now a purely internal responsibility – previously they were controlled by the Ministry in Madrid. The change has led to a tendency towards 'academic in-breeding' (*endogamia*). That is, departments tend to appoint their own ex-students and promote members of existing staff.

7.2.1.3 Competition

The results of the LRU were, at best, patchy. The government's response was to try and increase standards through competition between universities, in various senses. Probably the least significant step in that 'marketising' direction has been the establishment of new private universities. This step was envisaged in the LRU and its details finally regulated in 1990, with the first new institutions coming into operation in 1993/4.

Up to that time the only non-state institutions authorised to award higher degrees were the four given that privilege by the Franco regime. Of these, three were long-standing Church foundations (*see* Table 7.1); the fourth was the University of Navarre, set up in the 1960s by the Opus Dei [4.1.2.2]. All have small intakes and, in general, high academic reputations.

This is not true of the new private foundations, whose intake consists largely of students who have failed to pass the far from demanding entrance examination for the public universities [7.3.1]. The sole exception is the San Pablo University Centre; based on a Church-run former university college [7.3.2], this resembles the four older Church universities. Yet like them its standards are high because its intake is small – and for that reason it does not represent a meaningful competitor to the public sector.

Rather more important is the prospect of competition within this latter. One way it is being encouraged is by allowing universities to offer new degree courses of their own choice [7.3.2]. Another is by giving prospective students a wider choice of where to study. In recent years the relatively tight rules on catchment areas have been relaxed, so that universities can increasingly take in students from the country as a whole. At the same time economic and social changes are making it more practical and attractive for at least some young Spaniards to study away from home.

Other methods used by the government to promote competition recall those taken in the UK. Thus universities are being encouraged to seek funding from the private sector, a factor which has been apparent mainly at postgraduate level. There are also plans under way to evaluate universities' teaching and research performance. However, particularly in this latter area there have been signs of government despair that the university system can ever produce the goods unaided. Thus, in 1988 Prime Minister Felipe González threw his political weight behind a three-year National Scientific Research and Technological Development Plan (*Plan Nacional de Investigación Científica y Desarrollo Tecnológico*) coordinated by a Joint Government Science and Technology Committee (*Comisión Interministerial de Ciencia y Tecnología – CICYT*). In the same year a Centre for the Study of Advanced Technology (*Centro de Estudios de Tecnologías Avanzadas – CETA*) was also set up, in cooperation with private industry.

The only university involvement was through two of the country's Technical Universities [7.3.2], Barcelona in the Plan and Madrid in the Centre. Subsequent trends have pointed in the same direction. The clear intention seems to be to concentrate university-based research in a small group of leading institutions. Meantime it seems likely that the remainder will be left to face the problems of mass teaching, with neither a genuine research base nor adequate resources.

7.2.2 School provision

The second major education reform of the 1980s related to Spain's private schools, the great majority of them run by the Church. Reform of the private sector was to some extent driven by financial necessity. Over the decade before the Socialists came to power in 1982 maintenance grants to private schools had increased by a factor of over 70 [7.1.2]. Moreover, state support carried no strings, in the form of conditions on the nature of education provided.

Nor was the question merely one of control and finance. Notwithstanding the subsidies they received, over half the private schools charged fees (*tasas*), thus effectively restricting access on financial grounds. Measures passed in 1980 gave selection a legal basis, and allowed private schools to set criteria of their own choice, thereby further accentuating the socially divisive effects of private education.

7.2.2.1 The LODE

The Right to Education Act (*Ley Orgánica del Derecho a la Educación – LODE*) addressed the questions of public subsidisation and social division, as well as others related to the running of schools. Passed by Parliament in 1984, it implicitly recognised that private schools would continue to have considerable importance. But it also redefined the balance of power between them and both the government and parents, in such a way as strictly to limit their educational and social influence.

In order to receive public funds under the LODE, schools must sign an agreement (*concierto*) agreeing to fulfil a number of conditions. Most fundamentally, maintained schools (*centros concertados*) must provide compulsory education free of charge. They are also required to keep proper accounts subject to government scrutiny and to refrain from any supplementary profit-making activities. The LODE also stipulated that government approval was required for maintained schools' statement of educational philosophy (*ideario*).

The LODE also prohibits Church and other private schools from practising selection if they receive financial support. Access to maintained schools may be restricted only by the same resource considerations as in the public sector. In other words, where selection is unavoidable due to excessive demand for places it should follow only the criteria laid down by the state; that means giving priority to children of poorer families and those living close to the school concerned.

Maintenance agreements under the LODE also require a School Council (*Consejo Escolar*) to be set up. Some 40 per cent of the Council's members are elected by the teaching staff, and the same proportion by parents and pupils. Only the remaining 20 per cent represent the school's operators. Individual School Councils in turn elect the National Schools' Council (*Consejo Escolar del Estado – CEE*). The CEE's 80 members are drawn in specified proportions from representatives of the same three basic interests – staff, pupils and parents, and private school operators – and of the government.

The CEE, first constituted in 1986/87, has only advisory powers and in practice has not proved an effective channel of public input into education policy. The individual Schools Councils, however, have had a major impact, since they considerably reduce the absolute power previously enjoyed by private school operators over internal management. They elect the school's head-teacher (*director*) for a three-year term, and are responsible for appointing and dismissing staff. This latter provision in particular is intended to protect teachers' academic freedom (*libertad de cátedra*), restricting the ability of school operators, and specifically the Church, to influence the way subjects are taught.

The LODE provoked one of the most bitter political confrontations of the 1980s. At a time when the right was finding it hard to make any real progress in attracting popular support [2.4.2], the Act provided a rallying point for opposition to the government. It brought articulate, better-off parents reluctant to give up the privileges of private education into alliance with the Church and those close to it. Together these interests staged a mass campaign against the proposals. Eventually the case went to the Constitutional Court [1.1.3], which in 1985 found against the objections.

7.2.2.2 Freedom and diversity

Central to the debate over the LODE was the notion of educational freedom. The government held that the Act promoted the freedom not just of teachers but also of children and parents. Subject only to resource constraints, it ensured free access to all state-funded schools, and allowed greater public participation in their operation. The conservative opposition, on the other hand, argued that the LODE restricted freedom by placing constraints on the providers of education. Yet, despite these fundamental differences the Act's provisions are now, by and large, an accepted part of the Spanish education system.

There are a number of reasons for this acceptance. First, selective private schools have continued to function outside the LODE's framework. They receive no public support and continue to cater for a small but significant social group with the resources to pay the fees they charge. They provide not only a high level of education but also entry to a network of contacts in the business and political worlds. The best-known is Madrid's *Colegio del Pilar*, which has been described as Spain's Eton.

Second, it remains possible in practice for maintained schools to erect price barriers to access. For even within the public sector the notion of 'free' education relates only to teaching in the narrowest sense. Schools can and do charge for 'extras' such as sports and recreational facilities, meals and even supervised self-study.

The continuing existence of effective selection neutralised educational opposition to the LODE. As a result, the other main source of resistance to change, the Church, was left isolated – and alone it now lacks the influence to change policy. In any case, the Church now has significant problems in finding teaching personnel from within its own ranks [4.1.2.2].

With the dust over the LODE settled private establishments still account for a higher percentage of the Spanish school system than any other in Western Europe. In 1992/93 private schools made up 30 per cent of primaries and 23 per cent of secondaries. However, with public control over the bulk of such schools assured by the system of maintenance agreements some of the old divisions have been reduced, if not eliminated.

On the other hand, the 1980s brought a new source of diversity into the Spanish school system as a whole. By 1983 the seven regions enjoying the greatest degree of devolution had assumed responsibility for most education matters [3.1.4]. The Catalan government in particular used it to pursue policies significantly different from those of the central authorities. Until 1994 the remaining ten made up the so-called 'Ministry District' (*distrito MEC*) within which education policy continued to be controlled wholly from Madrid. More recently, however, they too have assumed education powers [3.5.1], further increasing educational diversity – or confusion, depending on one's viewpoint.

By the 1990s the Socialist government itself had come round to the view that diversity was to be encouraged. Among its last legislative measures was the 1995 Schools' Participation, Evaluation and Management Act (*Ley Orgánica de la Participación, la Evaluación y el Gobierno de los Centros Docentes – LOPEG*). The Act introduced an evaluation scheme for state and maintained schools. It also encouraged them to develop distinctive 'educational plans' (*proyectos educativos*), which would allow parents to exercise a degree of choice between them.

Like the LODE [7.2.2.1], the LOPEG caused considerable controversy. This time, however, the government received tacit support from maintained school operators, pleased at the partial return of control over their schools' educational philosophies. On the other hand, the new Act was bitterly opposed by the teaching unions and the Communist-led United Left, who had backed the reforms of the 1980s. And the conservative opposition People's Party (PP), which had resisted those, joined the left in rejecting the LOPEG. This realignment of forces indicated how the debate on school provision had moved on since the 1980s, but also the extent to which educational issues had become secondary to party political interests.

7.2.3 The LOGSE

Although it did not actually come into force until 1990, the last of the Socialists' major reforms was the product of work done in the 1980s. The Education System Structure Act (*Ley de Ordenación General del Sistema Educativo – LOGSE*) is a massive and ambitious piece of legislation which restructures the whole of Spanish education at secondary level and below [7.3.1]. As such, most of the changes it introduced were the subject mainly of technical debate. However, one of its provisions did give rise to controversy reminiscent of that surrounding the LODE [7.2.2.1].

Traditionally, Spanish schools offered instruction in religion, which in practice meant the Catholic faith. As part of the changes introduced by the LODE, all public and publicly maintained schools had been required to offer classes in ethics as an alternative to religious instruction. At the time that had been a further reason for the Church's opposition to the Act. However, its fears were subsequently assuaged by the fact that take-up of the alternative classes was low.

Taking this poor attendance as its reason, in the LOGSE the government abolished the requirement to offer alternative classes. Henceforth pupils not attending religious instruction would merely engage in private study. This move was regarded by the Church as a threat to the status of religious education, and it attempted to rally opposition to the LOGSE as it had to the LODE. However, on this occasion the issue directly concerned only the Church's interests; its calls for support met with a decidedly muted response and failed to change the LOGSE's provisions.

7.3 THE STRUCTURE OF EDUCATION

The reforms of the 1980s did not only affect the principles underlying the education system and its institutional structure. Far-reaching changes have also occurred in the structure and organisation of the studies themselves. Moreover, the inevitable need to introduce such changes over a period of years means that the situation is complicated by the existence of old and new structures in parallel – and will remain so for some time to come, especially in schools.

7.3.1 School education

It is in schools that the most complex changes are occurring. They derive from the 1990 Education System Structure Act (LOGSE) [7.2.3], but began even before it came into force, in the form of extensive tests in pilot schools (*centros piloto*). They, and other schools which have chosen to do so, are proceeding with implementation of the LOGSE's provisions ahead of the official timetable.

According to that, implementation began in 1991/92 and is currently due to be completed in the year 2000. However, the timetable has already been revised several times. In addition, the conservative government elected in 1996 has expressed grave reservations about the changes, and even suggested that they could be abandoned altogether. Whatever happens, into the next century some pupils will continue to be covered by the arrangements of the 1970 General Education Act [7.1.1].

The situation is least complicated in the 0–6 age group. Here the new arrangements for nursery education (*educación infantil*) are already largely in place, or at least those parts of them which are at all likely to be implemented. The LOGSE defines the whole of this age group as part of the educative process; however, there are as yet not even plans for introduction of the first stage (*ciclo*), covering the 0–2 age group.

On the other hand, near 100 per cent provision has already been achieved for the last two years of the second stage, i.e. 4- and 5-year-olds; for 3-year-olds it is around 60 per cent and rising. Under the old system many kindergartens (*jardines de infancia*) and infants schools (*escuelas de párvulos*) provided children of this age group with little more than supervision. Now, in theory at least, they are receiving education closely linked to that at primary level – hence the abandonment of the old denomination of 'pre-school education' (*educación preescolar*).

At primary level the LOGSE introduces radical changes. Formerly, 'basic' education (*Educación General Básica* – *EGB*) covered an unusually long period by international standards, from age 6 to 14. Under the new system primary education (*educación primaria*) runs from ages 6 to 12, in line with international norms, and is divided into three two-year stages (*ciclos*).

These arrangements are accompanied by other changes intended to correct many of the faults of the old EGB. In theory, at least, maximum class sizes have been reduced to 25, subject matter brought into line with contemporary requirements and more project work introduced. Implementation began with the first stage (ages 6–8) in 1992/93 and was completed in 1995/96.

Under the former LGE system, secondary education was divided and divisive. Only those pupils who passed the EGB final examination, obtaining the 'basic-level pass certificate' (*graduado escolar*), were allowed to proceed to academic secondary education, modelled on the French Baccalaureate (*Bachillerato Unificado Polivalente* – *BUP*). Those who failed received a leaving certificate (*certificado de escolaridad*) and were supposed to go on to vocational training [7.3.3]. Following BUP, pupils wishing to go on to higher education took a one-year pre-university course (*Curso de Orientación Universitaria* – *COU*). Together with BUP and the first level of vocational training, COU made up the secondary sector (*enseñanzas medias* – *EEMM*). Unlike the situation at primary level, none of its elements was provided free of charge.

The new arrangements, implementation of which should have begun in all schools by 1996/97, vary in all these regards. Under them, all pupils proceed to a common programme of compulsory secondary education (*educación secundaria obligatoria* – *ESO*), thus removing the old issue of primary school 'failure' [7.1.1]. Covering the 12–16 age group, ESO is free. As a result, in practice as well as theory, the school-leaving age is now 16. On completion of ESO pupils receive a 'secondary pass certificate' (*graduado en educación secundaria*), giving an attainment profile.

ESO consists of two two-year stages. The second will include a significant vocational element, the intention being to eliminate existing prejudices [7.3.3] and encourage more talented youngsters to follow the vocational path thereafter. The viability of this arrangement remains one of the question marks over ESO. Another is the fact that the two stages are to remain, to all intents and purposes, separate.

•The first will be taught in existing primary schools (*centros de educación primaria*), the second in secondaries (*institutos*). The staff involved, too, will be different; primary and secondary teachers respectively (*maestros* and *profesores de secundaria*). Especially given the different training received by these two groups [7.3.3] this will inevitably make the requisite coordination problematic.

Only at age 16 does the new system involve a division into academic and non-academic streams. The first will comprise a shortened Baccalaureate (*Bachillerato*), of two years' duration, which will take over the functions of the old COU. A further novelty is that the format will no longer be standardised for all pupils, who will now be able to choose between four options (*especialidades*): natural and health sciences, humanities and social sciences, technology and the arts. Pupils' choices in those schools where this part of the reform is already in operation provide one encouraging sign. It would appear that the technology option is the most prestigious of the four, raising hopes that it may now be possible to channel more able pupils into areas vital for Spain's economic future.

Finally, in order to go to university pupils completing the new Baccalaureate are required, as under the old system, to pass a university entrance examination (*selectividad*). The main issue here is not whether prospective students pass or fail; in fact the failure rate is under 10 per cent. More important are the marks (*notas*) obtained by candidates, since for some courses there is an intake limit (*Numerus Clausus*). Special arrangements exist for mature applicants.

7.3.2 Higher education

At higher level change in the structure of studies is part of the reform process begun by the 1983 Universities Reform Act (LRU) [7.2.1.1]. It involves the introduction of new qualifications (*títulos*) and degree courses (*carreras*) as well as changes to existing course structures (*planes de estudios*). As in schools, change is occurring gradually so that, at the time of writing, some students continue to be affected by old arrangements in the process of phasing out.

The greater part of the higher education system (*enseñanza superior*) is made up of the academic faculties into which each university is divided. Traditionally, these have offered undergraduate courses of five academic years (*cursos*), although these are a less rigid concept than in the UK. At any one time students may be taking subjects (*asignaturas*) from two or more years, and in practice many take considerably longer than five years to complete.

These old-style undergraduate courses are divided into two stages (*ciclos*). Passing the first, of three years, entitles students to leave with a diploma; most, however, continue to the second in order to obtain a degree (*licenciatura*). The faculties also offer studies at postgraduate level; a programme involving taught classes and a thesis leads to a doctorate qualification (*doctorado*), normally within five years.

In addition to the faculties, universities also incorporate various other types of institution. Some university colleges (*colegios universitarios*) acted in the past as local 'out-stations', enabling students to take the first stage of degrees without travelling to the main university. That function has mainly been superseded by the founding of new universities [7.2.1.1]. Others, in the larger centres, were and are distinguished by being privately run; the best known, the San Pablo college in Madrid, has now acquired full university status [7.2.1.3].

The university schools (*escuelas universitarias*) are also of a hybrid nature. Most of their three-year diploma courses (*diplomaturas*) are vocational or semi-vocational in nature, in specified areas such as nursing and primary teaching. Others, notably those in business studies and engineering, differ little from the early stages of courses offered elsewhere in the system. In general, however, they have enjoyed lower prestige.

This is decidedly not the case with the Advanced Technical Schools (*Escuelas Técnicas Superiores – ETS*). The ETS are broadly comparable to UK engineering faculties, offering a variety of undergraduate courses leading to a qualification as engineer in six years, or architect in five. Entry is subject to strict limits, and demand for places is high. Like the university faculties, the ETS also offer postgraduate studies. In Madrid, Barcelona and Valencia they are grouped together in separate Technical Universities. These have now lost their specialist nature by the addition of faculties where non-technical disciplines are studied.

The high reputation of the ETS is reflected in the fact that they have been left virtually unaffected by recent changes in course structures. In other parts of the system an attempt at rationalisation has been made, by distinguishing clearly between diploma and degree courses. The former continue to be of three years' duration (*carreras cortas*), and are offered by the university schools and colleges. They are intended explicitly to allow direct access to the job market.

On the other hand, undergraduate degrees offered by university faculties now last four years in total. They continue to consist of two stages, now each of two years, the first being intended to provide foundation knowledge and the second an element of specialisation. This is achieved through a system of core subjects (*troncales*), other compulsory subjects (*obligatorias*) and options (*optativas*), some of the latter to be drawn from a specified list and others to be chosen at will by the student (*optativas de libre elección*).

As well as this reform of degree structures, the range of degree subjects has been revised. In Spain official degree titles must, by law, be drawn from a listing established by the government. The age of the list valid in the 1980s was a major reason for the outdated nature of many degrees [7.1.3], and in 1986 the government gave the task of drawing up a new one to the Universities' Council [7.2.1.2].

The resultant deliberations proved lengthy; it was well into the 1990s before many of the degree titles finally received the Council's approval. Moreover, despite regional and university autonomy [7.2.1], new qualifications only have official status once their structures have been approved by the Council. This process is often a cause of further delay. Nevertheless, the range of officially recognised degrees offered by universities has been increased from 65 to some 150.

In addition, universities may now offer degrees without the Council's approval, although the corresponding qualifications lack official status. Thus various Catalan universities have pioneered degrees in environmental sciences. Such initiatives, if judged to be successful, may subsequently be incorporated into the government's approved list. Autonomy has also allowed further development of the trend towards shorter, practice-oriented postgraduate qualifications. These are known in Spain as *masters* and, as in the UK, normally involve a taught element followed by a dissertation.

7.3.3 Vocational training

Vocational training (*formación profesional – FP*) has long been a problem area within the Spanish education system. Although its importance was formally recognised by the 1970 General Education Act [7.1.1], vocational provision remained inadequate in terms of both quantity and quality. Although the 1970 Act in theory established a three-level system, in practice only the basic level (FP1), for 14- to 16-year-olds, was developed to any significant extent; the third, advanced level (FP3) was never implemented at all.

The main problem, however, was not paucity of provision but public perception. Because of the selective nature of secondary education [7.3.1], FP1 came to be regarded as a 'sink' for those who had failed to complete primary education successfully. As fewer and fewer able students opted for it voluntarily, FP acquired a poor reputation among employers as well as parents. A similar problem was apparent also at higher level. Despite the poor quality of many university courses, further aggravated by overcrowding [7.1.1], young Spaniards continued to display the traditional obsession with academic qualifications (*titulitis*), irrespective of the job prospects they offered.

By the 1980s these inadequacies were generally recognised, and attempts were made to address them in several of the 'social contract' agreements of 1980–84 [4.2.4]. Thus the 1984 Social and Economic Agreement (AES) set up a Solidarity Fund specifically to promote vocational training. A General Vocational Training Council (*Consejo General de Formación Profesional*) was established, with representatives of government, trade unions and employers. The AES also resulted in a National Plan for Vocational Training and Job-Creation (*Plan Nacional de Formación e Inserción Profesional*), which led among other things to the setting up of training workshops (*escuelas-taller*) and craft training centres (*casas de oficios*). In 1993 it was relaunched as a National Programme.

As a result of these and other *ad hoc* measures, the system began to lose all semblance of an overall structure. Restoration of logic to the vocational sector was an important aim of the 1990 reforms of school education. As part of them, basic vocational training (*FP de base*) is integrated into the new, unified secondary stage [7.3.1]. From there pupils may pass to an intermediate stage, designed to last two years and organised in the form of modules (*módulos*). Successful students become qualified technicians (*técnicos*).

There is also now provision for pupils to pass from the revised Baccalaureate [7.3.1] to an advanced level of vocational training. Access to this level involves an entry test (*prueba de acceso*); it in turn provides an alternative path into higher education. There both the advanced technical schools and university schools [7.3.2] provide vocationally oriented courses. In particular, training for primary teaching takes place in special university schools, still generally known by their old title *EU de Magisterio*. A number are run privately.

Secondary teachers are required to take a five-year degree and then obtain the Certificate of Teaching Aptitude (*Certificado de Aptitud Pedagógica – CAP*). Under the system established in 1970 this was done at a College of Education (*Instituto de Ciencias de la Educación – ICE*), attached to a university. The training offered at ICEs was unstandardised, often consisting of short intensive courses funded only through the fees paid by students.

In view of this, and the decentralisation of education responsibilities to the regions, the current intention is to phase out the ICEs. Their functions would be assumed by the regionally based Teachers' Centres (*Centros de (Encuentro de) Profesores*), which previously provided in-service training (*formación continua*) of various sorts. However, this reform has not yet been carried through in full. As in other Western countries, university teachers receive no formal training.

7.3.4 Further, continuing and special education

Several forms of further and continuing education are available in Spain. Some, like the people's universities [7.1.3], are community based: most are provided by official bodies, at national, regional and municipal level. The central government has attempted to coordinate these in a national programme of adult continuing education (*educación permanente*), with limited success.

A major part of continuing education consists of distance-learning programmes designed to allow adults to achieve conventional qualifications. Organisations dealing with the primary and secondary levels were set up during the Franco era. They were later joined by Spain's equivalent of the Open University (*Universidad Nacional de Educación a Distancia – UNED*). In addition, special arrangements, including a separate entrance examination, exist for those aged 25 and over who wish to enter the conventional higher education system.

A more recent innovation is the concept of 'compensatory education' (*educación compensatoria*). This comprises a wide range of programmes aimed at individuals who require to make up lost educational ground in order to enter the job market. Target groups include drug addicts and those who, for whatever reason, failed to complete normal school education.

Special education, on the other hand, is concerned with overcoming learning disabilities of various sorts. Traditionally provision for children affected by such disabilities, where it existed at all, tended to be strictly separated from mainstream education, and often had little genuinely educational content.

More recently the accent has been on overcoming such divisions. The Schools Integration Programme (*Programa de Integración Escolar*) aims at the teaching of disadvantaged children in mainstream classes wherever possible; only in extreme cases is separate provision now envisaged.

7.4 GLOSSARY

abandono m	dropping out
alfabetización f	basic literacy training
alumno m	(university) student; (school) pupil
asignatura f	subject
asociado m	teaching associate
aula f	classroom; lecture hall
autonomía universitaria f	university autonomy
ayudante m	junior lecturer; assistant
Bachillerato m	Baccalaureate
Bachillerato Unificado Polivalente (BUP) m	old-style selective Baccalaureate
beca f	student grant
carrera f	degree course
carrera corta f	three-year diploma course
casa de oficios f	craft training centre
cátedra f	professorial chair
catedrático m	professor
centro m	school
centro concertado m	grant-maintained school
centro no concertado m	non-maintained private school
centro piloto m	pilot school (for new teaching methods etc.)
certificado de escolaridad m	old-style school-leaving certificate
ciclo m	stage (of school/university course)
clase f	lecture; seminar; class
Colegio Mayor m	students' residence
colegio universitario m	university college
concierto m	maintenance agreement
Consejo Escolar m	School Council
Consejo Social m	(University) Court
Consejo de Universidades m	Universities' Council
cursillo m	short course
curso m	year of study
Curso de Orientación Universitaria (COU) m	pre-university year
desprestigio m	low reputation
diplomatura f	diploma (course)
director m	head teacher
docencia f	teaching
doctorado m	doctorate (course)
educación compensatoria f	compensatory education
educación especial f	special education

educación infantil f	nursery education
educación permanente f	continuing education
educación preescolar f	pre-school education
educación primaria f	new-style primary education
educación secundaria obligatoria (ESO) f	new-style secondary education
endogamia f	(academic) 'in-breeding', tendency for universities to recruit staff internally
enseñanza básica f	old-style basic education
enseñanza obligatoria f	compulsory education
enseñanza superior/terciaria f	higher/tertiary education
enseñanzas medias fpl	old-style secondary education
escolaridad f	school attendance
escolarización f	schooling; school attendance
escuela de párvulos f	infant school
escuela-taller f	training workshop
Escuela Técnica Superior f	Advanced Technical School
escuela universitaria f	university school
especialidad f	option
estudiante mf	student; (school) pupil
formación continua f	in-service training
formación profesional f	vocational training
fracaso escolar m	failure to complete compulsory education successfully
graduado en educación secundaria m	new-style secondary pass certificate
graduado escolar m	old-style basic-level pass certificate
gratuidad f	free provision
hora lectiva f	teaching/contact hour
ideario m	school's statement of educational philosophy
instituto m	secondary school
investigación f	research
jardín de infancia m	kindergarten
junta de gobierno f	(university) management board
libertad de cátedra f	academic freedom
licenciatura f	undergraduate degree (course)
maestro m	primary teacher
Magisterio m	primary teacher training
masificación f	overcrowding
master(s) m	postgraduate qualification offered without official government approval
matrícula f	(matriculation) fee
matriculación f	matriculation, registration
módulo m	module
nota f	mark
número de alumnos por aula m	class size
optativa f	option class chosen from specified list
optativa de libre elección f	unrestricted option class
plan de estudios m	course structure
posgrado m	postgraduate

profesor m	school-teacher; lecturer
profesor no numerario (PNN) m	temporary lecturer
profesor titular m	permanent lecturer
prueba de acceso f	entrance test/examination
rector m	vice-chancellor, principal
selectividad f	university entrance examination
subvención f	grant, subsidy
tasa f	fee
técnico m	qualified technician (new-style vocational qualification)
titulitis f	obsession with academic qualifications
título m	qualification, certificate, degree
troncal f	core subject
universidad popular f	people's university

8

SOCIAL WELFARE

One of the fundamental principles of Spain's 1978 Constitution is that free market capitalism must be tempered by a concern for social issues [1.1.2]. Implicitly the resultant responsibility for welfare provision lies with the state. Opinion polls have repeatedly confirmed that Spaniards, to a markedly greater degree than most Europeans, support this view. It is, however, one at odds with their country's recent history, which saw only the most rudimentary of welfare states develop. Coupled with the rapid socio-economic changes of recent decades, this situation has posed a number of problems for the country. This chapter examines these, and the solutions that have emerged in terms of social security, health care and social services provision. The final section considers five groups in Spanish society who, in various ways, have particular need for such provision due to their disadvantaged social situation.

8.1 SOCIAL SECURITY

The origins of social security provision in Spain go back to the beginnings of this century. In 1900 compulsory insurance against accidents at work was introduced; in 1907 the National Social Insurance Agency (*Instituto Nacional de Previsión – INP*) was created. Later, under the Primo dictatorship and the Second Republic, provision was extended in small ways. However, only under the Franco regime did a genuine social security system come into being. The unusual circumstances and nature of its development bequeathed substantial problems to the regime's democratic successors.

8.1.1 Francoism's legacy

Francoism's first attempt at establishing a unified system of social security came with the 1963 Social Security Framework Act (*Ley de Bases de la Seguridad Social*). This brought together a number of existing forms of benefit including old age, widows and invalidity pensions (*pensiones de vejez, viudez e invalidez*). Most of these were far from generous; nor was there any mechanism for adjustment in line with inflation. In 1970, flushed with the economic success of the intervening years [0.1.2], the regime decided to make good these deficiencies. The 1970 reforms improved a number of existing benefits (*prestaciones*) and extended coverage to new areas. In the medium term, their impact was disastrous. One reason was that they further accentuated the complexity and overlap which, despite supposed unification in 1963, characterised the francoist system. It included numerous special arrangements (*regímenes especiales*) for particular groups of workers, as well as other anomalies. Consequently, while significant sections of the population had no social security cover, some individuals were receiving multiple pensions from different parts of the system.

This bureaucratic complexity aggravated the second, and major problem bequeathed by the 1970 reforms – their high cost. Introduced without proper calculations of income and outgoings, they failed to foresee economic events. From 1973 on, economic boom turned to recession [5.1.1], causing a slump in the system's income, which was derived totally from the contributions (*cuotas*) paid by employers and employees. At the same time, the downturn also meant a rapid rise in the number of unemployed, for whom the 1970 reforms had increased the coverage and level of benefit.

The Franco regime's social security legacy thus turned out to be a considerable financial burden on its successors. In 1979 the system's outgoings exceeded its income for the first time. By 1986 its annual deficit had reached 24 per cent of budget. By European standards this figure was normal, or even low. In Spain, however, politicians and public were accustomed to the idea that the system should pay for itself.

The deficit accordingly gave rise to much talk of a 'crisis' in the social security system, and of a massive shortfall (*agujero*) in its finances. That there was, and is, a problem of how to finance the welfare state cannot be denied, but in essence it is one common to all developed countries. The distinctive issues facing the Spanish system in the early 1980s were, first, the alarming speed with which the financial situation was deteriorating and, second, the fact that welfare benefits remained relatively poor in a number of areas.

8.1.2 Reform and its limits

As in other areas of the economy, it was only when the Socialist Party (PSOE) reached power in 1982 that real steps were taken to tackle the social security 'crisis' [8.1.1]. The immediate problem was the system's financial deficit, which left the PSOE little option but to cut back on some existing benefits. Given that they accounted for the largest part of outgoings, the obvious place to start was with the various types of pension. In 1985 measures were introduced to rationalise them; some payments were reduced, and the number of years' contributions necessary to receive an old age pension increased.

Another area in which the government sought to make savings was unemployment benefit, by tightening up the requirements for entitlement and reducing the period of payment. The changes focused attention on those jobless (over 60 per cent) who received no support. In 1989 a number of regional governments introduced a form of income support, or social wage (*salario social*). The central government, however, refused to countenance a country-wide scheme because of concern about its potential cost. Instead, it addressed the problem as part of an attempt to restructure overall provision.

This was the intention of the 1990 Social Security Act (*Ley de Seguridad Social*). Like earlier legislation, the Act distinguishes between financial benefits (*prestaciones económicas*) and benefits in kind (*prestaciones técnicas*). However, it also introduced a new distinction, between contributory benefits (*prestaciones contributivas*) and non-contributory ones. The latter are paid out of the government's general budget. They cover benefits in kind, of which by far the most important is health care. Non-contributory benefits also include subsistence payments to those who, for various reasons, are in need of support, but have not paid into the system for long enough to qualify for the relevant form of contributory benefit.

The most important non-contributory financial benefits provide income support for the unemployed (*subsidio de desempleo*), as well as basic pensions (*pensiones asistenciales*) for the old and permanent invalids. These latter are paid out of the National Social Welfare Fund (*Fondo Nacional de Asistencia Social – FONAS*) originally set up in 1960, responsibility for which passed to the National Social Services Agency in 1985 [8.3]. Non-contributory unemployment benefit, on the other hand, is administered by the National Employment Agency [5.2.4].

Contributory benefits are payable only to those who have paid sufficient contributions into the system. They are administered by the National Social Security Agency (*Instituto Nacional de Seguridad Social – INSS*), which is attached to the Ministry of Employment. Because of the amounts involved, the system's accounts are kept separate from the general government budget and require parliamentary approval in their own right.

Payment of contributory benefit is made on the basis of a number of defined circumstances (*contingencias*). The most important is pensionable status, which covers old age, permanent invalidity, and the condition of widow or orphan. Payments under this head account for over two-thirds of the INSS budget. The other main ones are unemployment, temporary incapacity for work (*incapacidad laboral transitoria*), and non-permanent invalidity and its aftermath (*invalidez provisional y recuperación*). Family support (*protección a la familia*), which is essentially child benefit, is also a contributory benefit.

Undoubtedly, this rationalisation has ironed out some of the system's structural problems. However, it has not resolved those caused by the high level of employers' contributions [5.2.4]. Moreover, by increasing welfare coverage it has aggravated the underlying ones apparent in many Western countries. Indeed, in Spain these are more severe for two reasons, one being the seemingly endemic nature of mass unemployment, the other the rapidity with which the country's population is ageing [8.4.1].

8.2 HEALTH CARE

In international terms Spain continues to devote a relatively low share of national income to health care (*asistencia sanitaria*); at little over 5 per cent the figure is among the lowest in the EU. Nevertheless, health spending represents a major burden on public finances, and one that is rising fast. Part of the cause, as in other countries, is the speed of medical advance. However, the problem has been particularly acute in Spain, because until recently the level of health provision (*oferta sanitaria*) was extremely low.

8.2.1 The Spanish NHS

It is true that the Franco regime introduced compulsory health insurance (*seguro obligatorio de enfermedad – SOE*) for ever larger groups of workers; by 1975 nearly 80 per cent of the population was covered by it. Yet the resultant system was complicated, wasteful and prone to abuses, in particular the practice of doctors holding posts in both the public and private sectors simultaneously (*pluriempleo*). What is more, only around a fifth of hospital facilities (*instalaciones hospitalarias*) were in public hands, most being run by private organisations more or less directly linked to the Church.

The democratic governments of the late 1970s showed some awareness of the need for reform. In 1978 a National Health Agency (*Instituto Nacional de la Salud – INSALUD*) was created to coordinate provision. However, the move did not change the essential features of the system – high dependence on private care and inadequate services. For reasons of both ideology and efficiency this situation was unacceptable to the Socialist government elected in 1982. The new government introduced a series of reforms, the framework for which was set out in the 1986 General Health Act (*Ley General de Sanidad – LGS*). The LGS provided for the creation of a National Health Service (*Servicio Nacional de Salud – SNS*). As the name suggests, the model chosen by the Socialists was the British NHS rather than the contributory systems common in continental Europe.

Accordingly, the basic principle of the SNS is availability of care free of charge at the point of delivery. By the 1990s universality of free provision had effectively been achieved; only around 1 per cent of the wealthiest Spaniards are now required to pay for treatment under the SNS. However, users are required to bear 40 per cent of the cost of prescriptions (*recetas*), unless they are entitled to exemption. Charges also apply to dental and psychiatric care (*asistencia odontológica y psiquiátrica*).

The 1986 Act placed administration of the SNS in the hands of INSALUD. It provided for the creation of regional health services (*servicios autonómicos de salud*) and district health authorities (*Areas de Salud*), the latter serving a population of between 200 000 and 250 000. Each district is required to contain at least one district health complex (*Centro de Salud*), consisting of a general hospital and other facilities. In many cases these are based on the old 'health campuses' (*ciudades hospitalarias*) in which various general and specialist hospitals were grouped together.

These arrangements apply to hospitals and other facilities run by INSALUD. For those run by private operators the Socialists adopted a similar solution to the one they had already applied in education [7.2.2.1]. Private hospitals may receive public funding, but only if they sign a maintenance agreement (*concierto*) with the health authorities covering the conditions under which they provide care.

During the 1980s the government undertook a massive building programme which greatly reduced the importance of privately run facilities. Yet they still account for over 30 per cent of all hospitals, and about 20 per cent of available beds. Most have become maintained hospitals (*centros concertados*), but some continue to operate on a purely private basis.

Ironically, almost as soon as the SNS had been conceived other developments conspired to detract from its national character. Over the next few years responsibility for health care was devolved to the seven autonomous regions who, for various reasons, had acquired a higher level of autonomy than the other ten [3.1.4]. This difference persists, since health was the one significant policy area omitted from the 1992 agreement standardising regional responsibilities [3.5.1]. As a result, in seven regions – Andalusia, the Basque Country, the Canary Islands, Catalonia, Galicia, Navarre and Valencia – the regional health services not only exercise administrative functions but also have powers over policy and funding. In an attempt to ensure coordination, in 1987 the government set up the Joint National Health Council (*Consejo Interterritorial del Sistema Nacional de Salud*), which brings together representatives of central and regional governments. Its task has been difficult, due to the difference in political complexion between the central government and some of the regions with policy powers. In particular, Catalonia has tended to go its own way, placing considerably greater emphasis on the role of private care. For some years it did not even supply statistical information on the same basis as the rest, so that it became impossible to calculate key indicators for Spain as a whole. The conservative central government elected in 1996 is likely to take a line closer to that of its Catalan counterpart.

8.2.2 Resource problems

Despite spending relatively little on health care, Spaniards enjoy excellent health according to the most commonly used indicators. The country's infant mortality rate, which as late as 1960 stood at 43 per thousand, is now under 9 per thousand – lower than in several EU countries as well as the USA. Life expectancy (*esperanza de vida*) is the highest in the EU, having reached almost 80 for women and over 73 for men.

Yet for all the positive statistics, and despite the real achievements of recent years, the Spanish health service is widely perceived as being in crisis. The best-known symptom is the persistence of lengthy waiting lists (*listas de espera*) for many types of treatment. And certainly the system has significant resource difficulties.

Thus there is a shortage of qualified nurses (*enfermeras tituladas*) and nursing auxiliaries (*auxiliares de clínica*). Spain also continues to have insufficient hospital beds (*camas hospitalarias*) for its needs. Here a distinction must be drawn. Even excluding those in private hospitals, provision of acute beds (*camas de agudos*) is close to the EU average at around 3.5 per 1000 population. However, long-stay beds, especially for medical geriatric care, are in short supply. In addition, the available beds are unevenly distributed, being scarcer in rural areas and the south.

In the case of doctors, the problem is not quantity but quality. With over 330 per 100 000 population, Spain has proportionately more doctors than any other developed country, a situation which reflects the massive increase in those studying medicine since 1980. This same influx has aggravated the problem of poor doctor training; many graduates feel the need to work abroad after qualifying to acquire the practical experience which is virtually non-existent in most medical faculties. Expansion has led also to a maldistribution of specialists. Paediatricians are particularly abundant at a time when Spain's birth rate has plummeted. In addition doctors, like hospital beds, are poorly distributed across the country.

In 1987 doctors' own dissatisfaction with the system led them to go on strike. Ironically, the resultant publicity given to problems within the system prompted the government to act against their own abuse of it. At last it insisted on doctors' devoting themselves to a single job (*dedicación exclusiva*) instead of occupying several posts simultaneously [8.2.1].

The government's move reflected a growing concern with health costs, which have risen steadily since the 1986 Act. Thus between 1988 and 1994 hospital medical staff increased by 30 per cent. Over the same period there was a 68 per cent rise in the number of hospital managers and administrators. Alarmed at these trends, in 1991 the government set up a committee headed by Fernando Abril Martorell, Deputy Prime Minister in the late 1970s. The 'Abril report' recommended market-oriented reforms similar to those already under way in the UK. These recommendations were much discussed, then effectively ignored.

Nevertheless, the government remained determined to bring down public spending [5.1.2], to which health costs were an important contributor. To do so, in 1992/3 it introduced a National Health Service Consolidation Plan (*Plan de Consolidación del SNS*), whose basic principle is a clear division between policy-making and the provision of care. The intention is for the Health Ministry to define exactly the types of health care which Spaniards are entitled to receive free of charge. The Ministry also sets performance targets. These criteria are then incorporated in a services contract (*contrato-programa*) agreed with INSALUD [8.2.1], whose responsibility is to fulfil the targets and conditions set, within its assigned budget. Whether these measures are sufficient to stem rising health spending remains unclear. It must be doubtful, given that they do not address a key reason for it.

In most Western health systems doctors exercise a considerable influence on policy. Spain is no exception; the Medical Associations (*Colegios de Médicos*) act as expert advisers to the government. As elsewhere, this influence is an important factor in directing resources disproportionately towards specialist care. Since that is the sector where costs are rising most rapidly as the result of technical advances, the result is to increase still further the upward pressure on health spending.

8.2.3 Primary and specialist care

A further effect of the emphasis on specialist care [8.2.2] is that inadequate resources are directed to primary health care (*atención primaria de salud – APS*). Again, this is not a phenomenon unique to Spain. There, however, unlike in other Western countries, there was no established system of primary care in place before the rapid technological advances of recent decades. There has therefore been little in the way of a primary care lobby, to protect the sector's interests.

The 1986 General Health Act [8.2.1] recognised the obvious danger. Its aims explicitly included health awareness and the prevention of illness, and the Act stressed the importance of non-specialist care in achieving them. But these good intentions have been honoured more in the breach than the observance. Since 1986 the vast bulk of resources have continued to go on specialist care delivered in hospitals.

As a result, the local health centres (*ambulatorios*) through which primary care is delivered are underfunded by comparison with hospitals. Even more than the latter, they suffer from a lack of nursing staff. Moreover, few doctors wish to become GPs (*médicos de cabecera*). Until recently organisation of primary care was also poor; even now that an appointment system (*cita previa*) has been introduced waiting times are frequently long. Consultations, in contrast, last between 60 and 90 seconds on average. Small wonder that many Spaniards go directly to relatively well-equipped hospital accident and emergency units, thus increasing the pressures on them.

Such units, however, can do little to solve the biggest health problems facing Spain. They derive from the scope and depth of the social and economic changes the country has experienced over the last two or three decades. Alcohol consumption by the young has grown rapidly, as has the proportion of women who smoke. There has been a massive shift from manual labour to desk-bound employment. The country's traditional diet, thought to be the principal cause of good health and long life, is changing dramatically; young Spaniards now ingest as much cholesterol as their contemporaries in northern Europe.

The impact of these changes can be seen in a range of indicators, for example, the high incidence of circulatory and respiratory illness, and the large number of road deaths attributable to drunken driving. They mean that health awareness and illness prevention are even more vital than elsewhere as a factor in improving health levels, and, indeed, in maintaining existing ones. Yet, like other aspects of primary care, they continue to be the poor relations of the Spanish health system.

Like disparities in availability of doctors and facilities [8.2.2], neglect of primary care hits particularly hard at the worse-off in Spanish society, particularly rural dwellers. Moreover, research suggests that, in developed countries where health levels are already high, increased spending is generally reflected in the reduction of health inequalities. The poor are thus also likely to be the main losers from continuing downward pressure on health spending.

8.3 SOCIAL SERVICES

In some Western countries there is a long tradition of social welfare provision by charitable organisations (*sociedades benéficas*). In Spain, by contrast, the Church and the family remained virtually the sole providers into the 1970s. Since then, social and political change has radically reduced the social importance of both these institutions. Yet democracy has brought no significant flowering of interest or self-help groups [4.4]. As a result, it has been the public authorities which have been faced with the task of meeting rapidly increasing demand for social services.

Prior to 1975 public social provision was strictly limited, in both quantity and quality. Care facilities for the young, the old and the disabled or disadvantaged, where they existed, consisted almost entirely of large-scale, dehumanised institutions, reminiscent of the Victorian era in the UK. Significantly all tended to be referred to as 'asylums' (*asilos*), a name which reflected the degree of isolation from the rest of society they implied. Such conditions clearly demanded reform. At the end of the 1970s the restored democratic local authorities led the way in establishing alternative forms of provision. In 1978, to support and coordinate these efforts, the central government set up the National Social Services Agency (*Instituto Nacional de Servicios Sociales – INSERSO*).

Under the first round of regionalisation in the 1980s responsibility for social services was transferred to the seven regions which achieved a higher level of autonomy [3.1.4]. The remaining ten acquired similar powers in the second round after 1992 [3.5.1]. Throughout Spain it is now the regions which carry the main burden of social service provision.

Ironically, it was only once the central government had begun to shed its powers in this area that a separate Social Affairs Ministry was set up, in 1988. Responsibility for INSERSO, previously attached to the Ministry of Employment and Social Security, was transferred to it. Three years previously the Agency itself had undergone a revamp. Its remit was extended, not least by absorption of the National Social Welfare Agency (*Instituto*

Asistencia Social – INAS), responsible for payment of non-contributory pensions [8.1.2].

Notwithstanding these changes, social services remain very much the Cinderella of the Spanish public sector. Spending continues to be dwarfed by that on health, and on the financial benefits provided by the social security system. Throughout its life the Social Affairs Ministry was the smallest of the central departments; in the first cabinet formed by the conservative government elected in 1996, the portfolio was rejoined to that of the Employment Ministry.

8.4 DISADVANTAGED GROUPS

In any country, certain social groups suffer a degree of disadvantage (*discriminación*) relative to the population as a whole. In some cases these coincide with the major client groups who are the main recipients of welfare services. In others their disadvantage in part reflects the fact that provision largely fails to reach them. The concerns of five such groups structure much of the debate on social issues in Spain.

8.4.1 The elderly

Perhaps the most pressing demands which Spain's welfare services have had to face since 1975 result from the rapidity with which the country's population is ageing. Not only has life expectancy risen dramatically, the country's traditionally high birth rate is now among the world's lowest. One result is the urgent need for more geriatric hospital provision [8.2.2].

Equally great is the problem posed by the need for non-medical geriatric care. Not only are Spaniards living longer, but it is much less usual than in the past for younger relatives to be on hand. And even when they are it seems that they – like their contemporaries elsewhere in Europe – are increasingly unwilling to assume the task of caring within the family home.

Precisely because that was previously the norm, Spain had until recently virtually no public provision for the elderly. One advantage of this is that most publicly run old people's homes (*residencias de tercera edad*) are relatively new and in good condition. Unfortunately these currently only meet some 40 per cent of the demand, the rest being covered by private homes of much more variable quality. Over a third of these latter are still run by religious orders; although generally of a higher standard than other private homes these are threatened by the sharp drop in the number of nuns [4.1.2.2].

Residential facilities have been supplemented by provision of various types of community-based care (*asistencia comunitaria*). They include sheltered housing (*viviendas tuteladas*), a home-help service (*servicio de ayuda a domicilio*) and helpline facilities (*tele-asistencia domiciliaria*). In addition the existing network of pensioners' day centres (*hogares del pensionista*) has been extended. More innovatively, the Socialist governments of 1982–96 introduced a substantial programme of subsidised holidays for the elderly (*vacaciones de tercera edad*) and health cures (*termalismo*).

Given that their pensions have also been mainly unaffected by cutbacks since 1985 [8.1.2], all in all the elderly have been the major beneficiaries of the expansion of social provision. The 'grey vote' is, as in other Western countries, an increasingly important factor. In the so-called 'Toledo Pact', signed in 1995, all the major parties agreed not to make pensions an issue in the general election then looming. Once elected Prime Minister in 1996, José María Aznar explicitly excluded pensioners' benefits from the proposals he soon announced to reduce public spending across the board.

8.4.2 The young

Spain's young lack the electoral clout of the old. They are also probably the main victims of the massive rise over the last ten years in housing costs. Many have had little choice but to remain in the parental home until – and sometimes even after – marriage. Above all, the young are disproportionately affected by the scourge of unemployment [5.2.4]. It is thus scarcely surprising that, while the situation of younger children (*menores*) has not as yet been a major source of public concern, teenagers and young adults represent perhaps the most problematic group in Spanish society.

A number of initiatives have been taken by governments to address their situation. In 1985 a National Youth Bureau (*Instituto de la Juventud*) was created, responsibility for which was passed to the Social Affairs Ministry when this was set up three years later. In 1991 an Integrated Youth Plan (*Plan Integral de Juventud*) was launched. Its main thrust was to improve training and qualification levels among the young, and so attack the chronic problem of youth unemployment. But, while such measures may increase young people's chances of securing such work as is available, they do not of themselves create jobs.

Youth unemployment, it would appear, is closely connected with another problem which particularly affects the young; drug addiction (*toxicomanía*). Although notoriously difficult to measure, this seems to be especially widespread in Spain. Various causes have been suggested. Spain lies on the main routes into Europe of both marijuana (from Morocco) and cocaine (from Colombia). The Galician criminal families (*clanes*) who controlled the region's long-standing illicit trade in tobacco were well placed to move into the more lucrative business of narcotics smuggling. And the Socialist government elected in 1982 legalised all consumption, both public and private, a year later.

Perhaps rather more importantly it took a relaxed attitude, to say the least, to the provision of such things as clean needles, drug substitutes and rehabilitation facilities. The 1985 National Drugs Plan (*Plan Nacional sobre Drogas*) seemed to exist largely on paper. With the spectacular rise in the incidence of AIDS (*Síndrome de Inmunodeficiencia Adquirida – SIDA*), official concern grew and in 1992 public consumption of drugs was again made illegal.

However, at a time when even police authorities in some countries are arguing for decriminalisation (*despenalización*) of consumption, that hardly seems likely to resolve the issue. Generally, policy in recent years seems to have missed the point that, for many young addicts, drugs are only one link in a cycle of despair that also includes unemployment, crime and prostitution. The government appears to have been under the impression that addiction can be handled in isolation from these other issues; it is indicative that the Drugs Plan remained the responsibility of the Health Minister, and was never transferred to the Social Affairs Ministry during its short life [8.3].

Another way in which young people's frustrations have become apparent is in their rejection of compulsory military service. The reluctance of many young men to perform the *mili* is understandable. Every year around a hundred die while doing so, either through fatal accidents or suicide; many more suffer injury and humiliation in traditional initiation rituals. That has long been known, without provoking widespread rejection by young people.

In recent years, however, there has not only been a steady rise in the numbers of conscientious objectors (*objetores de conciencia*). There has also been a dramatic increase in those refusing to perform even the alternative community service (*servicio social sustitutorio*). These latter, known as *insumisos*, are in breach of the law, and a number have been imprisoned. Their plight has become a focus for young people's wider resentments.

It is no coincidence that by far the highest incidence of refusal to perform either military or community service (*insumisión*) has been in the Basque Country and Navarre. Especially in the former, youth joblessness is particularly severe. And there, too, radical Basque regionalists close to the terrorist organisation ETA [9.4.2] are ready and willing to channel resentment. In recent years the radical movement's youth wing, *Jarrai*, has repeatedly been involved in vandalism, street violence and physical attacks on political opponents.

A number of observers have made the point that in behaviour and appearance many of *Jarrai*'s followers closely resemble those of seemingly very different groups in other parts of Spain. Gangs of skinheads (*cabezas rapadas*) are now an established phenomenon in the Madrid area, and in a number of other centres. They show clear signs of influence by neo-Nazi groups, but as yet no real political cohesion. Notwithstanding the presence of some better-off elements, the last social remnants of francoism, most gang members are themselves victims of the marginalisation affecting so many young people in Spain today.

8.4.3 Women

Until relatively recently the situation of women in Spanish society was in important respects almost medieval. It was not until 1975 that the Franco regime abolished the legal requirement for married women to receive their husbands' permission before undertaking any activity outside the home. On Franco's death later that same year both divorce and abortion remained banned. During the transition period divorce was a tricky political issue. In 1981 the then government took steps to legalise it, but split apart in the process [2.2.2]. Some aspects of the measure, but above all the attitudes of the overwhelmingly male Spanish judiciary in applying it, led to dissatisfaction among women's groups about its efficacy.

Abortion was legalised in 1985, although only under three specified circumstances: danger to the life or health of the mother, rape or physical damage to the foetus. A 1991 decision by the Supreme Court, however, seemed to establish the possibility of using social grounds as a further justification. Even so the conditions are the strictest in the EU outside Ireland. And they are enforced – gynaecologists are periodically prosecuted for ignoring them. In practice many doctors still refuse to perform even legal abortions.

As a result, Spain's official abortion rate is very low indeed, less than a third of that in the UK. One effect is the rising number of single mothers (*madres solteras*). However, the official rate does not tell the full story. Many Spanish women travel abroad to receive abortions. Furthermore, it is estimated that up to 70 per cent of the abortions performed in Spain are illegal. In the light of the associated health dangers, there has been much discussion of possible legislation based on time limits (*ley de plazos*).

As well as tackling the abortion issue in 1983 the Socialists set up a National Women's Bureau (*Instituto de la Mujer*). The Bureau pioneered the establishment of centres for battered wives, and has produced two Women's Equal Opportunities Plans (*Planes para la Igualdad de Oportunidades de las Mujeres*), covering the periods 1988–90 and 1993–95. Yet both plans were characterised by a distinct lack of specific proposals, and it is hard to escape the conclusion that their main purpose was promotion of the government's image among women.

Cynics might see the same tokenism behind the creation of the Social Affairs Ministry [8.3]. It was the smallest in the government and, after the transfer of social service powers to the regions, had few obvious responsibilities other than the Youth and Women's Bureaux. Throughout its short life, however, the Ministry accounted for half the female representation in the cabinet through its successive political heads, Matilde Fernández and Cristina Alberdi.

That is not to say that there have not been real changes in the situation of Spanish women since 1975. However, it is debatable how far these are the result of deliberate government action as opposed to broader social forces. Perhaps the crucial point is that little official effort has been devoted to changing the entrenched attitudes of Spanish men. The results are to be seen in the hyperactive female characters in Almodóvar's films, tackling demanding jobs while still saddled with heavy responsibilities in the home.

8.4.4 Disabled people

Under the Franco regime state provision for the disabled (*minusválidos*), other than that in 'asylums' [8.3], was limited to social security payments for those most seriously affected. The only major exception was the Spanish National Blind Association (*Organización Nacional de Ciegos Españoles – ONCE*), set up by Franco in 1938 to support those blinded fighting (on his side) in the Civil War.

However, the ONCE has never been a drain on the state, since its activities are more than adequately financed through its various highly popular lotteries. In recent years its earnings have allowed it to become an important player in the Spanish economy and media [4.3.3]; its activities have also extended to groups suffering from other forms of physical disability (*minusvalía*). In effect, it represents an alternative means of tax-raising to pay for disabled provision.

The current framework for this is provided by the Disabled Persons Integration Act (*Ley de Integración Social de los Minusválidos – LISMI*), passed in 1982. As well as extending the system of payments to the disabled, and increasing their size, the LISMI introduced support for carers (*terceras personas*) and a mobility allowance (*subsidio de movilidad*). The Act also set guidelines for disabled access to public premises.

Over the next decade various type of smaller care units were opened with the aim of providing specialist and more personalised care for particular groups. Some serve the severely mentally handicapped and physically disabled (*centros de atención a minusválidos psíquicos/físicos gravemente afectados – CAMP/CAMF*). Others are rehabilitation centres for the physically disabled (*centros de recuperación de minusválidos físicos – CRMF*). Still others offer sheltered employment to those not in a position to deal with the world of work (*centros ocupacionales*).

More recently, the emphasis has been on the development of new forms of assistance for the disabled. INSERSO [8.3] now runs the National Centre for Personal Independence and Technological Aids (*Centro Estatal de Autonomía Personal y Ayudas Técnicas – CEAPAT*). Spain has also participated in various EU programmes aimed at the disabled. Nevertheless, provision remains highly uneven in quantity and quality across the country.

8.4.5 Ethnic minorities

For centuries, dating back to the Reconquest, many Spaniards' idea of their own nation has had strong overtones of racial purity. Franco, who deliberately likened his uprising against the country's legal government to the country's reconquest from the Moors, instituted an annual 'Day of the Spanish Race' (*Día de la Raza*). After his death any negative feelings associated with such ideas were swamped by enthusiasm for links with the outside world [0.2]. It became common to point to the relative racial tolerance characteristic of Spanish colonialism, and suggest that racism (*xenofobia*) was foreign to the Spanish character.

A more accurate view might have been that Spain was largely unaffected by the factors underlying rising racial tension in other Western European countries during the 1960s and 1970s. It had long since gone through the process of decolonisation; its economic backwardness made it a relatively unattractive destination for non-European immigrants, even after controls were relaxed after 1975. Today the country still has a comparatively small immigrant population by EU standards; an estimated 500 000 out of a total of 40 million.

Since the mid-1980s, however, important changes have occurred. Spain's location makes it an obvious point of entry from the south into a European Union increasingly concerned to close its borders. At the same time, the country is now sufficiently prosperous to be an attractive destination in its own right. As a result, recent years have seen a steep rise in immigration, much of it illegal. The North African enclaves of Ceuta and Melilla are one important entry route.

The other is the sea crossing from Morocco which, especially in summer, attracts a steady stream of would-be immigrants, usually in the tiny, unstable boats known as *pateras*. Many have paid considerable sums to unscrupulous agents. An unknown number die in the attempt; many more are caught and turned back by Spanish officials. Those who escape such hazards and remain in Spain are frequently exploited by employers in the country's large informal economy [5.2.3]. Others eke out a precarious existence as street-sellers of trinkets and other objects.

Unfortunately, the rise in immigration has come at a time when very high unemployment appears to have become endemic. As elsewhere in Western Europe resentment has sometimes been turned against immigrants, especially those easily distinguishable by skin colour. Of these the largest group consists of North Africans (*magrebíes*), mainly from Morocco; other significant ones are black Africans and Caribbeans.

It was one of the latter, a young woman from the Dominican Republic, who was the victim of the most serious incident to date. She was shot while sleeping in a disused warehouse on the outskirts of Madrid along with a number of compatriots. The most worrying aspect was that those responsible were linked to the security forces. More generally, immigrants provide a target for the skinhead gangs which have appeared in some areas [8.4.2].

These developments cast doubt on any notion of Spanish immunity to racism. In any case, one group which is effectively indigenous has long been the focus of tensions. Today gypsies still comprise Spain's largest ethnic minority, numbering over 300 000 in total. Popular antagonism towards them remains widespread, and in recent times has been given renewed vigour by the alleged involvement of gypsy gangs in drug dealing. In a number of cases this has led to reprisals against gypsy families or even whole communities.

In response to this situation, in 1988 the Social Affairs Ministry launched a Gypsy Development Programme (*Programa de Desarrollo Gitano*). Among other things it aims to integrate gypsies more closely into Spanish society, for example, by ensuring that all gypsy children receive the same education as other Spaniards, but also to preserve and promote gypsy culture and traditions. Unfortunately these laudable aims sometimes prove problematic and even contradictory.

Typically gypsies continue to live apart from non-gypsy society, often in shanty-like slums on the edges of towns and villages. Their traditional mode of life, which often involves a seasonal pattern of travelling determined by the farming year, can hamper efforts at integration. For instance, children's school attendance is frequently interrupted. And the desire to preserve gypsy traditions can come up against the uncomfortable reality that these may involve customs that seem to infringe contemporary norms, such as the treatment of women in gypsy society.

8.5 GLOSSARY

acogimiento familiar m	fostering
agujero m	deficit (in social security funding)
ambulatorio m	local health centre
Area de Salud f	district health authority
asilo m	asylum; old-style home (for children, the old, etc.)
asistencia comunitaria f	care in the community
asistencia odontológica f	dental care
asistencia sanitaria f	health care
asistencia social f	social welfare provision
atención especialista f	specialist (health) care
atención primaria de salud f	primary health care
auxiliar de clínica mf	nursing auxiliary
ayuda a domicilio f	home-help
cabeza rapada m	skinhead
cama de agudos f	acute bed
cama hospitalaria f	hospital bed
centro concertado m	private hospital publicly funded through a maintenance agreement
centro no concertado m	private hospital
centro hospitalario m	hospital
centro ocupacional m	sheltered training centre for disabled
Centro de Salud m	district health complex
cita previa f	appointment
ciudad hospitalaria f	'health campus', old-style health complex
Colegio de Médicos m	Medical Association
concierto m	(hospital) maintenance agreement
consulta f	(medical) examination, consultation; doctor's surgery
contingencia f	circumstance (giving entitlement to benefit)
contrato-programa m	services contract
cotización f	(*see cuota*)
cuota f	social security contribution
dedicación exclusiva f	ban on (doctors) filling several salaried posts simultaneously

derecho m	right; entitlement
despenalización f	decriminalisation
discriminación f	discrimination; disadvantage
enfermera titulada f	qualified nurse
esperanza de vida f	life expectancy
familia monoparental f	single-parent family
gratuidad f	free provision (of services)
hogar del pensionista m	pensioners' day centre
incapacidad laboral (transitoria) f	(temporary) incapacity for work
instalaciones (hospitalarias) fpl	hospital facilities
insumisión f	refusal to perform military or community service
insumiso m	person who refuses to perform military or community service
invalidez provisional f	non-permanent disability
juventud f	youth; young people; teenagers
ley de plazos f	abortion legislation based on time limits
lista de espera f	waiting list
madre soltera f	single mother
magrebí mf	North African
médico de cabecera m	general practitioner
menor mf	child
minusvalía f	disability
minusválido físico/psíqico m	physically/mentally disabled person
objetor de conciencia m	conscientious objector (to military service)
oferta asistencial/hospitalaria/ sanitaria f	welfare/hospital/health provision
patera f	small boat (used by illegal immigrants from North Africa)
pensión asistencial f	basic non-contributory pension
pensión de invalidez f	disability pension
pensión de vejez f	old age pension
pensión de viudez f	widow's pension
pluriempleo m	simultaneous filling of several salaried posts
prestación f	(welfare) benefit
prestación contributiva f	contributory benefit
prestación por desempleo f	(contributory) unemployment benefit
prestación económica f	financial benefit
prestación técnica/no económica f	benefit in kind
previsión f	social insurance
protección a la familia f	family support, child benefit
racismo m	(*see xenofobia*)
receta f	prescription
recuperación f	recovery (from illness); rehabilitation (of the disabled)
régimen especial m	special arrangements
residencia f	home
residencia de ancianos/tercera edad f	old people's home
salario social m	social wage, basic income support
sanidad f	health; health care

servicio autonómico de salud m	regional health service
servicio de ayuda a domicilio m	home-help service
servicio social sustitutorio m	community service alternative to compulsory military service
Síndrome de Inmunodeficiencia Adquirida (SIDA) m	AIDS
sociedad benéfica f	charitable organisation
subsidio de desempleo m	non-contributory unemployment benefit, income support
subsidio de movilidad m	mobility allowance
tele-asistencia domiciliaria f	helpline facility
tercera persona f	carer
termalismo m	health cure
toxicomanía f	drug addiction/dependence
vacaciones de tercera edad fpl	subsidised holidays for pensioners
vivienda tutelada f	sheltered housing (unit)
xenofobia f	racism

9

LAW AND ORDER

That Spain should be a 'state under the rule of law' is one of the three fundamental principles of the country's 1978 Constitution [1.1.2]. This chapter begins by examining the country's legal system, the safeguards of its independence and its functioning. The following sections look at the institutions charged with combating threats to the rule of law; the various police forces and the prison service. Since 1978 these have faced a considerable increase in the level of crime, and the last section considers the delicate relationship between protecting Spanish society from its effects and preserving civil liberties.

9.1 THE LEGAL SYSTEM

One aspect of Spain's limited experience of democratic politics [0.1.1] is that its judiciary has historically tended to be more or less directly controlled by the government of the day. Executive influence was especially widespread under the Franco regime and took a number of forms. Offences that would in most countries be considered a matter for the civilian courts fell under military jurisdiction; judges' career chances were under direct government control. As a result, the executive's role in the administration of justice was a thorny issue facing democratic governments after 1975.

9.1.1 The General Council of the Judiciary

The 1978 Constitution included provisions designed to ensure judicial independence. Modelled on similar arrangements in France and Italy, they envisaged creation of a General Council of the Judiciary (*Consejo General del Poder Judicial* – CGPJ). Two years later detailed arrangements for appointment and operation of the CGPJ were set out in the 1980 Judiciary Act (*Ley Orgánica del Poder Judicial* – LOPJ). In essence, the CGPJ's purpose was to remove from government control personnel decisions affecting the judiciary. Under the 1980 Act it had sole responsibility for all such matters, including the selection of members of the judicial service (*carrera judicial*), appointment to particular posts, and promotion to higher courts. Its remit also includes conduct of any disciplinary proceedings relating to members of the judiciary.

The CGPJ also has wide powers to propose changes in the organisation of the judiciary and court system. It examines proposed legislation of all types, advising the government as to compatibility with judicial procedures and the Constitution. It must be consulted by the government before the latter appoints a new Attorney General [9.1.2], and itself nominates two members of the Constitutional Court [1.1.3]. The Council is also responsible for nominating from among its own members the chairman of the Supreme Court [9.1.3], who in turn automatically assumes the chair of the CGPJ.

In addition to its chairperson, the Council contains 20 ordinary members appointed for a five-year period. Some eight must be lawyers with at least 15 years' professional experience; the remaining 12 are drawn from the judiciary itself. According to the 1980 Act the members were also elected in two different ways; 12 by the legal profession and eight by the two Houses of Parliament.

In effect, this last provision meant that control over the judiciary remained in the hands of lawyers appointed by the Franco regime. Most were conservative, even reactionary in outlook, a situation which led to conflict once the Socialist Party (PSOE) reached power in 1982. The PSOE believed the Council was blocking reforms which it had been democratically elected to carry out, both within the judicial system and more broadly, for instance over the limited legalisation of abortion.

In order to clear away what it regarded as unwarranted obstruction of the democratically expressed will of the people, in 1985 the PSOE passed a second Judiciary Act. Among its various measures, this removed from the CGPJ ultimate control over judicial appointments, which henceforth were required to be approved by the Ministry of Justice [9.1.2]. In 1993, however, a further reform reversed this change and returned sole control to the CGPJ.

The 1985 Act also included new arrangements for appointing the Council itself, under which all 20 ordinary members are elected by Parliament, with the support of 60 per cent of MPs. The effect of this change was to politicise all appointments to the Council. So long as the PSOE enjoyed a sufficient parliamentary majority it could appoint its own nominees at will; once its majority was eroded in the latter 1980s, filling vacancies depended on agreement between government and opposition.

For some three years following the 1993 general election this was not forthcoming and deadlock ensued. The opposition systematically blocked government nominations to the CGPJ and vacancies remained unfilled. However, after the 1996 election returned another minority government, this time of the right, the main political parties agreed to a compromise. In July of that year the Council was finally returned to its full complement of members.

9.1.2 Public interest

As required by the 1978 Constitution, various mechanisms exist to protect the public interest within the legal system. First, the elected government of the day has a number of responsibilities in this area. As in most continental European countries, these lie with the Ministry of Justice.

The Ministry has a number of different roles. In consultation with other bodies, including the Lawyers' Association (*Colegio de Abogados*), it drafts government legislation. It administers the legal system's physical infrastructure, such as court houses (*palacios de justicia*). The Ministry also runs the government's own legal service (*Servicio Jurídico del Estado*).

The Justice Minister is in an inherently delicate position when taking many decisions. As a member of an elected government he may, indeed must, bear in mind political criteria yet as head of the legal authorities he must adhere strictly to the law. Because of this special position the Justice portfolio is normally kept separate from other ministerial responsibilities. There was therefore considerable concern when, in 1994, the Justice and Interior Ministries were amalgamated [1.4.5]. The conservative government elected two years later opted to return to the practice of appointing a separate Justice Minister.

The second instrument of the public interest within the legal system is the government attorney service (*ministerio fiscal*). This body is responsible principally for acting as public prosecutor in criminal cases. As such, attorneys (*fiscales*) initiate the examination stage of cases [9.1.3], and thereafter cooperate with the police and the examining magistrate in assembling the evidence. At the subsequent trial they lead the prosecution case.

In addition, the attorney service has a general brief to monitor the functioning of the courts to ensure that verdicts are implemented and that procedures are properly carried out. Its members enjoy wide powers to intervene in cases where they have grounds to believe that the public interest is affected. The service is headed by the Attorney General (*Fiscal General del Estado*), nominated by the government after consulting the General Council of the Judiciary (CGPJ).

Particularly after the 1985 reform of the Council [9.1.1], this arrangement inevitably placed a question mark over the Attorney General's independence from government. At the same time, alleged breaches of the law by the governing party and executive itself [2.3.4] made his role as defender of the public interest particularly important. It was against this background that, in 1992, the Socialist government appointed as Attorney General a known party supporter, Eligio Hernández. The opposition challenged Hernández's appointment, on the grounds that he did not meet the constitutional requirement of 15 years' judicial experience. In 1994 the Constitutional Court upheld this challenge, a result all the more worrying since the original appointment had been approved by the CGPJ. By then, however, Hernández had resigned, and had been replaced by a less controversial candidate. Like the second reform of the Council in 1993, the move appeared to signal a more sensitive attitude on the part of executive.

Constitutional provisions for more direct public involvement in the judicial system have been less than fully implemented. Thus the Constitution allows for the possibility of trial by jury (*jurado*), yet measures to regulate its introduction were not passed until 1995. Even then there was very little preparation in terms of public education, giving rise to considerable concern among both lawyers and the public about the practical effects.

The Constitution also allows the possibility of a private prosecution (*acción popular*). If litigation can be shown to derive from a sufficient degree of public concern, then the costs must be borne by the state. Yet this provision too has had minimal impact, because of the highly restrictive conditions on its application. In practice, access to the courts continues to require the retention not just of a lawyer but also of an officially recognised legal representative (*procurador*), equivalent to a barrister or advocate. By law only the latter are permitted to present cases to a court.

9.1.3 Courts

Prior to 1975 several types of court enjoyed the power to impose legally binding decisions. They included Church courts (*tribunales eclesiásticos*), as well as the tribunals operated by certain professional organisations and by the military (*tribunales de honor*). The 1978 Constitution recognises the jurisdiction of these latter within the specifically military sphere. With this single exception, however, it explicitly denies legal jurisdiction to all organs other than the courts of the state's own judicial system. In Spain these comprise civil and criminal courts along with four other categories unknown in the United Kingdom (*see* Table 9.1).

As well as by their area of competence, Spanish courts are also structured on the basis of a conceptual division of the judicial process into stages. The central, indeed, the only one in many cases (*causas*), is that of trial (*enjuiciamiento*). Evidence is presented to and examined by the court which then announces its verdict (*sentencia*) and, where appropriate, any sentences

Table 9.1 Court types

Name	Type
juzgado de lo civil	civil court
juzgado de lo penal	criminal court
juzgado de lo social	employment court
juzgado de lo contencioso-administrativo	administrative court[1]
juzgado de vigilancia penitenciaria	prison supervision court[2]
tribunal titular de menores	children's court

Notes: [1] Deals with disputes between private individuals and state authorities.
[2] Deals with matters relating to the application of prison sentences imposed by the courts.

(*condenas*). If one of the parties has legitimate grounds to question the court's decision, the case may pass to a further stage, that of appeal (*recurso*).

In criminal cases the trial is also preceded by another stage, that of examination (*instrucción*). During it the court authorities are responsible for gathering the relevant evidence, in the form of exhibits and statements. The results are then presented to the court trying the case in a report (*sumario*). It is a fundamental principle of the system that, in a given case, no two of these stages should be handled by the same court.

The conceptual hierarchy of courts overlaps with a second, geographical one, higher levels of which cover larger areas as well as subsequent stages of procedure. It was subject to considerable reform by the 1988 Court Structure and Functions Act (*Ley de Demarcación y Planta Judicial*). The only tier left unaffected by the Act was the lowest, made up of the municipal courts (*juzgados de paz*) with jurisdiction over minor civil and criminal offences (*faltas*). They are presided over by a single Justice of the Peace (*juez de paz*), who is not required to have any legal training.

The fundamental change introduced by the 1988 Act was the establishment of new courts at the level of court districts (*partidos judiciales*) to replace the former district courts (*juzgados de distrito*). These so-called 'courts of the first instance and examination' deal with the bulk of cases. They act as appeal courts for cases tried before justices of the peace, a role in contradiction with their title. In other civil cases they act as a genuine court of the first instance, i.e. as the court by which the case is first heard. In most criminal cases they act as the examining court (*juzgado de instrucción*). These reformed district courts are again presided over by a single member of the judiciary (*juez*). Roughly equivalent to a Scottish sheriff, unlike JPs he or she must be a trained lawyer.

Another change brought about by the 1988 Act was the creation of special provincial criminal courts. They try lesser offences, that is, those subject to a maximum prison term of three years (*arresto menor*). Previously such trials had been heard by the district courts which had examined them, in violation of the principle that different stages of a case should be the responsibility of different courts. Along with the special provincial children's, prison, employment and administrative courts, they complete the category of lower courts.

Courts at higher levels of the system are distinguished in several ways. They are collegiate, that is, they are presided over by a bench composed of several members known as judges (*magistrados*). They consist of several divisions (*salas*), concerned with different types of cases. And they also generally deal with appeals from lower courts rather than with first hearings.

An important exception to this last distinction is provided by the provincial courts (*audiencias provinciales*) which, in addition to hearing appeals from below, also try criminal offences too serious to be heard by a lower court. The next level consists of the regional High Courts (*tribunales superiores de justicia*) established as a result of devolution in the 1980s, which replace the former regional courts (*audiencias territoriales*). For matters relating exclusively to the region concerned they provide the final court of appeal (*tribunal de última instancia*)

In cases where country-wide issues are involved, further recourse may be had to the High Court (*Audiencia Nacional*), established in 1977. Its criminal division also tries cases in certain fields, including falsification of the coinage, contamination of foodstuffs and medicines, and drug trafficking. To allow it to do so it has three special examining courts.

Finally, the Supreme Court (*Tribunal Supremo*) is concerned with resolving appeals relating to the interpretation of legislation. Its decisions in such cases constitute a body of case law (*jurisprudencia*). This is collected and published by the General Council of the Judiciary [9.1.1], for use by lower courts as a source of guidance, additional but subordinate to legislation. The Court consists of five divisions, four of which deal with civil, criminal, administrative and employment matters. The final one is a military division (*sala de lo militar*), to which appeal may be made from the separate military courts.

9.1.4 A system in crisis

Although there is concern in Spain about the relative ineffectiveness of provisions for public participation in the legal system [9.1.2], that is not the main reason why it is perceived to be in crisis. More worrying is the courts' inability to deal with the cases which come before them in a reasonable time period. Examples are numerous; perhaps the most notorious was the case of several hundred people poisoned by contaminated oil. Although the scandal was uncovered in 1981, government officials allegedly involved in it were not brought to trial until 1996.

A number of reasons can be identified for this serious situation. Crime has risen sharply [9.4.1], as has the volume of legislation. The judicial system has been starved of resources. In 1982 Spain spent only a tenth of the EC average under this heading and, despite considerable increases in the interim, spending remains relatively low. As a result, and again despite considerable increases in the 1980s, the judiciary is understaffed by Western standards.

The delays in the system can also be attributed to the complex separation of functions between the public attorney, the examining court and that responsible for the trial. Even simple cases can generate a lengthy interchange of judicial opinions (*autos*) between them. Yet another factor is the very steep rise in cases taken out against public authorities and coming before the administrative courts (*see* Table 9.1). This appears to reflect a continuing and regrettable tendency for such bodies to treat individual members of the public as subjects rather than citizens [1.5.1].

The Spanish courts also display an alarming propensity to commit errors, ranging from the loss of personal items submitted in evidence to wrongful imprisonment as the result of mistaken identity. Over the five-year period 1991–95 the Ministry of Justice received a total of 1038 claims for compensation in respect of these and other causes, 148 of which it found to be justified. In only one case has the Ministry attempted to recover the compensation paid from the member of the judiciary responsible. After several years the government's claim was awaiting examination by a Barcelona court.

The cost of compensation for delays and other injustices is, in financial terms, insignificant. Much more important is the effect of such problems on public attitudes. It is common knowledge that punishment is highly unlikely for many offences, especially traffic offences or failure to obtain various forms of official licence. The result is that the courts, the judicial system and the law itself are all drawn into disrepute.

In 1992 the government introduced an Emergency Court Procedures Reform Act (*Ley de Medidas Urgentes de Reforma Procesal*) in an attempt to address some of these issues. Implementation, however, has been problematic. For example, there has been little progress in reducing the bench in higher administrative courts to a single judge, in order to allow more cases to be tried.

9.2 THE FORCES OF PUBLIC ORDER

In Spain policing powers are exercised by a number of bodies. Under the Franco regime these included the country's military, and the overlap in functions was reflected by the prevalence of militarist and authoritarian attitudes throughout the various forces concerned. The 1978 Constitution drew a clear distinction between national security, a military responsibility, and the maintenance of public order. Nevertheless, vestiges of the past have remained.

9.2.1 Civil Guard

Spain's oldest public order force is the incongruously named Civil Guard (*Guardia Civil*). Set up in the last century to counter the problem of banditry on country roads, it retains a number of military characteristics. Not only do Civil Guard officers (*guardias*), like policemen in many countries, carry arms. They are deployed, often far from their home region, in barracks (*cuarteles*), and thus separated from the local population they serve.

Traditionally the Civil Guard's services to travellers in distress caused it to be known affectionately as *La Benemérita* ('The Admirables'). However, during and after the Franco era it became the subject of considerable public suspicion, because of doubts about its commitment to democracy. Mainly drawn from Spain's Military Academy, its officers have tended to share the reactionary views typical of their Army colleagues [4.1.1.1]. What is more, particularly in the early 1980s, the Civil Guard was the principal target of ETA terrorism [9.4.2].

These problems burst into the open with the participation of some Civil Guards in the 1981 attempted coup [0.1.3.3]. The Socialist government elected the following year placed the force under the command of Lieutenant-General Sáenz de Santa María, previously head of the National Police [9.2.2]. He was given the task of quelling unrest; once he was judged to have done so he was replaced by the Civil Guard's first ever civilian commander, Luis Roldán.

Only in time of war is the Civil Guard now responsible to the Defence Ministry, otherwise its political head is the Interior Minister. As a sop to officers' feelings – and in defiance of the EU's declared policy of phasing out all paramilitary police units – the Civil Guard's standing orders continue to reaffirm its military character. However, their detailed provisions are clearly closer to those of a police force.

These various moves have largely put a stop to overt insubordination, but not to all the Civil Guard's problems. They were aggravated by the activities of Roldán [9.4.1], which left the Civil Guard with an unnecessarily large and unwieldy central staff, infected with corruption. However, the force's problems go far beyond the influence of a single person.

Its officers have repeatedly been involved in human rights abuse of detainees, especially but not exclusively ETA suspects; the Intxaurrondo barracks in San Sebastián has been at the centre of a number of such allegations. Officers there and elsewhere have also been convicted of involvement in criminal activities; links to drug trafficking have been uncovered and more are suspected. There is evidence, too, of politically motivated violence by Civil Guard officers, one of whom was charged with Spain's first race killing [8.4.5].

In part the Civil Guard's problems can be traced to underemployment. Its numbers, larger than those of the National Police, reflect the fact that until recently most Spaniards lived in the rural areas for which it is responsible. Now population and, to an even greater extent, crime is concentrated in towns and cities. The government has attempted to combat this problem by extending the force's activities, previously mainly concerned with patrolling traffic and Spain's external borders.

In recent years specialist units have been created to deal with coastal patrolling and various environmental issues, such as forest fires, dumping of toxic wastes and protection of endangered species. It must be open to question whether such activities will serve to harness fully the energies and loyalty of highly conservative officers who continue to see themselves as soldiers. So too must be their effectiveness as a response to overmanning, as the changes have been accompanied by an increase in the Civil Guard's manpower.

9.2.2 Police

Spain's largest purely civilian policing agency is the National Police Force (*Cuerpo Nacional de Policía* – CNP). It was formed in 1986 by amalgamating two existing forces, the General Force (*Cuerpo General*) and the National Police (*Policía Nacional*), until 1978 known as the Armed Police (*Policía Armada*). Both of these were established by the Franco regime, and the second in particular was associated with the repression of civil liberties by it.

However, despite these unfortunate origins the CNP has been relatively successful in throwing off the burden of the past. To a large extent that is attributable to the work of Lieutenant-General José Antonio Sáenz de Santa María, commander of the National Police from 1979 to 1982. Under his leadership it took an active part in suppressing the 1981 attempted coup [0.1.3.3]. Sáenz de Santa María also set up the Special Operations Group (*Grupo Especial de Operaciones – GEO*), which has a good record in ending terrorist sieges and similar operations.

More generally, the operational effectiveness of the CNP has been constrained by a number of factors. One is the continuing presence in senior positions of officers promoted under the old regime. For a long time, even after the Socialists came to power in 1982, those known to hold more progressive ideas were persistently marginalised by the Interior Ministry, which has overall responsibility for the police. Not until 1994 did a new Interior Minister, Juan Alberto Belloch, take action to remove the old guard, and put younger officers in charge of the force. Perhaps significantly, Belloch was a lawyer who had served in the judiciary, and was already Minister of Justice. He was thus aware of the difficulties posed to the legal system by the lack of change in senior police personnel.

In the meantime considerable problems had built up at lower levels of the force, reflected occasionally in officers themselves turning to crime, and in widespread disillusionment. Such feelings were closely related to the acute problem of undermanning. With less personnel than the Civil Guard, the CNP has to deal with some four-fifths of crime, which itself has risen markedly since 1975. Especially for plain clothes staff stationed outside the Madrid headquarters, the burden is a massive one.

Operational efficiency is not helped by the existence of other police forces, in addition to the Civil Guard, whose operational fields overlap with those of the CNP. The most numerous of these are the local police (*policía municipal*) who operate in larger towns. They have responsibility for local by-laws, including parking regulations.

Considerably wider responsibilities are wielded by the forces under the control of the Basque and Catalan governments (*Ertzaintza* and *Mossos d'Esquadre*), which have partially replaced the CNP in their respective regions. In the Basque Country the situation was until recently complicated yet further by the existence of police forces responsible to the various provincial authorities; these have now been absorbed into the *Ertzaintza*.

9.3 THE PRISON SERVICE

Prisons in Spain are the responsibility of the Directorate General of Prisons (*Dirección General de Instituciones Penitenciarias*), which forms part of the Interior Ministry. Down the years the country has produced a number of notable penal reformers, and in general prison conditions have been fairly good. In recent years, however, there has been growing concern, for a number of reasons.

Like the courts and the police, prisons (*centros penitenciarios*) have been placed under an increasing burden by the steady rise in crime [9.4.1]. There has been a corresponding increase in the number of prison inmates (*reclusos*); between 1983 and 1991 alone this rose from under 15000 to nearly 40000. In a number of establishments the result has been severe overcrowding (*masificación*). Furthermore, there is a lack of adequate prison staff (*funcionarios de prisiones*). That in turn compounds the security problems posed by outdated facilities which have led to a number of spectacular escapes from custody, most notably by businessman-turned-politician José María Ruiz Mateos [2.6] and former Civil Guard commander Luis Roldán [9.4.1].

The problems are aggravated by the chronic slowness with which the courts operate [9.1.4], which means that prisons have to deal with many remand prisoners (*presos preventivos*). Their numbers first rose sharply during the transition period after 1975, due partly to a rise in offences. But the increase was also the result of a 1980 measure, which greatly tightened up the conditions governing release on bail (*libertad bajo fianza*). Specialist remand facilities proved quite inadequate to cope with these twin pressures.

As a result, remand prisoners – substantial numbers of whom would later be acquitted – were held in unsatisfactory conditions, and alongside convicted prisoners (*condenados*). The same problem applied to juvenile offenders, and to first offenders (*primeros*) who, in theory, should be kept separate from previous offenders (*reincidentes*). In 1983 the new Socialist government revoked the 1980 amendment to the bail regulations and placed a limit on the time which prisoners might spend on remand (three years for those accused of serious crimes, 18 months in the case of minor offences).

The change led to a massive exodus from the prisons, thought to have contributed to a further rise in offences. Subsequently the government introduced a third change, increasing the limits on remand time (to four and two years, respectively). It has succeeded in stabilising the situation to a considerable degree, although remand prisoners still account for around a third of the total.

The other main issues facing the prison system relate to inmates at the other end of the scale, that is, those convicted of serious crimes of violence. Spain has one high-security prison (*centro de alta seguridad*), located at Herrera de la Mancha. However, few of the most controversial prisoners convicted of violent crimes are held there. These are ETA members convicted of terrorist offences [9.4.2]. ETA and its supporters claim to regard these as political prisoners (*presos políticos*), and persistently demand special treatment for them. The government's policy towards them has varied, sometimes tending towards concentrating them in a small number of prisons, sometimes towards dispersal among many.

This latter policy was designed to make it easier for individual ETA members to renounce violence and opt for reintegration into society (*reinserción social*). A considerable number have done so; several have paid for 'betraying' ETA with their lives, the best-known being María Dolores Cataráin González, *Yoyes*, who was assassinated in 1986 after her release. At the same time, the reintegration measures have been criticised from the political right, since they involve early release of convicted terrorists.

That the courts should be able to require sentences to be served in full (*cumplimiento íntegro de penas*) has been a persistent demand of the right in recent years. In a sense the debate has the same symbolic significance as that in the UK over reintroduction of the death penalty (*pena de muerte*), which in Spain is forbidden by the 1978 Constitution. In drawing up the new Criminal Code approved in 1996 [9.4.4], the then Socialist government argued that the Constitution also outlaws full-term sentencing, although this is a matter of interpretation.

The government based its argument on the constitutional principle that one of the aims of imprisonment should be rehabilitation of offenders (*resocialización*). For one thing, full-term sentencing would mean prisoners staying locked up for longer periods, which in itself works against rehabilitation. Second, early release is one of the most important of privileges (*beneficios penitenciarios*) which act as an incentive for prisoners to join actively in rehabilitation programmes. On these grounds, the new Criminal Code passed in 1995 leaves the question of privileges, including early release and parole (*libertad condicional*), in the hands of the prison supervision courts [9.1.3]. The maximum prison term to be served in normal circumstances is set at 20 years. However, exceptions are allowed where consecutive sentences (*penas múltiples*) are involved, above all if any of the offences concerned is particularly serious.

The 1995 Code also includes a number of steps designed to address the problems of overcrowding and reoffending [9.4.4]. However, unlike full-term sentencing, these were not in the past supported by the conservative government elected in 1996. It must therefore be doubtful whether the necessary resources will be made available to implement them.

9.4 CRIME AND CIVIL LIBERTIES

Declining respect for the law is a common complaint among some older Spaniards, and it is true that the number of offences has risen sharply since Franco's death. On that basis it is sometimes argued that democracy has made Spain less safe and law-abiding. Such arguments ignore the fact that rising crime has been a widespread feature of Western countries since 1975. They also overlook abuses of human rights and the law by public authorities under the former regime. Even today, threats to civil liberties must constantly be balanced against the need to combat crime.

9.4.1 Changing nature of crime

Recorded crime has risen steadily in Spain since 1975. Despite an initial increase during the transition the number of offences (*delitos*) was less than 450 000 in 1982; by the end of the decade it was over 825 000 and rising. Yet the official level of crime (*delincuencia*) in Spain remains relatively low, at only around one-third of that in the UK. Even allowing for under-reporting it seems clear that crime is not a major problem there in comparative terms, especially as the increase appears to have levelled off in the 1990s.

On the other hand, overall figures for a particular year do not reflect two important aspects. One is the concentration of crime and its effects in specific areas, particularly the depressed outlying parts of larger cities (*barrios periféricos*). The other is the fact that crime was previously very little known in Spain, which inevitably conditions public perceptions of the present level.

For ordinary Spaniards the most immediate impact of crime is a so-called 'lack of public safety' (*inseguridad ciudadana*). By that is meant a generalised fear of offences affecting both individuals' property (e.g. house-breaking, car theft, bag-snatching) and their physical safety (muggings and other, more serious forms of assault). Whenever opinion pollsters ask about the issues that give Spaniards most concern, '*inseguridad ciudadana*' always features highly; in that sense the phrase has acquired roughly the same connotations as the 'law and order issue' in the British context.

Especially among the young, this sort of petty crime is closely associated with drug addiction. At the same time, drugs are also related to the more sinister phenomenon of organised crime. On the one hand, this involves indigenous gangs such as the Galician 'clans' [8.4.2]. On the other, there are fears that Mafia elements have established themselves around the Mediterranean coast. It should be pointed out, however, that the Spanish authorities lay considerable blame on their counterparts in Gibraltar, which they claim is a major centre for money-laundering (*blanqueo de dinero*).

Similar activities within Spain itself are part of a wider phenomenon, that of 'white collar crime' (*criminalidad de cuello blanco*). Recent years have seen a succession of major financial frauds. Perhaps the most notorious names are those of Mario Conde, one-time chairman of the *Banesto* bank, and Javier de la Rosa, who headed the Spanish operation of the Kuwait Investment Office (KIO).

Some have involved more or less leading figures in the public sector – in that sense the problem merges into that of political corruption [2.1.3]. One particularly spectacular case involved the former Governor of the Bank of Spain, Mariano Rubio, who was found to have engaged in various forms of insider dealing. Another was that of the first civilian head of the Civil Guard, Luis Roldán [9.2.1], who was discovered to have made a fortune from rake-offs on tenders for building new barracks and other projects.

The growth in crime has provoked a number of responses from government. In 1992 it introduced the Public Safety Act (*Ley de Seguridad Ciudadana*), better known as the 'Corcuera Act' after the then Interior Minister responsible for its drafting and passage through Parliament. The Act's main aim was to clamp down on drug-related offences. However, the methods it proposed provoked considerable controversy, and it was eventually declared unconstitutional [9.4.3].

Two years later Corcuera's successor, Juan Alberto Belloch, announced a Civil Liberty and Public Safety Plan (*Plan de Libertad y Seguridad*

Ciudadanas). The Plan's title betrayed a greater sensitivity to public concern about giving excessive powers to the police. Its approach was also different, based on getting more police on the streets in a preventive role. Whether adequate resources are available for such an approach to work remains to be seen.

9.4.2 Terrorism

In one respect Spain undoubtedly does face a particularly difficult law and order problem. Although so far relatively unscathed by international terrorism, it is the only Western country apart from the UK with a significant indigenous terrorist movement. ETA (*Euskadi ta Askatasuna*) (Basque Homeland and Freedom) was set up in 1959. It carried out its first killing in 1968; since then it has caused the deaths of nearly a thousand people, as well as wounding, kidnapping and intimidating many more.

Originally set up to oppose the Franco regime, it refused to lay down its arms on the restoration of democracy. Indeed, with the inevitable relaxation of security measures after the dictator's death it was enabled to step up its campaign of violence. The worst year for killings was 1980, when ETA assassinated 93 people. Since then the figure has fallen more or less steadily; on the other hand, the range of victims has widened. Initially ETA's victims came overwhelmingly from the security forces of the Spanish state, mainly the army and Civil Guard. After the Basque Country was granted autonomy in 1979 representatives of its new institutions, especially the regional police force (*Ertzaintza*) were also killed. More recently ETA has also undertaken more or less indiscriminate killing and maiming of private individuals.

On a number of occasions the organisation has been thought to be on the point of extinction. In 1983 France abandoned its policy of refusing to extradite suspected ETA members, and handed over a number of leading members to Spain. In 1992 the then leadership was captured *en bloc* at a hideout in the French Basque Country. Yet on each occasion ETA has proved able to rebuild itself. In the winter of 1995/96 it launched a new wave of bombings and killings, assassinating among others Francisco Tomás y Valiente, a former chairman of the Constitutional Court.

Yet, despite such incidents, there has been an undoubted change in the nature of the problems posed by ETA. Since the mid-1980s public opinion in the Basque Country, much of it previously supportive of or ambivalent towards ETA, has turned sharply against the organisation. Far more than in the past terrorism is now a genuine policing problem. On the other hand, ETA's apparent desire to sow discord within Basque society has given rise to new, and very serious issues. One is the intimidation to which those who speak out against ETA are subject, especially in smaller, rural communities. Another is the vandalism and street violence orchestrated by the youth wing of ETA's hardcore support, *Jarrai*. In a region which has been in political turmoil for 30 years and has one of the highest youth unemployment rates in Europe, this is indeed a worrying phenomenon.

Outside the Basque Country, Spain's two other regionalist movements have also spawned armed wings, but neither has ever posed a significant security threat. Indeed, in 1996 it is unclear whether the Catalan 'Free Homeland' (*Terra Lliure*) or the 'Galician People's Guerilla Army' (*Ejército Guerrilleiro do Pobo Galego*) are still in existence.

Another terrorist group, frequently thought to have disappeared, has repeatedly re-emerged to carry out new actions, mainly kidnappings. GRAPO (*Grupos Revolucionarios Antifascistas Primero de Octubre*) has always been shrouded in mystery; there have even been suggestions that it is in fact a front organisation for elements in the security forces. Whatever the truth, it poses no significant terrorist threat.

9.4.3 Civil liberties

The perceived need to take stringent action against crime has raised concern about the delicate balance between protecting some individuals' property and safety, and infringing the civil rights of others. It is a concern that is particularly pertinent in Spain because the country has so little tradition of limited, democratic government. Worries in this area were at the root of opposition to the 1992 Corcuera Act [9.4.1].

The Act proposed to give the police greatly increased powers to enter private premises in search of drugs; the phrase universally associated with it was 'kicking the door in' (*patada en la puerta*). Its opponents referred the measure to the Constitutional Court [1.1.3], which eventually found that it did indeed infringe constitutional safeguards for individual liberties and declared it invalid.

The Corcuera Act was by no means the first government measure to have awakened concern about civil liberties in recent years. Its provisions contained unfortunate echoes of the wide powers of deportation without recourse to the courts conferred by the Aliens Act (*Ley de Extranjería*). More generally, the governments of the post-Franco era have shown little desire to rein in or even investigate abuses by the security forces. Several scandals have occurred due to illegal telephone tapping (*escuchas telefónicas*) by national and regional police forces, and by the Defence Intelligence Service (*Centro Superior de Información de la Defensa* – CESID), the main Spanish secret service. In 1993 one such case forced the resignation of the Deputy Prime Minister, Narcis Serra.

The most flagrant abuses of civil rights have been associated with attempts to defeat terrorism. A number have been concerned with application of the Anti-terrorist Act (*Ley Antiterrorista*). Originally introduced in 1977 by the then centrist administration as an emergency measure, in 1985 it was normalised by the Socialist government in power at the time. The Act allows for the suspension of normal safeguards for the rights of detainees, such as access to a lawyer, where they are suspected of terrorist offences. In 1988, however, police officers were convicted of having used it in the case of a common criminal known as *El Nani*, who died in custody after suffering severe maltreatment. Moreover, on a number of occasions ETA members have died in detention.

Even more serious have been the revelations about government involvement in the use of counter-terrorism in the mid-1980s, when the shadowy Anti-Terrorist Liberation Groups (*Grupos Antiterroristas de Liberación – GAL*) were responsible for a number of murders and kidnappings of suspected ETA members and supporters. In the late 1980s and early 1990s successively more senior members of the Interior Ministry staff were indicted for involvement in this so-called 'dirty war'; in 1995 the chain reached a former Interior Minister [2.3.4]. The full details of this deplorable episode will probably never emerge despite the Socialists' removal from power in 1996, not least because it is common knowledge that earlier centre-right governments also indulged in similar activities.

More than anything, the failure to defeat ETA illustrates that in a democracy it is ultimately counterproductive for the government to abuse civil liberties as a means of combating crime. Time and again revelations of security force excesses have diverted attention from ETA's own atrocities. Moreover, they have rekindled old sympathies for ETA among Basque opinion, and confirmed its hardcore supporters in their intransigence. To give just one example among many – in 1995 two mutilated corpses found a decade earlier were finally confirmed as belonging to ETA members who had disappeared in police custody; within months the organisation, which had been thought on the verge of extinction, had launched a bloody offensive [9.4.2].

9.4.4 The 1995 Criminal Code

A need long recognised by all shades of political opinion in Spain was a thorough revision of the country's criminal code (*código penal*), which in essence dated from the last century. It was a theme of the 1982 election campaign which brought the Socialist Party (PSOE) to power. The following year the PSOE introduced changes covering about a sixth of the relevant provisions, including the decriminalisation of soft drug usage. However, it was not for over a decade that a full revision was carried out, in November 1995. The substantial changes introduced by the new code reflect changes in the nature of crime [9.4.1], as well as the consolidation of democratic values over the foregoing 20 years.

Thus a new category of corporate offences (*delitos societarios*) has been introduced, in an attempt to counter white-collar crime. They relate to company directors and carry a maximum penalty of three years' imprisonment, as well as heavy fines. Specifically covered are the falsification of company accounts, and the use of a majority holding to decide on actions contrary to the interest of other shareholders.

In the area of political corruption [2.1.3], the new code mainly increases the penalties for existing offences. Those involved in bribery of public employees (*cohecho*) may receive a fine and six-year prison term, as well as disqualification from public office (*inhabilitación*) for up to twelve years. One new provision relates to conflict of interest; public employees who act as advisers to private persons or companies may now be heavily fined and barred from office for three years.

Other changes introduced by the code relate particularly to young offenders [8.4.2], and place the emphasis on preventing reoffending rather than punishment. Incapacity due to drug or alcohol addiction can now, under certain circumstances, exempt individuals from criminal responsibility, thus opening the way to rehabilitation outside prison. Those who refuse to perform compulsory military or community service are now more likely to be fined than imprisoned.

The new code also includes a number of measures designed to reduce prison overcrowding and aid rehabilitation by keeping offenders out of prison as far as possible. They extend the opportunities for courts to impose a suspended sentence (*suspensión de pena*), a possibility first introduced in 1983. A completely new concept is that of weekend imprisonment (*arrestos de fin de semana*), which may replace terms of up to two years at the rate of two weekends per week of sentence. With the agreement of the offender, fines or community service (*trabajos en beneficio de la comunidad*) may also be substituted.

Finally, the new code widens significantly the civil responsibility of the state for the actions of its employees. Compensation to members of the public for the errors and omissions of public bodies is now payable under much less stringent conditions. No longer must a claimant prove the direct responsibility of a particular employee, merely show that he or she was prejudiced by the 'operation of public services'. Moreover, responsibility now extends to unintended acts (*delitos culposos*) and is not limited to intentional ones (*delitos dolosos*). This last change was introduced during the code's passage through Parliament, against the government's will. That, like the provision itself, was a welcome check on the executive [1.4.1], and a reassuring indication of Spanish democracy's good health.

9.5 GLOSSARY

acción popular f	private prosecution
antecedentes penales mpl	criminal record
arresto de fin de semana m	weekend imprisonment
arresto mayor m	custodial/prison sentence of over three years
arresto menor m	custodial/prison sentence of up to three years
Audiencia Nacional f	high court
audiencia provincial f	provincial court
audiencia territorial f	old-style regional court
auto m	judicial opinion
barrio periférico m	(deprived) outlying area of city
beneficios penitenciarios mpl	privileges granted to prisoners
Benemérita f	Civil Guard
blanqueo de dinero m	money-laundering

carrera judicial f	judicial service
causa f	case
centro de alta seguridad m	high-security prison
centro penitenciario m	prison
código civil/penal m	civil/criminal code
cohecho m	bribery of public employee
Colegio de Abogados m	Lawyers' Association
condena f	sentence
condenado m	convicted prisoner
Consejo General del Poder Judicial (CGPJ) m	General Council of the Judiciary
contencioso m	case, legal dispute
criminalidad f	crime; criminality
criminalidad de cuello blanco f	white-collar crime
Cuerpo Nacional de Policía (CNP) m	National Police Force
cumplimiento íntegro de penas m	full-term sentencing
delincuencia f	crime
delito m	offence
delito culposo m	unintentionally prejudicial act
delito doloso m	intentionally prejudicial act
delito societario m	corporate offence
destino m	post (in judicial service)
director m	governor (of prison)
enjuicamiento m	(process of) trial
Ertzaintza f	Basque police force
escuchas telefónicas fpl	phone-tapping
falta f	minor offence
fiscal m	state attorney
Fiscal General del Estado m	Attorney General
funcionario de prisiones m	member of prison staff; prison warder
Grupo Especial de Operaciones (GEO) m	Special Operations Group (of National Police)
Guardia Civil f	Civil Guard
guardia (civil) m	civil guard officer
inhabilitación f	disqualification (from office)
inseguridad ciudadana f	lack of public safety
instrucción f	examination (stage of legal process)
juez m	member of judiciary
juez de instrucción m	examining magistrate
juez de paz m	justice of the peace
juicio m	trial (of a particular case)
jurado m	jury
jurisprudencia f	jurisprudence, case law
juzgado m	court
juzgado de lo civil m	civil court
juzgado de lo contencioso-administrativo m	administrative court
juzgado de distrito m	old-style district court
juzgado de paz m	municipal court
juzgado de lo penal m	criminal court

juzgado de primera instancia m	court of the first instance
juzgado de primera instancia e instrucción m	new-style district court
juzgado de lo social m	employment court
juzgado de última instancia m	final court of appeal
juzgado de vigilancia penitenciaria m	prison supervision court
lavado de dinero m	(*see blanqueo de dinero*)
libertad bajo fianza f	release on bail
libertad ciudadana f	civil liberty
libertad condicional f	parole
magistrado m	judge
masificación de presos f	prison overcrowding
ministerio fiscal m	government attorney service
Mossos d'Esquadre m	Catalan police force
órgano colegial m	court presided by bench with several members
órgano unipersonal m	court presided by single-person bench
palacio de justicia m	court house
partido judicial m	court district
pena f	sentence
pena de muerte f	death sentence
penas múltiples fpl	consecutive sentences
poder judicial m	judiciary
preso m	prison inmate, prisoner
preso preventivo m	remand prisoner
primero m	first offender
procurador m	officially recognised legal representative, barrister
recluso m	(*see preso*)
recurso m	appeal
reincidente mf	reoffender
reinserción social f	reintegration into society; rehabilitation of offenders
resocialización f	rehabilitation of offenders
sala f	division (of court)
sala de lo militar f	division of Supreme Court dealing with appeals from military courts
sentencia f	verdict
Servicio Jurídico del Estado m	government legal service
suburbio m	(*see barrio periférico*)
sumario m	report from examining court/magistrate
suspensión de pena f	suspended sentence
trabajos en beneficio de la comunidad mpl	community work
tribunal m	(*see juzgado*)
tribunal eclesiástico m	Church court
tribunal de honor m	military court; tribunal of professional association
Tribunal Superior de Justicia m	regional high court
Tribunal Supremo m	Supreme Court
tribunal titular de menores m	children's court

FURTHER READING

Amodia, J. 1990 Taxonomía e inestabilidad del sistema de partidos en España. *Journal of Association for Contemporary Iberian Studies* **3** (1).

Amodia, J. (ed.) 1994 *The resurgence of nationalist movements in Europe.* Bradford, Bradford University Press (Chaps 10, 11).

Anuario El País (annual produced by newspaper of same name).

Balcells, A. 1996 *Catalan nationalism: past and present.* London, Macmillan.

Bangs, P. 1995 The European Union and the Spanish environment. In Cooper, T. (ed.) *Spain in Europe.* Leeds, All Saints College.

Bell, D. (ed.) 1993 *Western European Communists and the collapse of Communism.* London, Berg (Chap. 6).

Berger, S. and Broughton, D. (eds) 1995 *The force of labour: the Western European labour movement and the working class in the twentieth century.* London, Berg (Chap. 7).

Boyd-Barrett, O. and O'Malley, P. (eds) 1995 *Education reform in democratic Spain.* London, Routledge.

Brenan, G. 1990 *The Spanish labyrinth.* Cambridge, Cambridge University Press.

Carr, R. 1980 *Modern Spain: 1875–1980.* Oxford, Oxford University Press.

Deacon, P. 1994 *The press as the mirror of the new Spain.* Bristol, Bristol University Press.

España/Spain (annual Spanish government publications).

Ferner, A. and Hyman, R. (eds) 1992 *Industrial relations in the new Europe.* Oxford, Blackwell (Chap. 15).

García Cotarelo, R. and López Nieto, L. 1988 Spanish conservatism 1976–87. *West European Politics* **11** (2).

Gillespie, R. *et al.* 1995 *Democratic Spain: reshaping relations in a changing world.* London, Routledge.

Graham, H. and Labanyi, J. (eds) 1995 *Spanish cultural studies: an introduction.* Oxford, Oxford University Press (Chaps. 18, 20).

Harrison, J. 1993 *The Spanish economy: from the Civil War to the European Community.* London, Macmillan.

Heiberg, M. 1989 *The making of the Basque nation.* Cambridge, Cambridge University Press.

Hernández, A. 1995 *El quinto poder: la iglesia de Franco a Felipe.* Madrid, Temas de hoy.

Heywood, P. 1991 Governing a new democracy: the power of the Prime Minister in Spain. *West European Politics* **14** (2).

Heywood, P. 1992 The Socialist Party in power. *Journal of Association for Contemporary Iberian Studies* **5** (2).

Heywood, P. 1995 *The government and politics of Spain.* London, Macmillan (Chaps. 5, 7, 10).

Hollyman, J. 1995 The tortuous road to regional autonomy in Spain. *Journal of Association for Contemporary Iberian Studies* **8** (1).

Hooper, J. 1995 *The new Spaniards.* Harmondsworth, Penguin.

Hopkin, J. 1993 Reflections on the disintegration of UCD. *Journal of Association for Contemporary Iberian Studies* **6** (2).

International Journal of Iberian Studies formerly: *Journal of Association for Contemporary Iberian Studies.*

Longhurst, A. 1995 The Spanish labour market. In Cooper, T. (ed.) *Spain in Europe.* Leeds, All Saints College.

Newton, M.T. and Donaghy, P.J. 1996 Institutions of modern Spain: a political and economic guide. Cambridge: Cambridge University Press.

Román, P. (ed.) 1995 *Sistema político español.* Madrid, McGraw Hill.

Ross, C. 1996 Nationalism and party competition in the Basque Country and Catalonia. *West European Politics* **16** (3).

Salmon, K. 1995 *The modern Spanish economy.* London, Pinter.

Sánchez Goyanes, E. 1989 *Constitución española comentada.* Madrid, Paraninfo.

Tamames, R. 1993 *Estructura económica española.* Madrid, Alianza.

Tamames, R. 1995 *La economía española 1975–1995.* Madrid, Temas de hoy.

Tusell, J. and Sinova, J. 1992 *La década socialista: el ocaso de Felipe González.* Madrid, Espasa.

Wagstaff, P. (ed.) 1994 *Regionalism in Europe.* Oxford: Intellect (Chap. 6).

INDEX